Beyond Complementary Medicine

Beyond Complementary Medicine

Legal and Ethical Perspectives on
Health Care and Human Evolution

By

Michael H. Cohen, J.D., M.B.A., M.F.A.

Ann Arbor

THE UNIVERSITY OF MICHIGAN PRESS

Copyright © by the University of Michigan 2000
All rights reserved
Published in the United States of America by
The University of Michigan Press
Manufactured in the United States of America
⊚ Printed on acid-free paper

2003   2002   2001   2000   4   3   2   1

A CIP catalog record for this book is available from the British Library.

Library of Congress Cataloging-in-Publication Data

Cohen, Michael H.
   Beyond complementary medicine : legal and ethical perspectives on health care and human evolution / Michael H. Cohen.
       p.   cm.
   Includes bibliographical references and index.
   ISBN 0-472-11135-3 (cloth : alk. paper)
   1. Alternative medicine—Moral and ethical aspects. I. Title.
R733.C644   2000
174'.2—dc21   99-50870

Portions of this book appeared in a different form as: "Toward a Bioethics of Compassion," 28 *Ind. L. Rev.* 667 (1995); "Malpractice Considerations Affecting the Clinical Integration of Complementary and Alternative Medicine," 2 (4) *Current Practice of Medicine* 87 (1999); "Do Clones Have Souls and Other Medicolegal Mysteries," 5 (3) *Alt. & Comp. Therap.* 177 (June 1999); "Medicine in 'Flatland': A Tale of Two Dimensions," 5 (2) *Alt. & Comp. Therap.* 110 (April 1999); "Complementary and Alternative Medicine Policy: The Future of Regulation," 5 (1) *Alt. & Comp. Therap.* 50 (Feb. 1999); "Sex, Scandal and Spirituality," 4 (6) *Alt. & Comp. Therap.* 435 (Dec. 1998); "Yoga, Medicine, and the Law," 2 (3) *Alt. Healthcare Mgt.* 16 (1999); "Changing U.S. Dietary Supplements Regulation: Belief, Values, Policies," 2 (2) *Alt. Healthcare Mgt.* 16 (March 1999); "An Indigenous Mexican Healer: A Personal Encounter," 2 (2) *Alt. Healthcare Mgt.* 24 (March 1999); "Examining the Legal Status of Energy Healing," 1 (2) *Alt. Healthcare Mgt.* 14 (Nov. 1998) and 2 (1) *Alt. Healthcare Mgt.* 16 (Jan. 1999); "Integrating Complementary and Alternative Therapies: Strategic Advice for Health Care Institutions," 1 (1) *Alt. Healthcare Mgt.* 10 (Sept. 1998).

   All the royalties from the sale of this book will be donated to an international charitable organization that focuses primarily on the health care needs of children and their families.

Contents

Introduction

The close of the nineteenth century witnessed the rise of a system of scientific medicine that established medical orthodoxy (or "biomedicine") and, for better or worse, the exclusion or suppression of all philosophical and economic competitors in the sphere of professional health care.[1] This exclusion resulted from a growing division between the "regular" physicians, who relied on technological discoveries that enabled them to systematize diagnosis and quantify the patient's condition, and the so-called irregular physicians, who advocated therapies connected to larger, humanistic or social frameworks, which included ideas about human emotion and spirit in diagnostic and therapeutic categories.[2] Such modalities as homeopathy, naturopathy, and folk and community-based healing were expelled from the mainstream and/or condemned as charlatanry.[3] Simultaneously, biomedicine's consolidation of political power and influence resulted in statutes and a regulatory structure that secured the professional dominance, if not monopoly, of biomedicine within the national and even international health care market.[4]

Since the late nineteenth century, the biomedical community persistently has criticized therapies outside its ken as unscientific, irrational, unsubstantiated, and potentially dangerous to health care consumers. Such therapies have been called "unconventional," "nonconforming," and "unorthodox." Proponents have countered that these terms define the therapies from the perspective of biomedicine, which concurrently determines which scientific paradigms and methodologies satisfactorily establish proof of safety and efficacy.[5]

In any event, by the mid-1960s, consumer interest in such therapies as herbal and nutritional care, chiropractic, massage, body-oriented psychotherapy, homeopathy, and spirituality and prayer led to a resurgence of these approaches. Consumer interest cultivated what came to be known as the "holistic health care" movement, with a focus on the "whole person," whose health was seen to depend not only on genetics and biochemistry but also on physical, emotional, mental, environmental, nutritional, and even spiritual factors. When President Nixon opened the door to China in the early 1970s, the movement grew, as acupuncture and traditional oriental medicine—and later, Ayurvedic medicine—gained popular use in the U.S. health care system. In this way, the medical systems, traditions, and knowledge indigenous to other peoples and populations began to challenge biomedical dominance of U.S. health care. This movement was paralleled in Europe and elsewhere abroad with increasing penetration of "complementary medicine" in mainstream regulatory and reimbursement structures, together with continuing medical and legislative recognition of the importance of "traditional" health care practiced outside the confines of biomedicine.[6]

In the last two decades, there have been increasing efforts to subject such therapies, as much as possible, to rigorous scientific investigation. In 1992, Congress created the Office for the Study of Unconventional Medical Practices, with the mandate that it investigate such practices and provide a clearinghouse for information regarding their use. Subsequent studies revealed the extent to which such practices pervade the social fabric of U.S. health care, showing that they are performed alongside, as well as outside of, conventional medical care.[7] In the United States, the term *complementary and alternative medicine* has entered general usage and now describes a collection of therapies that are sometimes used to complement conventional care (for example, acupuncture and massage therapy to relieve nausea following chemotherapy) and sometimes employed as substitutes (for example, nutritional therapies in attempts to forestall chemotherapy). In 1998, the Office for the Study of Unconventional Medical Practices (by then renamed the Office of Complementary and Alternative Medicine) became the National Center for Complementary and Alternative Medicine at the National Institutes of Health.

I use the term *integrative health care* to describe a system of medicine that integrates conventional care with complementary and alternative medicine and seeks to provide *safe, effective, and appropriate* care in the best interest of the patient. While firm proponents and staunch opponents of complementary and alternative medicine represent the poles of belief about the role, safety, and efficacy of such therapies, the term *integrative health care,* as just defined, expresses an achievable and desirable goal in the future of U.S. health care. Integration requires responsible investigation, informed judgment, and open-minded, yet critical, study and analysis of various systems of healing, so that divergent philosophies, paradigms, and practices may be bridged.

This book addresses the growing interest in legal, ethical, and regulatory aspects of integrative health care. In so doing, the book is a sequel to *Complementary and Alternative Medicine: Legal Boundaries and Regulatory Perspectives* (Baltimore: Johns Hopkins University Press, 1998). That book exhaustively researched federal and state law to explore the legal and regulatory authority on which future health care, integrating conventional with complementary and alternative medicine, can rest. The web of legal issues explored therein included credentialing and licensing, scope of practice limitations, provider malpractice and institutional liability, patients' right to receive nonconventional treatments, professional discipline (premised on the use of modalities outside prevailing professional norms), and the availability of third-party reimbursement.

This book selectively explores, in greater depth, several of these legal, ethical, and regulatory issues. It further addresses the broader foundational questions surrounding the integration of complementary and alternative medicine into clinical care. For example, when integrating such therapies, how should physicians structure their clinical practice to avoid malpractice liability exposure? And what would such structural changes, in turn, imply for the evolution of the regulatory structure? Similarly, should informed consent disclosure include complementary and alternative medicine? If so, on what basis? What effect would such disclosure, in turn, have on legal ideals of informed consent?

Turning to medicine and spirituality, can paradigmatically foreign therapies, such as spiritual healing, have a place in medical care, and if so, should they be treated as religion or as medicine? What legal and ethical responsibilities accrue to spiritual leaders and advisors who touch on health and to their followers? As a final example, what systemic changes or paradigmatic shifts might evolve in biomedical ethics if foundational beliefs from complementary and alternative medicine take root in biomedical tradition?

These kinds of questions aim to stimulate and inform at least five interrelated groups: (1) physicians practicing conventional medicine who are integrating or considering integrating various complementary and alternative therapies; (2) complementary and alternative medicine

providers (such as acupuncturists, chiropractors, herbalists, homeopaths, naturopaths, healers, massage therapists, reflexologists, nutritional consultants) and companies commercializing nutritional therapies; (3) medical schools and other health care educational institutions
(for example, schools of public health, of public policy, and of chiropractic, massage therapy, and acupuncture), law schools, and other
academic institutions; (4) health care executives, institutions, and insurance organizations, attorneys, policymakers, legislators, and adminis-
trators in fields touching on integrative medicine; and (5) patients and
their families.

The chapters of this book, which vary in length and style, are unified in their exploration of the potential frontiers of health care. These
frontiers may transcend our experience or imagination, if we merely
extrapolate based on existing technological and biomedical models.
While pursuing this unified and transcendent theme, the book is
designed so that its range mirrors the integrative process itself, a
process of grappling with and meaningfully assimilating disparate traditions and unfamiliar ways of thinking about the significance of health
and body in human affairs.

The topics I have selected hone in on three major areas likely to
inform providers and policymakers assessing integrative medicine in
this new millennium: liability issues, ethical issues, and bioethical
issues. The section on liability issues addresses questions involving credentialing, malpractice, and referrals. More specifically, chapter 1
assesses the effectiveness and appropriateness of licensing as a key regulatory control to protect the public against dangerous complementary
and alternative practitioners and practices. Chapters 2 and 3 address the
way malpractice and informed consent disclosure are likely to frame an
integrative clinical practice. Chapter 4 discusses liability for physician
referral to complementary and alternative medicine practitioners.
Chapter 5 discusses certain legal risks facing health care institutions.

The section on ethical issues addresses the ways in which a new scientific understanding of the human being, as existing beyond the confines of the body, will shape health care and the practice of medicine.
This new understanding shapes *energy medicine,* a term I use to describe
systems of diagnostics and therapeutics based on the use of human consciousness and intentionality (for example, prayer, visualization, and
mental healing). Chapter 6 specifically explores legal and ethical questions surrounding biofield therapeutics, also known as spiritual healing

or energy healing and under the names of specific modalities, such as Polarity Therapy, Pranic Healing, Reiki, Therapeutic Touch, and *chi gong*. The chapter addresses use of energy healing to affect the health of the human organism by physicians, nurses, and licensed complementary and alternative providers (including, for example, licensed chiropractors employing "network chiropractic"), as well as independent practitioners. Chapter 7 describes an encounter with an indigenous Mexican healer. This chapter will help illuminate the experiential component of the legal, ethical, and clinical debate. Chapter 8 then turns to the liability exposure of a spiritual leader whose influence has reached into followers' personal health decisions. Chapter 9 analyzes the role of belief systems in determining values, policies, and regulatory proposals governing consumer access to dietary supplements.

In the section on bioethical issues, chapter 10 articulates a bioethics of compassion. The chapter employs narrative in an attempt to determine whether the experiential and mystical side of complementary and alternative medicine, so often criticized within mainstream scientific models, can add to bioethical traditions that primarily derive solutions from reasoned, logical, and philosophical explorations. Chapter 11 views some of the bioethical issues raised by complementary and alternative medicine from the perspective of Flatland, a mythical society in which intuition, body wisdom, and personal revelation disrupt political and medical hierarchies and create challenging new paradigms for the existing social order. Chapter 12 explores some of the bioethical implications of understanding the human organism as dwelling within a larger human energy field, which carries biosocial information of value to each individual's medical history, condition, and treatment, as well as to each individual's personal evolution.

In moving from liability, to ethics, to bioethics, the book's structure embodies a gradual progression from examinations of more readily accessible concerns, such as licensing, malpractice, informed consent, and criminal liability, to more challenging explorations of new paradigms of thought and belief that relate to integrative health care. These explorations will push legal, ethical, and clinical boundaries. The intention is to stimulate and, if necessary, provoke, in order to help bridge these divergent worlds. May these essays present a basis for further discussion concerning the way integrative care will impact medicine, health care regulation, and health care policy, as foundational views of disease and health continue to unfold in the new millennium.

PART 1

Liability Issues

CHAPTER 1

Credentialing Concerns

Legal and regulatory structures governing complementary and alternative medicine emerged out of the sectarian factionalism, competition, and professional monopolies of the nineteenth and twentieth centuries. Expulsion of nonconforming providers from medical societies, public campaigns against such "irregular" practitioners, ethical codes forbidding association and consultation with these providers, and the establishment of the American Medical Association as the dominant voice in U.S. health care all contributed to the suppression or decline of health care practices outside the stream of scientific medicine (or biomedicine). These activities coincided with the rise of regulation insulating the "regular" physicians from their economic and philosophical competitors through medical licensure.[1]

The medical licensing laws, ostensibly aimed solely at protecting the public from untrained physicians, ensured that only those meeting the criteria set by practitioners of scientific medicine could legally practice. All others—such as naturopaths, homeopaths, chiropractors, massage therapists, and even spiritual healers—could be prosecuted under these laws and jailed for practicing "medicine" without a license. Biomedicine thus established legal as well as political dominance, and it suppressed rivals through enforcement of the regulatory structures it had encouraged or created.

By the early twentieth century, "Go to jail for chiropractic!" was a popular slogan for the profession, and chiropractors earned political mileage largely by performing spinal manipulations on fellow prisoners, on their wardens, and, upon release from prison, on legislators. Other providers were less successful in achieving legislative recognition, and although naturopaths, acupuncturists, massage therapists, and others ultimately earned licensure in many states, prosecution for the unlicensed medical practice of such diverse providers as midwives, hypnotherapists, iridologists, and even those offering such services as ear piercing and tattooing continued well into the end of the twentieth century.[2]

Most medical practice acts have provided limited exemptions for those engaged in healing services of a religious nature. The exemption, however, typically has been limited to those practicing under the tenets of an established church and has not been extended to complementary and alternative medicine providers. Indeed, some claims by providers purporting to be practicing "religion" rather than "medicine" have been rejected, on the grounds that patients have come seeking health improvement[3] and that the concepts of "diagnosis" and "treatment" in the definition of practicing "medicine" are broad enough to encompass such providers.[4] Moreover, while spirituality plays an important role in many complementary and alternative medicine therapies, typically it is neither necessary nor appropriate to relegate a specific therapy or complementary and alternative medicine in general to the realm of belief (religion) rather than health care.[5]

The law provides no standard definition of the term *complementary and alternative medicine.* No court or legislature has defined the practice of complementary and alternative medicine or set its legal parameters and boundaries generally. Rather, individual groups of providers are subject to different licensing laws, and providers and practices fall within several interlocking areas of law. While there has been no systematic attempt to bring unity and coherence to these different aspects of regulation, debates have continued regarding the appropriateness and efficacy of credentialing rules and other methods of regulating various complementary and alternative medicine providers.

Three levels of analysis can help frame the assessment of any form of regulation or policy relevant to clinical integration of complementary and alternative medicine. The first is paradigmatic: how do these diagnostic and therapeutic systems fit into health care as a whole? How do we assess safety and efficacy, when some therapies lack the kind of rigorous research base to which we are accustomed, while some even challenge conventional paradigms? More important, how do, or how should, these methodological and paradigmatic issues affect regulatory perspectives, such as the desire for reliable credentialing?

The second level involves consumer protection concerns. Typically, legal rules have been concerned with preventing fraud, abuse, and mistreatment of patients who trust in therapies outside biomedicine. Can this goal be achieved while still permitting appropriate clinical exploration of complementary and alternative therapies and keeping the patient's best interest in mind? Does existing law satisfactorily control dangerous or deviant practitioners, or does it stifle health care freedom and the health care system's ability to adapt and innovate to changing perceptions of disease and health? In general, should regulatory controls be loosened or tightened? To what extent should legal rules grant less deference to medical paternalism—the notion that patients must be protected against their own ill-advised choices? To what extent does the advent of complementary and alternative medicine herald a final shift from paternalism toward the recognition of deep autonomy as an important and countervailing, if not overarching, value?

The third level deals with the evolution of legal authority. How are courts and legislatures handling the integration of complementary and alternative medicine into mainstream health care? How can they continue to protect patients from dangerous practitioners and treatments yet allow access to a fuller range of therapies than conventional medicine to date has found comfortable?

These three levels of analysis can begin to open some of the ethical, legal, and even perceptual issues arising when health care paradigms of different cultures and subcultures clash. While these questions are pertinent to each area of law, this chapter focuses on the credentialing process for nonphysician providers of complementary and alternative medicine.

Regulators increasingly have looked to provider credentialing, primarily through state licensure, as a means of ensuring that health care professionals outside the biomedical paradigm have sufficient levels of training and competency to provide the public with safe, effective, and appropriate health care services. Adequate credentialing gives assurance to regulators as well as health care executives, insurance companies, clinicians, and patients that such providers have authority and capability to practice within definitely circumscribed, legally sanctioned boundaries. The effectiveness and appropriateness of such regulatory controls, however, must be scrutinized in the context of a larger shift from a health care system based on biomedicine to one moving toward integration of complementary and alternative medicine.

Shifting Paradigms and Regulatory Values

With its emphasis on standardized, quantifiable, objectively validated methods of diagnosis and treatment, the biomedical orientation toward health and disease has been characterized by *mechanism*—the notion of the body as a machine composed of separate parts—and *reductionism,* the reduction of illness to a set of physical symptoms.[6] Mechanism and reductionism tend to separate diagnosis and treatment from the patient's subjective and social experience of disease, distance patient from caregiver, and sever personal meaning from the process of healing.[7] On the whole, complementary and alternative therapies aim toward an opposite ideal, *holism.* This view attempts to account for patients as whole persons, exercising autonomous choices and seeking health in terms of a larger pursuit toward an irreducible, unified, physical, emotional, mental, and spiritual wholeness.[8]

Although biomedicine historically regarded usage of complementary and alternative medicine as marginal or fringe, a 1993 study in the *New England Journal of Medicine* challenged this assumption, reporting that one American out of every three uses complementary and alternative medicine.[9] Five years after this survey, a 1998 Landmark Healthcare study showed the figure was up to 42 percent of Americans;[10] the 40 percent range was confirmed in a follow-up survey to the 1993 study.[11] A follow-up to the *Journal* study revealed a 47.3 percent increase in total visits to complementary and alternative medicine practitioners, from 427 million in 1990 to 629 million in 1997, with total 1997 out-of-pocket expenditures relating to alternative therapies estimated at 27.0 billion dollars.[12] The study suggested that use of complementary and alternative medicine is likely to continue to increase, particularly as insurance reimbursement for alternative therapies grows. Further, the study suggested that complementary and alternative therapies displace biomedicine, or at least become the preferred first route of diagnosis and treatment, for many patients with chronic disease, back problems, anxiety and depression, and other conditions.

These and other surveys have demonstrated that attitudes that dominated medical control of regulatory and reimbursement structures in the twentieth century no longer accord with patient values, attitudes, beliefs, and desires. Medical sectarianism no longer provides an adequate model for regulation of health in this country, and the notion that extreme medical paternalism should dominate legal rules and liability surrounding, as well as patient access to, therapies outside of biomedicine is anachronistic.[13] Moreover, such paternalism demonstrates medical chauvinism: worldwide, some 80 percent of the world's population relies on non-Western, "traditional medicine" (such as acupuncture and traditional oriental medicine, Ayurvedic medicine, and folk medicine) and considers biomedicine to be "alternative" health care. To respect the patient, as person, the legal system, like medicine, must engage with paradigms beyond mechanism and reductionism and move toward a holistic understanding of the human being's journey toward health on all levels.

Legal authority can draw on efforts within the government and health care communities to obtain a fuller understanding of complementary and alternative medicine than has been traditionally canvassed. One foundational effort occurred during a meeting of leaders of complementary and alternative medicine in 1992, which culminated in the publication of what has come to be known as the Chantilly Report, a document bearing the parenthetical subtitle *A Report to the National Institutes of Health on Alternative Medical Systems and Practices in the United States.*[14]

Although the report is not definitive, it represents a preliminary, quasi-governmental effort to systematically catalog fields of practice for complementary and alternative medicine. The seven major fields (and some of the subfields) include (1) mind-body interventions (including psychotherapy, support groups, meditation, imagery, hypnosis, biofeedback, yoga, dance therapy, music therapy, art therapy, and prayer and mental healing); (2) bioelectromagnetics applications in medicine (including applications of nonthermal, nonionizing electromagnetic fields for bone repair, nerve stimulation, wound healing, treatment of osteoarthritis, electroacupuncture, tissue regeneration, immune system stimulation, and neuroendocrine modulations); (3) alternative systems of medical practice (including home health care, traditional oriental medicine, acupuncture, Ayurveda, homeopathic medicine, anthroposophically extended medicine, naturopathic medicine, environmental medicine, Native American medicine, and Latin American community-based practices); (4) manual healing methods (including osteopathic medicine, chiropractic science, massage therapy, and biofield therapeutics); (5) pharmacological and biological treatments not yet accepted by mainstream medicine (including antineoplastons, cartilage products, EDTA chelation therapy, and immunoaugmentative therapy); (6) herbal medicine (including European phytomedicines, Chinese herbal remedies, Ayurvedic herbal medicines, and Native American herbal medicines); and (7) treatments focusing on diet and nutrition in the prevention and treatment of chronic disease.[15] Chapter 6 will reexamine this classification by using the concept of the biofield (here in category 4, under manual healing) as a unifying concept for some of the groupings.

While addressing some of the complex methodological issues involved in researching such therapies, the Chantilly Report's detailed exploration of these therapies also suggested the difficulty that legal authority must encounter in generalizing regarding proof, efficacy, and overall relevance to prevention and treatment of disease. The report noted that while many therapies are backed by solid research,[16] some therapies continue to challenge conventionally accepted models of health and disease or even purport to render conventional categories dubious. As one example, according to Chinese medicine, *chi* circulates through channels in the body known as "meridians," yet the meridians have no known anatomical counterpart in Western science. Even if some anatomical correlations can be found or appropriate mechanisms of action adduced, theories of *chi* are not expressed in Western terms and purport to transcend mechanistic and reductionistic explanations of acupuncture's effects. Although traditional oriental medicine has earned legislative recognition by virtue of organized lobbying in many states, acupuncture has not received general medical acceptance beyond a narrow range of uses; the legislatively authorized scope of practice varies widely across the states; and many licensing statutes require referral from or supervision by a medical doctor in order for the patient to receive acupuncture and other traditional oriental medicine modalities.

A second example comes from Tibetan medicine. Tibetan physicians place little emphasis on Western scientific methods of analysis, technology, and proof, but Western physicians have little awareness of Tibetan knowledge of subtle energies and the role of consciousness in the creation and maintenance of health. Thus, at the outset, the clash in culture and temperament raises barriers to the possibility of dialogue, then research, then acceptance, and finally, integration. The more estoteric therapies within complementary and alternative medicine face significant hurdles when judged by the standards of biomedicine. Ethnocentrism is particularly acute when dealing with such a foreign medical tradition as Tibet's—yet this is one world medical tradition against whose longevity biomedicine seems hardly a blip on the screen.[17]

While a Western scientist might attempt to match a Tibetan doctor's pulse and tongue diagnosis against a diagnosis made with sophis-

ticated modern instrumentation—assuming a translation of disease
categories is possible—much of Tibetan medicine remains esoteric,
mysterious, and impervious to mechanistic, conventional explanations.
For instance, the Tibetan Book of the Dead is written as a manual for
how to help the soul on its journey immediately following death.[18]
Although Western scientists may consider this unprovable religion,
Tibetans view the book as a code or protocol, establishing specific steps
for postdeath care as an integral part of their medicine.

Therapies that challenge Western medical convention raise an
important question for regulatory bodies: should the regulatory system
solely be based on the evaluation of these therapies by dominant medical communities and scientific paradigms? Or should regulatory bodies take into account the historical, economic, political, and paradigmatic differences between these various systems and providers?
Moreover, to what extent should paradigmatically foreign therapies
and biomedicine's unreadiness, inability—or outright lack of competence—to comprehend such therapies influence legal rules and regulatory structures? For example, what light can Tibetan medicine's views
of immediate postdeath procedures shed on legal rules governing end-
of-life decision making[19] or even on such seemingly mundane details as
how many days the corpse should be left in the hospital bed before
being disturbed?[20] Such questions frame legal and ethical explorations
in this chapter and in succeeding chapters.

Consumer Protection and Health Freedom

In the context of integrative health care, enhanced credentialing of
complementary and alternative medicine providers potentially serves
three significant objectives: (1) increasing consumer access to complementary and alternative therapies being provided in a safe, effective,
and appropriate manner; (2) increasing the availability of a system-
atized framework that can be relied on by the clinician making referrals, the health care institution and/or third-party payer, and the
patient seeking specific complementary and alternative treatments or
providers; and (3) increasing global, systemic integration of biomedicine and complementary and alternative medicine.

The dominant form of state-sanctioned credentialing is mandatory
licensure. Professional licensure is governed by state law pursuant to

the Tenth Amendment to the U.S. Constitution, which leaves states free to regulate matters of health, safety, and welfare affecting their citizens.[21] The medical licensing laws enacted in the late nineteenth century now exist in every state. In prohibiting the unlicensed practice of medicine, these statutes typically define "medicine" as including one or more of the following: (1) diagnosing, preventing, treating, and curing disease; (2) holding oneself out to the public as able to perform the preceding; (3) intending to receive a gift, fee, or compensation for the preceding; (4) attaching such titles as "M.D." to one's name; (5) maintaining an office for reception, examination, and treatment; (6) performing surgery; and (7) using, administering, or prescribing drugs or medicinal preparations.[22] The breadth of these definitions reflects the presumption in favor of biomedical control of professional healing.

Health care providers who lack licensure have been viewed as "diagnosing" and "treating" patients and thus as practicing medicine unlawfully.[23] Nonlicensed providers have had little success arguing that the prohibition in medical licensing statutes against unlicensed medical practice exempts a nonmedical, holistic healing practice.[24] Thus licensure is a growing trend for complementary and alternative professionals. For example, chiropractors are licensed in every state, acupuncturists in well over half the states, massage therapists in over half the states, naturopaths in at least eleven states, and homeopathic physicians in three states;[25] and over a dozen states have or are considering statutes purporting to insulate physicians from professional discipline merely for offering their patients complementary and alternative therapies.[26]

The public benefits of licensing such providers are easy to identify. Licensure elevates professional competence, reputation, and image and furnishes a recognized gateway to hospital privileges, third-party reimbursement, and other marks of regulated health care professions. Further, licensing develops once specific professional communities of complementary and alternative providers develop sufficient cohesion to create standards of professional practice, codes of ethics, and strong mechanisms for internal regulation, thus accentuating public and regulatory confidence in the profession.

Licensing laws also maintain standards and help address one of the key questions raised by regulators—how to protect consumers from overreliance on complementary and alternative therapies and from overbroad claims of cure by such providers. Among other things, licensing statutes for nonmedical professionals, such as chiropractors, acupuncturists, and massage therapists, are limited to the specific scope of practice authorized in their licensing laws; such statutes also typically echo the provision in medical licensing statutes that nonmedical providers are expressly prohibited from practicing "medicine"— from diagnosing, curing, and treating disease.[27]

Even as complementary and alternative medicine providers gain increasing legislative recognition, credentialing embraces a shadow side that cannot be underestimated. Although state law credentialing— particularly licensure—is intended to protect the public from charlatans and ignorant practitioners, it is a double-edged regulatory tool. Licensure largely protects those entrenched practitioners who control the profession and whose interests define the licensing boards' agenda; further, licensing fails as an effective safeguard of public safety and unnecessarily increases barriers to professional entry.[28]

The argument against licensure has particular force when considering the integration of biomedicine and modalities based on concepts that lack conventional scientific understanding or validation, such as *chi* or the biofield.[29] The power and capacity of such phenomena to create a therapeutic encounter that is sacred, healing, and utterly transformative requires protection from unduly intrusive regulation.[30]

The regulatory history of biomedicine's relationship to complementary and alternative medicine and of subgroups within each camp has been anything but "complimentary." At every step, leaders of health care movements have retraced the rivalries, labeling, expulsions, and other efforts designed to neutralize, incorporate, or extinguish competing camps of providers.[31] In biomedicine, the litigation between podiatrists and orthopedic surgeons over whether treatment of the ankle is within the authorized scope of podiatric practice in Connecticut provides a salient example.[32] In complementary and alternative medicine, questions have arisen as to whether energy healers require massage licensure to provide noncontact energetic therapies (see chap. 6) and whether services by hypnotherapists, energy healers, and even licensed providers offering consultations that touch on the mind and emotions constitute "counseling" and require licensure in the field of psychology or mental health counseling.[33] Such questions are emblematic of the failure of licensing and scope-of-practice rules to harmonize competing claims to state recognition of professional healing services.

Regulation of integrative health care in the twenty-first century requires wisdom and vision, or it well may re-create the rivalries, factionalism, and destructiveness of the late nineteenth and most of the twentieth century. Because of these dark tendencies, a large portion of humanity's resources for healing was suppressed or deleted from legally and politically sanctioned medicine. At its worst, excessive requirements for and standardization of credentialing can represent a Faustian bargain in which legitimacy and credibility are achieved at the expense of the integrity underlying healing therapies. One could argue that the same unholy alliance between health care and the "dark side" of the regulatory structure tainted the integrity of biomedicine, invaded the integrity of the practice of medicine, distorted the therapeutic relationship, and created such regulatory nightmares for the honest clinician as the possibility of criminal liability for innocent coding or billing errors.[34] Any regulatory structure easily becomes a multi-headed hydra whose appetite, once whetted, cannot easily be sated or appeased. Thus, the desire to protect the public from charlatans, fakers, and frauds must be balanced against the wish to grant patients every opportunity to access healing, alleviate suffering, and move toward wholeness at every level of being.

The Evolution of Legal Authority

Historically, debates surrounding complementary and alternative medicine have been characterized by such terms as "snake-oil salesman," "charlatan," "quackery," "bogus treatments," and other dismissive and unflattering epithets. Such language is unfair to the many legitimate professionals who are dedicated to alleviating human suffering[35] and to the numerous individuals turning to such therapies in a legitimate quest for wholeness and health. Further, such a war of epithets does not create any realistic policy solutions.

The concern for fraud and abuse, while important and valid, has dominated regulatory structures and attitudes and caused legal authority to undervalue concern for patient access to a fuller range of treatments.[36] The primary goals of health care regulation in the area of integrative medicine must include not only patient protection but also health promotion and respect for intelligent and informed patient choices. With the advent of integrated medicine, the regulatory environment should balance all three goals—health protection, health promotion, health freedom. Thus, while concern for overreaching by unscrupulous practitioners is important, addressing the "best interest of the patient" requires a realistic appraisal of all the regulatory controls already in place to prevent overreaching, deception, and danger.

In fact, when considering energy medicine as well as integrative medicine, the taxonomy of regulatory values can be expanded as follows. Historically, the regulatory system has focused on *fraud control* and *ensuring competence* (see chart 1). Presently, the meaning and focus of these terms are shifting away from insulating medical orthodoxy and toward permitting consumers to make their own decisions. This calls for an expansion of paternalistic goals into regulatory objectives that represent the changing scope of clinical practice. Thus, *fraud control* expands into *quality assurance*, and *ensuring competence* into *safeguarding information flow*. With this shift, the regulatory system of the future also will incorporate at least three additional values: *health care freedom, functional integration of medical systems*, and *transformation*.

The ultimate goal, *transformation* (both individual and collective) can be viewed as a pinnacle in a hierarchy of values governing medicine. Just as the evolution of the human being and humanity toward the Godhead (known in some traditions as God-realization, enlightenment, the Christ Self, or the Buddha nature) is an explicit objective in the spiritual technologies used in energy healing (see chap. 6), similarly, the goal of transformation supports an evolutionary process within the legal and regulatory framework.

Some courts and legislatures have adopted a more patient-centered approach toward evaluating health care choices that involve complementary and alternative medicine. For example, in *Schneider v. Revici*, the U.S. Court of Appeals for the Second Circuit affirmed the patient's right to choose, stating: "[W]e see no reason why a patient should not be allowed to make an informed decision to go outside currently approved medical methods in search of an unconventional treatment. While a patient should be encouraged to exercise care for his own safety, we believe that an informed decision to avoid surgery and conventional chemotherapy is within the patient's right to 'determine what shall be done with his own body.'"[37]

Similarly, in *Rogers v. State Board of Medical Examiners*, in response to a disciplinary action against a physician integrating complementary and alternative medicine, the Florida District Court of Appeals stated:

CHART 1. Regulatory Values Governing Medical Providers
and Therapies

Historic

1. *Fraud control:* protecting patients by eliminating practices and practitioners contravening known principles of medical science.

2. *Ensuring competence:* protecting patients by controlling access to
   providers and setting standards for professional competence.

Future

1. *Quality assurance:* protecting patients by monitoring known dangerous practices and providers and ensuring that patients are free
   from inadvertent toxicities.

2. *Safeguarding information flow:* protecting patients by promoting professional standards and providing consumers with full information
   regarding risks and benefits of various providers and therapies.

3. *Health care freedom:* promoting consumer autonomy and choice and
   providing access to a broad spectrum of therapies and providers
   spanning time and drawn from many cultures and belief systems.

4. *Functional integration:* promoting the safe, effective, and appropriate integration of biomedicine with complementary and alternative
   medicine and balancing scientific technologies with intuitive
   knowledge and nonscientific sources of wisdom.

5. *Transformation:* promoting mind-body-spirit health of person and
   community and moving toward individuation and the fulfillment
   of human evolution.

"Orthodoxy in medicine is like orthodoxy in any other professional
field. [I]t starts as a theory or tentative belief in some particular course
of action . . . [and] begins to be held as a passionate belief in the absolute
rightness of that particular view. Right or wrong, a dissenting view is
regarded as a criminal subversion of the truth and the holder is frequently exposed to slander and abuse by his orthodox colleagues . . . .
[and] these same oppressive forces may shackle the advancement of
medicine."[38] The court's language here stands in contrast to other judi-

cial opinions referring, for example, to "voodoo or alternative medicine."[39]

Parallel developments have occurred in state legislation. For
example, a bill in the Hawaii legislature to develop a more integrated
medicine noted that Hawaiians emphasize "the belief that health,
which comes from the same root as 'wholeness,' involves the body,
mind, and spirit of the whole person."[40] A similar respect for provider
and patient interest in therapies outside biomedicine is demonstrated
in rules adopted by the State Board of Medical Examiners in Texas to
establish standards for physicians practicing "integrative and complementary medicine."[41] The standards aim "to recognize that physicians
should be allowed a reasonable and responsible degree of latitude in
the kinds of therapies they offer their patients" and that "patients have
a right to seek integrative or complementary therapies."

The rules established in Texas define "integrative and complementary medicine" as "those health care methods of diagnosis, treatment or
interventions for which there is support within the peer reviewed scientific literature or generally accepted methods."[42] The rules provide
that a physician may not be found guilty of unprofessional conduct or
be found to have committed malpractice solely on the basis of providing an integrative or complementary therapy, "unless it can be demonstrated that the therapy has a safety risk for the patient that is unreasonably greater than the conventional treatment."[43] The guidelines
require a thorough medical history and physical examination, documentation as to whether conventional medical options have been tried,
and fully informed consent for the nonconventional treatment, including patient notification of any possible adverse effects of the treatment.

Although these rules govern physicians rather than complementary and alternative medicine providers, they suggest a balance
between the different regulatory values identified earlier in this chapter and thus serve as one potential model for future regulatory efforts
in this arena. The overt reference to "integrative medicine," the lenient
standard requiring *some* support (rather than general acceptance), and
the tolerance for benign or moderately risky therapies (unless their
safety risk is "unreasonably greater" than biomedical therapies) all
suggest an openness to a new paradigm of health care. As this openness continues to expand, it is likely that more and more complementary and alternative medicine modalities and providers will find viable
avenues into the regulatory structure.

A regulatory system that historically has focused on protecting biomedicine should move toward the notion of protecting humans, who are seeking optimal health and care, at the deepest levels of being. The law thus will fulfill its highest potential, in supporting human essence and the heart of healing.

CHAPTER 2

Reconceptualizing Malpractice

At first glance, malpractice and credentialing require distinctive analysis—violation of malpractice rules leads to civil liability, while violation of licensing laws leads to criminal liability. Further, each supports an enforcement structure that addresses different aspects of consumer protection: credentialing through licensure is used by regulators to control entry of health care professionals and to ensure that providers are practicing within parameters established by the legislature or professional governing board, whereas malpractice litigation is used by patients to curb irresponsible and dangerous providers. The two, however, are related, as, for example, a civil malpractice claim by a patient can lead both to professional discipline and to questions regarding the provider's licensure. Moreover, while both areas of law aim to protect patients from dangerous and overreaching practitioners, both require rethinking since relevant legal rules impose constraints on integrative health care and undermine the notion of addressing the patient as a whole being.

Few, if any, sources of legal authority describe the application of medical malpractice rules to physicians' integration of complementary and alternative medicine. Few cases have come through the courts to date, as providers have only begun the process of integration in everyday clinical practice. Moreover, legal authority largely has followed medical authority in considering as illegitimate those therapies and treatments outside the mainstream, resulting in a lack of innovative thinking about changes in legal rules.[1] Furthermore, to date, courts by and large have failed to recognize the paradigmatic shifts occurring within professional practice toward expanded patient choice, in which some nonconventional treatments are included.[2] This chapter aims both to set forth legal guidelines for the medically responsible integration of complementary and alternative medicine in clinical practice and to support the evolution of legal authority toward a more integrative system of medicine that is safe, effective, and appropriate to the patient.[3]

Malpractice Per Se

Medical malpractice is defined as occurring when a physician deviates from the standard of care and when that deviation causes patient injury. The initial question is whether the physician commits malpractice merely by incorporating into the therapeutic regimen therapies that fall outside biomedicine. This question arises because the legal elements of medical malpractice have not yet been adapted to such therapies.

The Standard of Care

Standards of care develop from professional journals, meetings, and peer discussions over time and, in the litigation context, typically are established by expert medical testimony as to generally accepted, national standards for physicians in the same specialty. Thus, for example, standards of care in Europe or Japan, where certain forms of herbal medicine are routinely prescribed, would not match standards of practice governing physicians in the United States. However, practice guidelines developed by national medical organizations, by government agencies, and by hospitals may help establish the standard of care in a medical malpractice case.[4]

To date, few therapies have been identified as being definitively indicated for treatment of a specific condition, and indeed, medical pronouncements regarding efficacy have been relatively conservative. For example, the consensus panel convened by the National Institutes of Health recently concluded that there is clear evidence that acupuncture is effective for only a few conditions, such as chemotherapy nausea and vomiting.[5] Similarly, few professional journals, meetings, and peer discussions have concluded that a particular herb should routinely be used to treat a particular condition (for example, echinachea for the common cold); in fact, some case reports of adverse drug-herb reactions have been published. Thus, most complementary and alternative therapies will remain outside the standard of care for some time.

More problematic is the legal implication of defining complementary and alternative medicine in terms of treatments not commonly taught in medical education or used in U.S. hospitals. Historically, the notion of "complementary and alternative" evolved precisely to distinguish such therapies from biomedically accepted modalities, and hence to define such therapies as those outside biomedical standards of care. This suggests that physicians integrating such treatments *by definition* deviate from conventional standards of care and thus risk malpractice liability.[6] Even as alternative therapies become more widespread in medical schools and hospitals,[7] integrative care remains bounded by failure of malpractice law to treat therapies that deviate from prevailing professional standard but are nonetheless selected and executed with due care.

In *Charell v. Gonzales*,[8] the physician used hair analysis and nutritional care to diagnose and treat a cancer patient. The cancer cells metastisized; the patient developed blindness and back problems. The patient sued, presenting two claims: (1) negligence, arguing that the physician persuaded her to forgo conventional care and to rely solely on the nutritional protocol, and (2) failure to obtain informed consent. The patient also sought punitive damages.

The jury found that the physician had departed from accepted medical practice and that this deviation had caused the patient injury. It awarded $4.5 million for pain and suffering, $200,000 for loss of earnings, and $150,000 in punitive damages. The decision, though, arose out of arguably unusual facts: the physician used hair analysis and nutritional care to diagnose and treat cancer; the court found that the physician was "motivated by greed and reckless in his care"; and the jury accepted expert testimony on behalf of the plaintiff that if the patient had not been improperly dissuaded from conventional treatment, the cancer probably would not have metastasized, and that the defendant's treatments were "bogus" and "of no value."[9] Nonetheless, in denying the physician's motion to set aside the verdict, the court noted that practitioners of complementary and alternative medicine necessarily deviate from accepted medical standards and thus might not be able to prevail against claims of malpractice liability.[10] This is malpractice per se.

This court's conclusion is not asymptomatic: courts historically have treated nonbiomedical therapies as suspect in cases where fraud or lack of due care has not been proven.[11] The definitional conundrum leaves the physician who integrates complementary and alternative medicine but lacks support through consensus standards at risk of liability, irrespective of any actual lack of due care in selecting or utilizing the nonconventional treatment.[12]

Causation and Injury

The second element of medical malpractice, patient injury, remains problematic if a judge or jury finds causative injury in the complementary and alternative treatment when the plaintiff is deceased or debilitated. The problem is exacerbated by the fact that many, though not all, patients seek complementary and alternative medicine as a last resort, when conventional care has failed. The physician may be asked, for example, to administer untested remedies to a terminal patient. This can put the physician in a dilemma: treat the patient with complementary and alternative care, knowing the patient or the family may sue if the patient's disease continues its natural course, or refuse to provide, refer for, or disclose the existence of such a treatment, telling the family that no further accepted treatment is possible.

Although judicial guidance is rare, judicial opinions involving nonconventional therapies to date suggest that in determining causation and injury, some courts look askance at the physician's decision to steer patients toward nonbiomedically accepted treatments and view this as "medical chicanery."[13] Historically, some courts' views of complementary and alternative medicine have gone beyond the kind of skepticism associated with neutrality.[14] In a malpractice case, injury might be presumed from the fact that the patient, whose disease has progressed, has relied on the physician's trust in methods outside the known and accepted boundaries of conventional care.

Defenses

One long-term solution is to reformulate judicial thinking about medical malpractice so as to alleviate the definitional conundrum. Unless and until courts adopt doctrinal changes providing greater leeway for responsible incorporation of integrative therapies, traditional malpractice defenses must be adapted to physicians' integration of therapeutic choices.

Traditional Malpractice Defenses

The traditional defenses are the respectable minority defense, the clinical innovation defense, and assumption of risk. The first defense protects the physician who follows a "respected minority" within the profession. The second defense authorizes physicians to make innovative (but not "experimental") therapeutic choices where justified by necessity in specific cases or as a last resort. Because the law is underdeveloped, however, and because the level of medical acceptance for various complementary and alternative therapies is in flux, it is difficult to draw broad-based conclusions regarding the availability of these first two defenses in integrative care. The respectable minority defense is especially problematic, since the size and content of a respectable minority varies by jurisdiction, and since no court yet has had occasion to decide whether a particular group or population of physicians using a complementary and alternative treatment constitutes such a minority.[15]

The leading case on assumption of risk is *Schneider v. Revici*.[16] The patient sought nutritional and other nonsurgical treatment for breast cancer. She signed a detailed consent form releasing Dr. Revici from liability. Following the treatment, the tumor spread; the patient sued. The jury found Dr. Revici liable for malpractice but halved the award, finding the patient 50 percent comparatively negligent.[17] The U.S. Court of Appeals for the Second Circuit, reversing the decision, held that the trial judge should have instructed the jury that express assumption of risk was a complete defense to malpractice.[18]

The court distinguished express assumption of risk (in which the patient agrees in advance that the physician need not use reasonable care for the patient's benefit) from implied assumption of risk (which is founded on the patient's reasonable, voluntary, and intelligent consent to the risk of harm from the physician's conduct).[19] Under New York law, express assumption of risk completely exonerates the physician and "dissolve[s] the physician's duty to treat a patient according to medical community standards," whereas implied assumption of risk triggers comparative negligence, in which the physician's liability is reduced to the extent of the patient's responsibility or fault.[20]

A complete defense (express assumption of risk) serves physicians better than a partial defense (implied assumption of risk). In jurisdictions authorizing express assumption of risk, physicians will benefit from a clear, written agreement documenting the patient's consent to, and express assumption of, risks relating to the selection and professionally responsible execution of complementary and alternative treatments. The physician offering the patient such an agreement should, of course, be sensitive not to allow consideration of legal risk to intrude unduly into the therapeutic encounter. Further, the physician should maintain clear documentation as to literature and symptoms relied on for any therapeutic choice, so as to help deflect claims using inadequate record keeping as a basis for proving substandard care.

In any event, many courts will honor agreements that show an express assumption of risk, in order to uphold the physician's freedom of contract to provide the patient with appropriate care. Courts should find contracting principles especially appropriate where complementary and alternative modalities emphasize patient responsibility for such tasks as nutritional and lifestyle changes.[21] Such agreements are consistent with the premise that holistic health care implies a departure from paternalistic, authoritarian models of health care in favor of broader patient choice and greater patient responsibility for and participation in the healing process. Through such agreements, physician and patient become collaborators in disease management and the restoration of wholeness. Further, irrespective of judicial approval, express assumption of risk agreements may reduce litigiousness by clarifying patient expectations and documenting patient participation in the choice of innovative treatments.

Limitations on Assumption of Risk

Many jurisdictions follow the distinction between express and implied assumption of risk, with minor variations. Hawaii, for example, distinguishes between express assumption of risk (in which a plaintiff contracts to assume and release the defendant from liability for specific risks), primary implied assumption of risk (in which the plaintiff enters voluntarily and reasonably into some relationship with the defendant, which the plaintiff knows to involve risk), and secondary implied assumption of risk (where the plaintiff knows of the danger presented by the defendant's negligence and proceeds voluntarily and unreasonably to encounter it).[22]

As patients turn to new journals on alternative therapies, to the Internet, and to other sources outside traditional physician-patient channels, the informational swell has the potential to make judges and juries increasingly sympathetic to the defense of an implied assumption of risk. Physicians will point to the patient's awareness of sources describing risks associated with complementary and alternative therapies. This can soften a potentially adverse verdict by invoking the doctrine of comparative negligence and assigning a portion of the fault (liability) to the patient.

Even where the doctrine is available, assumption of risk cannot be regarded as a panacea. The verdict in *Charell* suggests that the physician facing comparative negligence can incur substantial monetary liability even if the jury finds that the patient bears significant responsibility for the harm.[23] Furthermore, some courts reject assumption of risk entirely as a defense to medical malpractice. For example, in *Morrison v. MacNamara*, the U.S. Court of Appeals for the District of Columbia stated that because of the physician's expertise and fiduciary obligation to the patient, patients cannot appreciate risks, and that therefore, "save exceptional circumstances, a patient cannot assume the risk of negligent treatment."[24] In a later case, *Weil v. Seltzer*, this court applied the same principles to the related defense of contributory negligence.[25] Still other courts have criticized assumption of risk as controversial, deceptive, and "adding 'nothing to modern law except confusion'"; some commentators have advocated abolishing the defense and substituting such concepts as duty.[26]

It is doubtful, as well, that the doctrine will relieve a physician of malpractice if the physician, while providing complementary and alternative medicine, disregards obvious warning signs of disease progression, fails to continue conventional diagnostic monitoring methods, or egregiously neglects the patient's basic treatment needs. In other words, the patient may assume the risk of an unconventional treatment, but not the risk that the physician will abandon good medical practice by forgoing necessary conventional diagnostic monitoring and treatment.

Courts tend to disfavor waivers of liability or other attempts by providers to exculpate themselves from conduct that fails to show an exercise of due care.[27] Even *Schneider*, while recognizing a potential defense based on a signed "covenant not to sue," held that such a covenant would be strictly construed against the physician and would have to be "clear and unequivocal" to provide protection.[28] A similar result was reached in *Gonzalez v. New York State Dept. of Health*, upholding disciplinary proceedings against Dr. Gonzalez for using nutritional therapy with patients having advanced and incurable cancer.[29] The court noted that a patient's "'consent to or even insistence upon a certain treatment does not relieve a physician from the obligation of treating the patient according to the usual standard of care.'"[30] Thus, physicians cannot immunize themselves from malpractice liability (or, potentially, from related professional disciplinary proceedings) merely because the patient has agreed to waive all risk; the immunity only goes to risks of modalities selected and administered in the exercise of sound professional judgment—even though such treatments may be outside conventional medicine.[31]

For example, suppose the physician offers the patient acupuncture to alleviate stress and imbalances relating to a stomach upset. The physician may have obtained an agreement from the patient in which the patient expressly waived all risks relating to acupuncture treatment, provided that such treatment was executed with due care (for example, that the physician followed clean needle technique, using only safe and sterile needles). The agreement further may have specifically authorized the physician to utilize acupuncture in treatment of stomach imbalances, together with any appropriate conventional treatment for conditions (such as an ulcer) within conventional diagnostic categories. Suppose, however, that the physician, in palpating the patient's stomach, misdiagnosed the imbalance as an ulcer and missed the fact that the patient was developing serious abnormalities in the tissue, leading to cancer. Express assumption of risk probably would not protect the physician against potential liability for the negligent misdiagnosis. The reason is that, whether using Western diagnostic tests or evaluating the flow of *chi*, the physician would be held to the standard of care of conventional medicine for related diagnoses and treatments. If a similarly situated physician would have found the abnormalities, the physician would be negligent for having failed to do so, even though acupuncture was added to the treatment regimen.[32] Thus, even as physicians take advantage of contractual means to limit liability for the incorporation of complementary and alternative treatments, common sense and good medical judgment provide the best legal protection.

For these reasons, the defense of assumption of risk remains a precarious bulwark against malpractice liability in integrative care and, as currently developed, leaves many policy questions. Does malpractice law adequately balance concerns for consumer protection, on the one hand, against the patient's interest in autonomous choices, on the other? Or should courts adopt stronger controls on patient acquiescence to complementary and alternative therapies? Is it appropriate to define malpractice in a way that makes physicians who offer complementary and alternative therapies liable per se? At what point do therapies previously considered "complementary and alternative" fall within conventional standards of care? If such therapies continue to fall outside biomedicine, should the defense of an express assumption of risk be allowed if the patient is given full information about risks and benefits of therapies outside of medical orthodoxy? Concerning the treatment of chronic and/or incurable diseases, how should the doctrine evolve to accommodate the integration of therapeutic responses that are currently outside biomedicine? Courts and legislatures doubtless will wrestle with such questions as increased litigation and media attention continue to shift the boundaries of accepted therapeutic practice.

Evolution of Legal Authority

Ultimately, legal authority must evolve commensurate with changes occurring in the medical profession and marketplace. Certain trends within the law provide an argument for the evolution of malpractice law toward responsible professional integration of complementary and alternative medicine. Further, such evolution may be necessary in order for medical malpractice insurance to more meaningfully cover physicians' exploration of useful therapies currently considered outside mainstream medicine.

Deviation from Conventional Standards

With the caveat indicated earlier—that physicians act with due care in the selection and execution of complementary and alternative treatments and do not fail to exercise due care in making diagnoses and providing treatments within conventional medicine—the physician integrating complementary and alternative treatments should not risk malpractice liability per se merely for utilizing such treatments. Furthermore, conventional medicine should not dictate the standard of care for integrative medicine. The very rivalry between orthodox medical practitioners and complementary and alternative practitioners suggests the need for judicial flexibility in evaluating "deviance." To decide otherwise would stifle clinical innovation and perpetuate medical authority, as well as its dominance over legal authority involving complementary care. Only by refashioning the criteria for standards of care can malpractice jurisprudence incorporate the nascent changes in clinical practice.

A minority of courts have criticized judicial reliance on conventional standards of care to determine malpractice liability, and scholars likewise have argued that in assessing malpractice, conventional medical authority should not serve as "its own judge."[33] In *Helling v. Carey*, the Supreme Court of Washington rejected conventional medical custom and required ophthalmologists to perform routine glaucoma tests, even though the incidence of the disease was only one in twenty-five thousand persons over forty.[34] The court thus substituted its judgment for that of the ophthalmologists regarding the applicable standard of care and imposed a stricter standard on physicians than medical custom permitted.

Although many courts have rejected *Helling*'s risk-benefit balancing as an unwarranted judicial intrusion on medical authority, a minority have adopted the perspective that physicians must adhere to a different standard than that set by the profession.[35] This provides one possible model for changing malpractice definitions to accommodate appropriate integration of complementary and alternative treatments. To date, medical acceptance of such treatments lags behind patient demand, government-sponsored research, and insurance and market forces. Therefore, courts should accept expert testimony regarding evolving standards of care that incorporate complementary and alternative modalities. In so doing, courts may reject medical custom and include within the standard of care those therapies not yet generally accepted in the medical community at large but supported by significant research and used responsibly according to existing studies and protocols.

Although it is difficult to predict the limits to which courts will permit such deviation from conventional medicine, one may imagine that such treatments as dietary and lifestyle changes are acceptable, assuming basic conventional diagnostic and therapeutic approaches are covered. For example, the program developed by Dean Ornish, M.D., for cardiac disease has found a home in many hospitals and reimbursement programs and should not be deemed negligent merely because it has not yet reached majority acceptance or involves yoga, meditation, lifestyle changes, and therapeutic support.[36] Similarly, recommending chiropractic care (over pharmaceuticals and surgery) for low-back pain should be considered good medicine and nonnegligent.[37] These treatments, among others, have support in the literature and are gaining ground in clinical practice and in third-party reimbursement practices.[38]

In fact, when such treatments gain sufficient support in the medical literature and among physicians, incorporating such treatments can either become part of the standard of care or surpass conventional standards of care, even though the complementary or alternative treatments have not yet been generally recognized. At this point, the possibility arises that failing to offer to provide or refer for such treatments could trigger malpractice liability. Relying on conventional treatment alone would be equivalent to utilizing an obsolete technology and would fall below accepted professional standards.[39] This development in the law would lead to a proposition many presently would consider radical and controversial: that physicians could be liable in malpractice for failing to provide complementary and alternative treatments.

This proposition has foundation: arguably, physicians should at least know about viable approaches outside biomedicine; they may, in fact, have a duty, under current rules on informed consent, to inform patients about such approaches.[40] Further, irrespective of such a duty, market forces may dictate such flow of information: future patients (and health care institutions) are likely to employ physicians who are educated as to useful nonconventional therapies, including dietary supplements, lifestyle choices, and modalities within the patient's control and responsibility. The increase in third-party reimbursement for such practices also lends credence to the argument that failure to incorporate such approaches could constitute negligence, thus stimulating physicians to expand their therapeutic armamentarium beyond strictly biomedical approaches.

Causation and Patient Injury

To return to the second element of medical malpractice—resulting patient injury—notions of complementary and alternative medicine as inherently suspect or injurious can lead to overgeneralized, conclusory labels justifying the imposition of liability.[41] Future courts will unpack the different therapies brought under the rubric of complementary and alternative medicine, as identified in such documents as the Chantilly

Report, and will evaluate causation and injury irrespective of historical biases or labels.

One way courts might evaluate causative injury is to assess the following three factors: (1) the risk of danger or injury created by the specific therapy, (2) the extent to which the patient's condition was likely to result in death or disability irrespective of complementary and alternative care, and (3) the extent to which the complementary and alternative therapy displaced conventional care and the extent to which the neglect of conventional care was the actual and proximate cause of the injury.

In assessing the first factor (risk), courts should consider that a low risk of injury is carried by many complementary and alternative therapies (for example, acupuncture, using clean needle technique; aromatherapy, using scents to stimulate emotional well-being; or a highly diluted homeopathic remedy). Many therapies carry definite risks (for example, an herb—such as ephedra—may produce toxic side effects, or a caregiver using an unsterile acupuncture needle may infect the patient), while for other therapies, the risks may be unknown or may not be definable in conventional scientific terms (for example, the potential adverse effects—defined in terms of homeopathic principles—from taking the wrong homeopathic remedy). In any case, the risk must be identified and not presumed.

In assessing the second factor, inducing patients to forgo necessary conventional care can, in some cases, be dangerous, if not deadly.[42] Yet in many other cases it may be difficult to determine whether the harm has resulted from the complementary and alternative treatment or would have occurred regardless (for example, in cases where death follows a prolonged and terminal illness or where there is recurrence of a malignant tumor that conventional therapies could not destroy). The mere fact that an injured patient or deceased patient's family has brought litigation and that a nonconventional therapy has been used should not indicate negligence per se. A required finding of the second factor is especially significant when a complementary and alternative therapy (for example, homeopathy) is used as a treatment of last resort.

In assessing the third factor, courts should evaluate whether the physician, in providing complementary and alternative treatment, has neglected to provide (or to refer the patient to another physician specialist to receive) conventional diagnostic monitoring and treatment in conjunction with the complementary and alternative therapy. For example, if the physician presents nutritional care in an attempt to limit the spread of a tumor, the physician should ensure that the patient's condition is properly monitored using available conventional diagnostic resources (for example, CAT scans and MRIs) and that known, efficacious conventional therapies are available in case the nutritional treatment fails to produce the desired result.

When physicians utilize complementary and alternative therapies as adjuncts to conventional care, they are less likely to be viewed as taking the patient down a fruitless, diversionary, and possibly dangerous road. For example, some therapies are used in adjunctive or complementary ways that do not unduly threaten conventional care: these therapies include acupuncture and massage therapy to treat nausea following chemotherapy, hypnosis to reduce postoperative pain and complications, and proper nutritional and herbal support prior to hospitalization or surgery. However, some treatments purport to displace conventional care: these treatments include the use of saw palmetto over Proscar to treat benign prostatic hypertrophy, of St. John's wort over Prozac to treat depression, and of EDTA chelation therapy over bypass surgery. These therapies range from the more accepted to the more controversial. Yet a third category of therapies may serve as a first line of defense: this category includes a pediatrician's initial choice to treat ear infections with homeopathic remedies over antibiotics[43] and the treatment of allergies and asthma with homeopathic remedies.

It is impossible to forecast in advance exactly what integrative medicine will look like or which combinations of biomedical and complementary and alternative therapies courts and juries will later find acceptable as opposed to negligent. Thus, while courts may regard the displacement of conventional care as a significant factor in the assessment of causative injury, courts still should be required to identify, rather than assume, neglect of the conventional therapy as the actual and proximate cause of the injury. Further, ideally, clinical judgment and legal prudence will dovetail, and the best interest of the patient will not be sacrificed for fear of liability.

Conclusion

Whether incorporating traditional oriental or Ayurvedic medicine, homeopathy, herbal and nutritional care, or another complementary and alternative modality, physicians must assess the risk of malpractice liability if treatment results in a claim of patient injury based on use of complementary and alternative medicine. Courts examining such claims must assess the extent to which application of current malpractice rules inhibit or promote responsible exploration of nonbiomedical therapies in integrative practice.

Currently, the paucity of written legal guidance makes any transition to integrative medicine problematic for physicians, even if supported by satisfactory research and some scientific consensus. The three factors identified in the preceding section of this chapter provide an initial basis for avoiding the imposition of malpractice per se; the process of evoking appropriate questions regarding safe, appropriate, and effective integration is likely to continue to unfold. In this way, evolving legal rules can continue to seek to shield patients from unsafe or ineffective therapies while promoting responsible exploration of complementary and alternative medicine in the interest of patient and public welfare.

CHAPTER 3

The Informed Consent Obligation

Informed consent presents one of the major unresolved areas in the integration of complementary and alternative therapies into the health care system.[1] Legal requirements of informed consent aim to protect the patient against nonconsensual interference with his or her body in medical matters. Informed consent requires the physician to disclose, and ensure that patients (or authorized surrogates) comprehend, all information material to the patient's decision to undergo or reject a specific medical procedure.[2] Inclusion of complementary and alternative medicine in any such requirement is likely to have a significant impact on clinical practice.

This chapter evaluates physicians' legal obligation to disclose the availability of complementary and alternative modalities in clinical practice. In attempting to determine whether and when such an obligation exists—or should exist—this chapter first examines whether disclosure would be (1) consistent with informed consent ideals generally, (2) appropriate for paradigmatically foreign therapies, and (3) of benefit to the physician-patient relationship. This chapter then analyzes cases framing disclosure.

Disclosure and Informed Consent Ideals

To satisfy informed consent, physicians must disclose the nature of the problem, the purpose of the proposed treatment and the probability of its benefits and risks, and the probability of benefits and risks that would be incurred in alternative treatments or by doing nothing.[3] Whether such disclosure must or should encompass complementary and alternative modalities has not yet been addressed in the literature. The question of appropriate disclosure becomes especially troubling where treatments are supported by results of studies published in medical literature but are not generally accepted or adopted by physicians nationwide.

For example, is a surgeon obligated to advise the patient that there are reports that chiropractic care may be more effective and less invasive than surgery for certain cases of lower-back pain?[4] Is a gynecologist obligated to inform patients about the possible effect of acupuncture on reduction of pain medication in dysmenorrhea?[5] Should neurologists afford patients the opportunity of taking ginkgo biloba for improving dementia due to circulation problems[6] and possibly that due to Alzheimer's?[7] To what extent must primary care physicians disclose information about the possible benefits of nutritional therapies, such as treatment of benign prostatic hypertrophy with saw palmetto and other herbal preparations[8] and treatment of depression with St. John's wort?[9] Should they inform patients with irritable bowel syndrome that Chinese herbal formulations may in some cases offer improvement in symptoms?[10] Such questions likely will multiply as studies are conducted with increasing rigor by research centers, including those funded by the National Center for Complementary and Alternative Medicine.[11]

The argument against disclosure of the risks and benefits of such therapies stems from the lack of satisfactory scientific evidence and medical consensus to support regular use of such therapies. Since complementary and alternative treatments normally fall outside conventional medical education and clinical practice, these treatments by definition are not within the therapeutic armamentarium of the conventional physician and therefore are unlikely to be considered or raised. Moreover, the physician's promise to "do no harm" militates against giving the patient false hope based on irresponsible or incomplete information. Prevalent also are concerns about presenting therapies with uncertain benefits and unknown risks, creating false expectations, or diverting patients from needed conventional care to inefficacious or dangerous therapies.[12]

Arguments favoring disclosure of such therapies stem primarily from deep respect for patient autonomy interests.[13] The premise of informed consent—that patients have the right to *all* information material to their medical decision making—arises from the notion of bodily integrity: the patient's "right to determine what shall be done with his [or her] own body."[14] This right arguably transcends majoritarian medical views of certain therapies and should include the right to receive information about nonconventional therapies that are not fully accepted yet are supported by a material and credible body of evidence.[15]

It may be relevant in this regard that medicine historically has expressed opposition or outright hostility toward "irregular" practitioners and nonconventional therapies. It also may be relevant that many of these therapies challenge dominant medical paradigms or methodologies. To demand that such therapies receive general medical acceptance before requiring their inclusion in informed consent disclosure effectively will cut off many patients from access to information about the therapies' risks and benefits. To broaden the disclosure obligation, in contrast, would counter the historical medical parochialism toward complementary and alternative therapies and enhance patient access to the information being filtered through their physicians about such therapies.

Consumer demand has led to the recommendation that physicians routinely ask their patients about use of such therapies.[16] This recommendation has included such therapies as imagery and spiritual healing, which are foreign to conventional paradigms, supported largely by anecdotal reports, and not yet amenable to generally accepted methods of validation.[17] Beyond asking what patients use, the forgoing arguments suggest that physicians should initiate discussion of available evidence regarding various therapies. In this way, the informed consent doctrine can offer a potential bridge to integrative care—an arena in which physicians are obligated to satisfy patient demand for information about complementary and alternative therapies.[18]

Disclosure of Paradigmatically Foreign Therapies

Assuming informed consent disclosure of complementary and alternative medicine becomes appropriate in any given situation, such disclosure may require an evolutionary synthesis in the way physicians discuss the benefits and risks of integrative treatment plans. Among the trademarks of holistic health care are its emphasis on factors outside biochemical, pharmacological, and other scientifically accessible explanations and its reliance on different paradigms concerning health and the disease process.[19] Examples include the manipulation of *chi* in acupuncture and the use of highly diluted homeopathic remedies for constitution and disposition. As noted, informed consent requirements are framed in terms of what a reasonable patient (or, in some jurisdictions, reasonable physician) would find material to a treatment decision. Under conventional scientific methodologies, the therapeutic vagueness of many complementary and alternative therapies makes it difficult to determine precisely what risks and benefits require disclosure. For example, although one can describe a series of physical risks involved in using acupuncture needles (for example, the risk of inserting an unsterile needle) as a practical matter, risks relating to such traditional oriental medicine concepts as altering the flow of *chi* lend themselves less easily to disclosure. Similarly, while homeopaths insist that low dilutions have subtle effects on disease and healing[20] and that it is disadvantageous to take too many remedies or the wrong remedy, it may be difficult to describe the risks of doing so.

More significantly, it is difficult to conceive what kind of disclosure would be appropriate for integrative care, in which homeopathy, acupuncture, and other such modalities are appropriately blended with conventional medical practices, when such a synthetic system of health care has not yet fully emerged. The pharmacological interactions between Western drugs and Chinese or Tibetan herbs, for example, have not been studied—let alone interactions within the paradigm of traditional oriental medicine. While future studies might quantify some risks in Western medical terms, other risks might have to be expressed in terms of Chinese medicine. Similarly, what kind of comprehensible disclosure is material to a patient's decision to accept acupuncture and hypnotherapy to reduce postoperative pain? Should a physician warn patients not to do yogic headstands following open-heart surgery?[21] What risks are foreseeable and describable?

Such questions suggest that informed consent doctrine may not, at first, find an easy adaptation to therapies that rely on concepts foreign to conventional medicine. In this respect, the informed consent issue differs from situations in which physicians either offer a therapy approved by the federal Food and Drug Administration and employ it for an off-label use or engage in clinical innovation using conventional modalities. In these situations, physicians at least have the benefit of existing foundational assumptions about the therapies and about their conventionally accepted uses. Ultimately, integrative health care may require still deeper collaboration between physicians and alternative healers to create comprehensible disclosure, capable of maximizing patient understanding of the therapeutic routes presented yet also of capturing paradigmatically foreign ideas about disease processes and health management.

Disclosure and the Physician-Patient Relationship

Whether the complementary and alternative therapy in question fits within existing medical guidelines or challenges current paradigms, appropriate disclosure of the risks and benefits of such a therapy may serve an additional role beyond satisfying patient autonomy interests: that of improving the physician-patient relationship. Such disclosure ideally would protect physicians by satisfying patient interest in information and by broadening patient choice and would enhance patient confidence in the physician's knowledge and willingness to describe what lies outside such knowledge. Such disclosure also may loosen medical intolerance for therapies outside of orthodoxy, increase medical innovation (or at least patient perception of openness), reduce misunderstanding, and thus lower malpractice risk. Indeed, one court has suggested that adequate informed consent could shield a physician from malpractice liability for providing a complementary and alternative therapy.[22]

Informed consent has received praise for respecting patient autonomy and equalizing the balance of power in the physician-patient relationship. Yet scholars have urged a shift from the authoritarian, formulaic, and inflexible disclosure of informed consent, to a partnership between physician and patient in an atmosphere of conversation and shared exploration.[23] This shift suits complementary and alternative medicine's emphasis on patient responsibility for self-care. Such increased responsibility can enhance shared insights into the therapeutic possibilities—and limits—of procedures in each domain of knowledge.

As suggested in surveys of patient usage of complementary and alternative therapies, many patients are demanding treatments and modalities beyond the training, education, and therapeutic inclination of many primary care physicians. Patients will continue to extend the boundaries of the therapeutic arsenal, while physicians, faithful to good science, will challenge therapies through conventional knowledge. In the process, informed consent can move further from doctrinal rigidity and toward its ideal of dialogue.

Precedent for Disclosure

While no court to date has expressly ruled that a physician must disclose the availability of complementary and alternative medicine alongside conventional medical care, existing cases provide ground for the evolution of legal authority in this area. Typically, courts have required disclosure only of less invasive alternatives within conventional medicine. Within these parameters, courts have shown reluctance to expand the limits of what must be disclosed. For example, in *Thornton v. Annest*, a Washington appellate court held that informed consent did not require the physician to disclose the possibility of an X ray and consultation with a gynecologist as alternatives to removing the patient's fallopian tubes during an exploratory surgery.[24]

Some courts have held nonconventional alternatives to be outside the realm of required disclosure. For example, in *Madsen v. Park Nicollet Medical Center*, the Minnesota Supreme Court held that disclosure of an in-home birth as an alternative to managing pregnancy in the hospital was not required.[25] Similarly, in *Plumber v. State Dept. of Health and Human Resources*, a Louisiana appellate court held that disclosure of cancer treatments alternative to chemotherapy was not required.[26] The court reasoned that in "conventional medical wisdom, the alternative to chemotherapy in this situation would be simply to not undergo chemotherapy."[27] Commentators have criticized such reasoning as being unduly dismissive of the patient's right of bodily self-determination,[28] overly protective of biomedical dominance, and inadequately attentive to patient interests outside a narrow range of orthodox choices.[29]

In *Moore v. Baker*, a patient sued for malpractice based on the physician's failure to disclose the possibility of EDTA chelation therapy as an alleged safer, equally effective alternative to a carotid endarterectomy.[30] The U.S. District Court for the Southern District of Georgia held that the plaintiff failed to show that reasonably prudent physicians generally recognized and accepted the treatment. The U.S. Court of Appeals for the Eleventh Circuit affirmed the ruling, based on a finding that the mainstream medical community did not recognize the claimed alternative in treating coronary blockages.[31] The Eleventh Circuit suggested that it would have decided the case differently had medical education and testimony been more favorable toward the therapy in question.

In *Moore*, the Eleventh Circuit did not delineate exactly what would qualify as sufficient validation of a complementary and alternative modality to justify its required inclusion in informed consent disclosure. One wonders whether one randomized controlled trial would suffice or whether several studies in nontraditional or foreign medical journals would satisfy the requirement. One strategy is to look to the current tests for informed consent: what kind of disclosure would a reasonable patient (or in some jurisdictions, a reasonable physician) find material to a decision to undergo or forgo treatment?

For example, the Ornish program, which, as noted, incorporates yoga, meditation, and lifestyle changes, is being widely adopted by medical centers and reimbursed by insurance companies for the prevention and treatment of cardiac disease.[32] A cardiologist's failure to disclose the possibility of such a treatment approach could conceivably serve as a basis for a malpractice claim when the patient is injured by a conventional therapy that is more invasive or more toxic than such a program. Similarly, some studies have shown that social support could play a meaningful role in recovery from breast cancer and other medical problems.[33] Presumably, this is the kind of information that both a reasonable patient and a reasonable physician would want to see disclosed. Failure to disclose the availability of such therapies (together with potential risks and benefits) could give rise to a malpractice claim based on lack of adequate informed consent—provided that the patient can show causative injury (for example, that the patient would have declined the conventional treatment had he or she received full information about the risks as compared with nonconventional alternatives).

The proposed expansion in informed consent in no way would substitute for the obligation to disclose and discuss all material treatments available through conventional medicine. A thorough discussion of conventional choices would be necessary as usual. Moreover, disclosure of complementary and alternative treatments material to patient decision making would not relieve the physician of liability if the physician induced patient overreliance on the alternative therapy in lieu of necessary conventional care and failed to exercise due care, with the result that the patient suffered injury or died. Further, even jurisdictions accepting an express assumption of risk defense will tend to look toward a full and fair disclosure of risks and benefits by the physician and thus to find liability if such disclosure has been incomplete.

To avoid such legal risk, physicians may be tempted in their informed consent disclosure to heighten warnings regarding particular therapies or concerning their use in lieu of conventional treatment. Such warnings might include, for example, the physician's own beliefs about a particular therapy or course of treatment, or they might emphasize the fact that the therapy challenges conventional scientific models. Presumably, such warnings would reflect available research and change as new information becomes available. Warnings may or may not make sense under prevailing models—for example, the possibility of a "kundalini awakening" or spiritual crisis for patients who are especially sensitive to energy healing may not presently find explanation in contemporary medical and scientific terms.[34]

Whether such heightened warnings make legal and ethical sense in any given situation requires deeper consideration of the balance between autonomy, beneficence, nonmaleficence, and the physician's interest in medical innovation, on one hand, and professional integrity and standards, on the other. While, as noted, some of the boundaries for informed consent disclosure governing complementary and alternative medicine follow the parameters of existing law, others must await more specific unfoldment of integrative care and energy medicine.

Conclusion

Informed consent rules to date have failed to address the medical profession's growing exploration of complementary and alternative medicine. Yet, as specific therapies garner credible levels of scientific validation, physicians' duty to obtain informed consent will evolve. In light of existing malpractice rules, such disclosure has the potential to manifest increased respect for patient autonomy and the physician-patient relationship, without encouraging inappropriate reliance on nonconventional care or the forgoing of appropriate conventional care. Such disclosure thus has the potential to increase clinicians' awareness of possible patient benefit from complementary and alternative medicine approaches and to advance and diversify integrative methods of managing disease and maintaining health.

In sum, although no court yet has articulated a duty to disclose the risks and benefits of complementary and alternative therapies as part of the informed consent obligation, such a duty well may arise as well-designed and well-executed trials furnish sufficient evidence of efficacy such that a reasonable patient or reasonable physician would find the information material to a treatment decision.

CHAPTER 4

Referrals to Complementary and Alternative Medicine Providers

The question of referring patients to complementary and alternative providers raises complex issues. The physician risks liability both by choosing to refer, and, potentially, by failing to refer.[1] Accurate information regarding the nature of these risks will enable the physician to combine sound clinical judgment and good medical practice, on the one hand, with the ability to manage and minimize potential legal exposure, on the other.[2] Further, a thorough understanding of the legal rules governing referrals suggests the ways in which the law, to date, has created rules adverse to integrative care, stymied the patient's interest in access to nonconventional treatments, and forced an untenable balance between the various theories of liability.

Civil Liability

Legal rules governing referrals to providers within biomedicine, such as allied health professionals and specialists, presumably will extend to situations involving referrals to complementary and alternative medicine providers. Ordinarily, a physician bears no malpractice liability merely for referring the patient to a specialist or other health care practitioner. There are several exceptions. First, liability attaches if the decision to refer itself reflects a lack of due care and results in patient injury.[3] This is known as direct liability. Second, liability attaches under a theory of vicarious liability if the treating practitioner is viewed as an agent of the referring physician. In these situations, the practitioner's negligence can be imputed to the referring physician. A third possibility is that the courts will impose joint and several liability on the referring physician and treating practitioner on the theory that the two providers, although acting independently, have inflicted an indivisible injury on the patient.[4] Yet a fourth possibility is that the court will regard the physician's duty as one of continuing care and responsibility, which is not extinguished by referral to the complementary and alternative medicine provider but requires ongoing supervision and oversight.

Direct Liability

Direct liability for referrals results when the selection of the specialist or other treating practitioner itself is negligent.[5] Thus, a physician could face liability for referring the patient to a complementary and alternative medicine provider if the condition is not amenable to the complementary and alternative therapies offered by the designated provider or is aggravated by such therapies, and if the referring physician knows or has reason to know of such facts.

Given the breadth of complementary and alternative medicine fields of practice, a risk management specialist can only speculate about whether direct liability will be incurred in any given situation. Complementary and alternative medicine treatments that are noninvasive and nontoxic, such as aromatherapy and guided imagery, usually do not raise this specter. Not enough information has accumulated regarding various forms of herbal medicine, EDTA chelation therapy, and other such treatments to determine whether it would be considered negligent to refer for such modalities. A court could view the referral as responsible for unnecessary delay or as inducing the patient to forgo necessary conventional treatment and thus as negligent.

Direct liability requires proof of causation: the patient must show that the negligent referral was responsible for the injury.[6] As noted, though, courts could lean toward tracing the injury to the complementary and alternative therapy, holding the physician liable for failing to take due care in making the referral. The prospect of direct liability, whether clear or remote, suggests that physicians should increase their knowledge of the potential benefits and pitfalls of different complementary and alternative therapies and the ways these therapies might interface with existing conventional modalities within their specialty. This will be an ongoing process of investigation and peer discussion. Presently, many clinicians dabbling in "integrative" medicine utilize a smorgasbord of complementary and alternative therapies, for example, a little nutritional adjustment here, some energy healing there, plus a colonic to purge the system and counseling to clean up any underlying emotional stagnation. The caregivers lack defined clinical pathways for combining conventional and complementary and alternative therapies in ways that maximally help their patients. Knowing that nutrition, lifestyle choices, relaxation therapies, and self-care in general generate holistic healthiness is different than being able to target specific combinations of interventions for specific diseases and conditions.

Physicians should not abdicate responsibility to patients, especially those who are critically ill, for finding the right combinations or best way to integrate the different streams of health care practice. This would be clinically irresponsible and potentially disastrous. Ideally, physicians will work closely with the complementary and alternative medical practitioners to whom they refer so that the patient's condition can continue to be monitored through conventional means and so that some sensible road map for "integration" can be constructed. Synergistic as well as adverse interactive effects should be documented. The necessary level of research and dialogue among the biomedical and complementary and alternative medicine professions necessary to achieve such a synthesis, on a worldwide basis, may take years. At the same time, understanding the proper role of intuition and guidance in therapeutic decision making may take time. So, as well, will the paradigmatic philosophical and cultural shifts that are necessary to assimilate the balance between objective and subjective information in the management of health (see chap. 6).

Good clinical practice ideally should equate with good legal protection: the more the referring physician knows about the treating practitioner's methods, the greater is his or her chance of detecting any decisions by that treating practitioner that could trigger a malpractice lawsuit against that practitioner and the consequent imposition of direct liability on the referring physician. Unfortunately, however, increased physician involvement with the treating practitioner also can lead to the conclusion that the two are engaged in "concerted action for a common purpose"—a conclusion that, while potentially beneficial to the patient's well-being, could lead to the imposition of vicarious liability.

Vicarious Liability

Courts have imposed vicarious liability under several scenarios. The first involves a treating practitioner who is an actual agent, employee, or assistant of the physician and thus is answerable to the physician's supervision and control. For example, attending physicians have been held responsible for negligent medical care delivered by residents.[7] Similarly, physicians have been held responsible for the negligence of nurses and operating assistants under their control.[8]

Many of these cases have arisen in the operating room or within the hospital and thus, at first blush, would seem inapplicable to referrals to independent complementary and alternative medicine practitioners. But courts may decide to apply the same principles when analyzing the integration of complementary and alternative medicine services with biomedical services through different kinds of vertical and horizontal arrangements (for example, integrated medicine clinics; HMOs with referral networks to complementary and alternative medicine providers; benefit plans permitting referred-to visits to chiropractors, acupuncturists, and other such providers).[9]

The second situation involves referral to a provider that the referring physician knows or has reason to know is incompetent. Although some courts consider this a case of vicarious liability,[10] referral to a known incompetent also may be considered a variant on direct liability (the referral itself is negligent). The question that arises is, when will courts consider a provider of complementary and alternative medicine to be a known incompetent? Since many of the modalities indicated in the Chantilly Report and elsewhere in the literature exceed the bounds of known science or purport to operate on principles neither validated nor accepted in Western science, the issue of competence again could become a conclusory label justifying the imposition of liability.

The third situation involves concerted action for a common purpose, such as a joint treatment plan.[11] Among other things, courts look to whether the referring physician and treating practitioner are employed jointly and diagnose and treat the case together.[12] Courts may infer joint employment where the two providers diagnose and treat the patient together, reach the same conclusion, consider the patient their joint patient for whose progress each is responsible, and act together to achieve a common therapeutic goal.[13]

Where two providers have acted concurrently but independently, courts have declined to find vicarious liability, unless, in the exercise of ordinary care, one should have observed the other's negligence.[14] Similarly, in a group practice in which providers advise each other of the status of patients under their care, mere consultation and the rendering of an informal opinion, without undertaking to supervise the patient's care, has not rendered the provider vicariously liable.[15] Similarly, sharing an office and agreeing to serve each other's patients for a shared fee also has been held not to generate vicarious liability, in the absence of legal or actual control of the treating physician by the other physician.[16]

Once again, though, the many different ways in which physicians, health care institutions, and insurance organizations are partnering with complementary and alternative medicine providers suggest the possibility that courts will extend vicarious liability under the theory of concerted action. Courts have held that where physicians enter into partnership for practice of medicine, for example, all may be held liable for the negligent actions of one member of the partnership.[17] Physicians employed by the same hospital or health plan or within an integrated health care clinic could find themselves liable under this theory.[18] As one judge has warned: "Recent developments in the health care industry have diffused the chain of medical authority for the sake of containing costs and increasing profits. . . . Unless the Legislature acts in a comprehensive way to address this issue, courts will be forced to re-think traditional notions of duty and standards of care, leading to fundamental doctrinal shifts gauged both to protect victims of medical malpractice and to shield physicians from frivolous malpractice claims."[19] Thus, efforts to create the illusion of clinical and legal separation between such providers, or to characterize the affiliation as one of independent contractors with no liability for each other's negligent acts, may not necessarily succeed.

The prospect of vicarious liability under a theory of concerted action suggests keeping referrals at arm's length and ensuring that any practitioner receiving a referral will be deemed an independent contractor with no supervisory or conceivable employment ties to the referring physician. In practice, as noted, the latter may be difficult, given the many different interlocking structures being created for the delivery of health care services that integrate biomedicine and complementary and alternative medicine. Further, to the extent that the physician establishes clinical distance from the activities of the complementary and alternative medicine provider, such distance creates the possibility of direct liability for making a negligent referral, if the patient is later injured by using or overrelying on the complementary and alternative therapy. Finally, even if physicians are in fact operating within a loose affiliation that does not have a high degree of institutional cohesion, concerted action—the creation of a treatment team involving biomedical and complementary and alternative medicine professionals—may be in the patient's best interest. Because the law in this area is undeveloped, legal protection and good patient care thus may diverge, suggesting a need for professional organizations, institutions, and regulators to consider what further evolution direct and vicarious liability must take to accommodate new patterns of health care practice.

Joint and Several Liability

Some courts have imposed joint and several liability on physicians whose independent negligence caused the patient an allegedly indivisible injury, even though the physicians did not act in concert or concurrently.[20] In joint and several liability, each tortfeasor can be held responsible for all of the damages, regardless of any apportionment of fault (although a plaintiff cannot have a double recovery). Other courts, imposing joint and several liability, have insisted that liability be apportioned according to fault. In any event, patients have been permitted to sue for damages for the entire course of conduct where there was a continuum of medical care related to a single condition.[21] Certainly a plaintiff's attorney's first impulse would be to join all potentially responsible and financially viable defendants.

In *Samuelson v. McMurty*,[22] the plaintiff came to his physician with a boil under his arm; he subsequently developed a fever, inflammation around the boil, and back pain. Thereafter he visited a chiropractor; the next day, he died of pneumonia, which had not been diagnosed by any of his health care providers. The lower court severed the chiropractor as a defendant. The Supreme Court of Tennessee held this to be error, since all potentially responsible persons were to be brought before the jury for an apportionment of fault.

The facts in *Samuelson* may be unusual: the patient had made several emergency room visits; during one such visit, he was discouraged by hospital personnel from seeing a physician. These facts indicate potentially direct negligence by the institution (in the form of negligent emergency room care), if not a more attenuated form of corporate negligence in failing to properly supervise the plaintiff's physician. Doubtless, the physician's failure to make a proper diagnosis was a factor in the court's decision. More troubling, however, is the suggestion that

joint and several liability could arise out of mere visits to the chiropractor. Moreover, although the different doctrinal bases for liability are
distinct, where an injured plaintiff confronts an array of providers—
physicians, specialists, allied health providers, and complementary
and alternative medicine practitioners—involved in a single health
condition, it is tempting to allege negligence up and down the chain of
providers; and state rules of civil procedure, like the federal rules, typically entertain the broadest possible joinder of parties, at least at the
pleading stage.[23]

Continuing Duty

The expression "the exceptions swallow the rule" may be apt in relation to the principle that referral in itself does not result in liability.
Although many courts have attempted to draw lines so as to insulate
referring physicians from liability where appropriate, as noted, remain-
ing uncertainties regarding the meaning of a "known incompetent,"
ambiguous and conflicting application of agency principles, the accel-
erating integration of health care providers and services, and shifting
lines of employment, authority, and responsibility for patient care all
make the prospect of malpractice liability much more fluid and unsta-
ble than providers and institutions might wish.

To add to this uncertainty, yet a fourth potential line of liability
exists in the notion that the referring provider remains "on the hook"
and does not discharge the duty of care toward the patient even though
he or she neither knows nor has reason to know of the specific therapeutic approach the treating provider will take.

In *Joyce v. Boulevard Physical Therapy & Rehabilitation Center*,[24] the
patient alleged that the surgeon's failure to instruct a physical therapist
that a knee immobilizer was not to be removed resulted in a fall in
which the patient suffered further injury. The trial court held that the
surgeon's duty to his patient was "severed" (so to speak) once the surgeon prescribed physical therapy. The appellate court disagreed and
analogized the surgeon's legal relationship with the physical therapist
to that between physician and pharmacist.

The court noted that the physician's duty to a patient in prescribing medicine is "not extinguished once the prescription sheet is
handed to the pharmacist" and that therefore the physician "cannot
. . . escape liability by hiding behind the negligence of a pharmacist."[25]

For example, if the physician fails to prescribe the proper dosage and the pharmacist negligently fills the prescription, the physician remains liable. The court emphasized: "We will not condone the negligent conduct of one as an escape valve for the negligent conduct of the other . . . [nor allow the surgeon to] wash his or her hands of any patient merely by asserting that he had sent his patient to a physical therapist."[26]

Since the court in *Joyce* emphasized the surgeon's independent negligence for failing to provide proper instructions to the physical therapist, the case could be viewed as a variant on liability for "negligent referral." The court, however, expressly declined to characterize the relationship between the surgeon and the physical therapist as one between a general physician and a specialist and thus declined to invoke the general rule governing referrals. Indeed, the court expressly stated that this was *not* a case of referral to another medical doctor; rather, the court noted, the patient remained under the surgeon's care during his physical therapy sessions: "Physical therapists, while highly trained, are not medical doctors; rather they are akin to pharmacists and can treat only that which the doctor orders."[27] Further, as regards causation, the court held that all the plaintiff had to show was that the surgeon's negligence was a "substantial factor" in causing the plaintiff's injury.[28] Finally, the physical therapist's removing the immobilizer from the plaintiff's knee was held not to be an independent intervening cause.[29]

The relationship between referring physician and complementary and alternative medicine provider bears some resemblance to the relationship between surgeon and physical therapist. For example, even though the chiropractor is a licensed, independent provider, one can imagine referral to a chiropractor for services analogous to those provided by the physical therapist. In many cases, the referral will be for services adjunctive to medical care—for example, acupuncture, massage therapy, and nutritional counseling to stimulate vital energy and improve immune response and mood. Yet physicians are likely to be less familiar with the range of modalities offered by complementary and alternative medicine providers than with those offered by the physical therapist. The medical doctor may be at a loss as to what to caution against or prescribe. The admonition to avoid Chinese medicinal herbs or chiropractic, on one hand, or to "go ahead if you think it will help," on the other, both are inadequate and unsatisfying from both clinical and legal standpoints. Again, the lacuna in the law points to the need for clinicians, judges, legislators, and members of other professions to come together toward understanding a new kind of medicine and its profound implications for health care and public policy.

Criminal Liability

Aiding and Abetting

Aiding and abetting the crime of the unlicensed practice of medicine can give rise both to professional discipline and, in serious cases (such as grievous bodily injury to or death of the patient), to criminal liability. In such cases, the physician could be deemed criminally negligent for the injury to the patient. In general, accomplice liability does not require any agreement between the parties.[30] Although there is disagreement about the mental state required, in some jurisdictions it is sufficient that the accomplice either knows that the principal is committing a crime (for example, unlicensed medical practice) or encourages the crime.[31]

Aiding and abetting means furnishing assistance to an individual who is engaged in unauthorized medical practice. Aiding and abetting may occur in two scenarios: (1) when the physician refers the patient to an unlicensed practitioner, such as a lay homeopath or an energy healer, who is deemed to be practicing medicine; and (2) when referral is made to a licensed provider, such as a licensed acupuncturist or chiropractor, and the provider exceeds his or her legally authorized scope of practice.

Referrals

As an example, homeopathic licensure currently exists in only a handful of states, and generally the individual who acquires such licensure must first be a licensed physician. In all other states, the nonphysician homeopath who has no other licensure is practicing illegally. Suppose that the physician refers the patient to a nonlicensed homeopath to help the patient alleviate a chronic condition for which conventional medical treatment has been unsuccessful. An example would be chronic allergies. The homeopath takes the patient's history and assesses the complaint, the patient's constitution, and relevant physical and emotional factors. The homeopath then makes a series of recommendations, including the suggestion that the patient go to the local health food store and purchase a certain homeopathic remedy.

At this point, the homeopath would argue that what is being practiced is not medicine per se but rather a holistic assessment and recommendation that takes into account overall emotional and spiritual health in addition to well-being. The homeopath's skills, tools, and recommendations are different from and outside of what we know as conventional medicine; moreover, the remedies are not prescription drugs but items commonly available in any health food store. As noted, though, courts have interpreted medical practice acts broadly against practices not specifically and independently licensed.[32] Even activities such as offering "celestial water" and "special pillows" to cure stomach pains[33] and supervising severe fasting at a "health sanctuary" have been found to fall within the definition of practicing medicine without a license.[34] Further, under many state statutes, misrepresenting oneself as a physician and falsely using such titles as "doctor" or "M.D." also constitute the unlicensed practice of medicine.[35]

If the lay homeopath is found guilty of practicing medicine without a license—a criminal conviction—then the referring physician potentially has been an accomplice to the crime. The physician's intent, knowledge of the homeopath's practices, and level of involvement in these practices all would be relevant to a determination of liability.

In the case of referral to or co-management of patient care with a licensed provider who exceeds the legally authorized scope of practice, this, too, may constitute aiding and abetting unlicensed medical practice. For example, in advising a cancer patient regarding nutritional therapies to help shrink the tumor, a chiropractor or acupuncturist may be deemed to have crossed the line separating chiropractic or acupuncture diagnosis and treatment from medical diagnosis and treatment. The referring physician then may have aided and abetted unlicensed medical practice by the nonphysician complementary and alternative medicine practitioner.[36]

Legal Risks, Legal Reform

The preceding assessment of risk is not meant to imply that physicians should *never* refer to unlicensed providers. There may be cases in which such referral is appropriate and, indeed, vital to the patient's health or even survival. For instance, there may be times when a movement therapist (for example, a Feldenkrais practitioner) or a hypnotherapist can help unlock areas of distress based on emotional patterns that manifest in certain postures or behavior. Hypnotherapy, for example, has been utilized successfully with dental and other patients who cannot tolerate regular anesthesia. Similarly, many healers, who occupy the boundary between spirituality or religion and the physical or medical, have helped patients who found no relief in conventional medicine. Though rigorous and systematic studies have not been published, and research is in its infancy (see chap. 6), numerous personal experiences are recorded of patients who have visited healers and found their condition so improved that physicians could not explain the change or that later surgery was unnecessary. To describe such experiences as "spontaneous remissions" or "miracles" is simply to acknowledge that their origin exceeds the present known boundaries of medicine and science.

Should a physician withhold a referral where the physician sincerely believes the referral is medically necessary? Should referral generate legal risk simply because the practitioner receiving the referral lacks state licensure and, therefore, while having evidence of some professional training and respect for patient boundaries, faces risk under medical practice acts? Finally, does the question become more complex if the patient has a chronic or terminal condition?

So long as unlicensed providers do not induce overreliance on the unlicensed modality, do not make implied promises of cure or overbroad claims, and do not purport to provide or substitute for biomedical care, arguably they should not be subject to prosecution under medical practice acts. For example, suppose a healer uses therapeutic touch or Reiki to create balance and harmony in the energy field of a cancer patient or to help remove the residue of chemotherapy in the energy field.[37] These activities are not likely to induce a patient to forgo the kind of conventional care provided by an oncologist, are not typically taught in medical school or used by U.S. physicians, and arguably should not fall within medical practice acts as constituting the practice of "medicine." Yet providers and referring medical doctors remain at risk.

While recognizing the arguments within existing legal structures, not only malpractice, informed consent, and medical practice acts but *all* of health care regulation must account for new understandings of the human organism. For example, what positive role can yoga and meditation instructors play not only in helping patients relieve or manage stress and pain but also in bringing patients to a state of greater total health in which disease is affected on the physical level? Similarly, what legal rules take account of the phenomenon that healers, *chi gong* practitioners, and some yoga and meditation teachers call the human energy field or simply the biofield (see chap. 6)?[38] How can healers practice and physicians refer to healers without triggering potential liability under medical licensing statutes?[39]

As a beginning, medical licensing statutes should be amended to reflect a century of experience and an opening to new systems of thought about disease and health. Beyond questions of interpreting specific legal rules and implementing specific legal reforms, larger and more universal questions call for contemplation and discussion.

Conclusion

The astute physician must understand both the sources of liability that apply to the practice of medicine generally and ways in which prosecutors, disciplinary committees, and injured patients might seek to extend current legal rules to integrative practice. Statutes and cases vary by jurisdiction. Further, the issues differ when the physician is directly providing a therapy deemed to fall within complementary and alternative medicine, as opposed to merely referring for such a therapy. Within this maze of rules and structures, legal counsel that is sensitive to patient care can help structure practice so as to minimize legal risk yet preserve the sacredness of the healing enterprise.

CHAPTER 5

Liabilities of Health Care Institutions and Insurers

Hospital-based facilities, freestanding clinics, academic medical centers, nursing homes, insurance companies, and managed care institutions are increasingly seeking ways to integrate complementary and alternative medicine into health care practices in a legally safe and medically appropriate manner. Many hospitals, for example, have integrative medicine centers that coordinate complementary care involving nutritional and herbal therapies, acupuncture, hypnotherapy, and therapeutic touch.[1] Similarly, many insurers are adding visits to acupuncturists, massage therapists, and other complementary and alternative medicine providers as part of standard benefit packages or are experimenting with various means of incorporating such providers and therapies, such as furnishing access to discounted networks or providing reimbursement for dietary supplements.

One of the major issues such institutions face is the risk of malpractice liability for the negligent actions of providers within the institution—or, potentially, within its referral network. The question of liability changes as new cases narrow old doctrines or create new bases for the imposition of liability. Further, few, if any, cases have arisen involving the liability of a health care institution or insurer for delivery of complementary and alternative medicine or referral to a complementary and alternative medicine provider. Thus, the law has not had to determine whether cases involving complementary and alternative medicine should be treated any differently than cases involving negligence by practitioners working within the biomedical model.

Some institutions currently rely on strict credentialing mechanisms, while others insist on such additional layers of quality control as on-site visits to providers within a referral network, strict utilization review, and peer review of any definite plan for treatment involving complementary and alternative medicine. Again, the law is fluid, and as cases arise, institutions are likely to alternate between the Scylla of excessive legal caution and the Charybdis of excessive attention to changing market preferences.

Traditionally, health care institutions have faced direct liability (also known in this context as "corporate negligence") for their own failure to take due care and vicarious liability for the negligent acts of their employees when employees have been found to be acting as agents for the institution. Presumably, like principles will apply to situations involving complementary and alternative medicine, with the possible caveat that in the transition to a more integrated system of health care, some courts might more readily impute negligence to institutions offering therapies that are riskier or less understood.

Direct Liability

Health care institutions have been held directly liable for negligently hiring or failing to take due care in supervising health care professionals. The principle likely will be applied to institutions utilizing complementary and alternative medicine providers or biomedical providers offering complementary and alternative medicine therapies.

The landmark case in direct negligence is *Darling v. Charlston Community Memorial Hospital.*[2] The plaintiff broke his leg in a college football game. He was taken to the hospital emergency room and treated by the physician on call. Shortly after the physician placed the leg in a cast, complications developed. Among other things, the nurses failed to monitor the plaintiff's protruding toes for changes in color, temperature, and movement; and the physician, in the course of cutting the cast, cut the plaintiff's leg. Ultimately, the leg had to be amputated. The Supreme Court of Illinois held that the hospital had a duty to ensure proper care for the patient and that violating this duty was negligent. The court noted at least two possible bases for the imposition of liability. First, the hospital had failed to have a sufficient number of trained nurses capable of recognizing a gangrenous condition and of bringing this condition to the attention of appropriate members of the hospital administration and medical staff so as to secure adequate consultation and rectify the situation. Second, the hospital had failed to require the emergency room physician to seek consultation with or examination by members of the hospital surgical staff skilled enough to assist in treating the patient.

One well can imagine extension of *Darling* to situations in which the provider offers the patient a complementary and alternative medicine therapy that, while not in itself dangerous, can create serious complications if the patient's use or condition is not monitored. For example, it may be appropriate, as an initial matter, to try homeopathic remedies for recurrent ear infections in children, but if the condition becomes chronic or severe, conventional medication becomes appropriate. Thus, the hospital does not necessarily incur liability merely by allowing its hospital staff to use homeopathic remedies, but it may be liable for failure to ensure that conditions are conventionally monitored and treated when necessary.

Subsequent cases have affirmed and elaborated on the principle of corporate negligence articulated in *Darling*. For example, in *Thompson v. The Nason Hospital*,[3] the Pennsylvania Supreme Court held that the hospital has a duty to take reasonable steps to ensure the patient's safety and well-being. This duty includes employing due care in maintaining safe and adequate facilities and equipment, using competent staff and overseeing such staff, and implementing rules and policies to ensure quality care. Violation of any portion of this duty constitutes negligence.

Although courts have imposed such duties on hospitals, the courts recognize that health care institutions are not absolute guarantors or insurers of patient safety.[4] All hospitals are required to do is to take reasonable steps toward quality care. What constitutes "reasonable" or due care, however, is left to the jury. This leaves institutions integrating complementary and alternative medicine at considerable risk.

Safe and Adequate Facilities

The first requirement in *Thompson*, safety and adequacy in facilities and equipment, is more readily understood in some complementary and alternative modalities than others. Some of the mind-body interventions (such as meditation, imagery, hypnosis, and prayer and mental healing) rely on intuition, subtle energies, and dimensions of human experience that are not readily measurable in existing scientific terms.

It is one thing to protect a patient's body from unnecessary exposure to X rays, another to prevent the patient from experiencing "bad *chi*" in the hospital or to inhibit disturbing bioenergy fields during a Reiki treatment. Similarly, ensuring that contrast dyes are safe in a biomedical procedure may be easier than assessing the effects of Chinese herbs whose constituent parts and pharmacological effects on the body may be unknown. Neither the language nor the paradigm of relevant legal rules has caught up to the shifting and multidimensional currency of a system of care in which consciousness and intention are viewed together with biochemical, pharmacological, and physiological perspectives as crucial factors in patient healing.[5]

In part, certain basics can be observed. For example, any equipment used by a complementary and alternative medicine professional should be safe and adequate to the modality being employed. Thus, the chiropractor who uses a machine for X rays should comply with any applicable safety standards, and the techniques any provider uses should be well documented and accepted in the profession, rather than those the profession itself considers dangerous or fringe. Similarly, the herbs or dietary supplements being used or recommended should have no known unduly dangerous side effects or contraindications. Similarly, any instructions given to the patient before, during, and after the session should be reasonably related to treatment. The cleanliness and sterility of acupuncture needles should be ensured. All these aspects of the complementary and alternative treatment come within the purview of the health care institution's supervision to ensure safety and adequacy.

While the need for standards, safety, and adequate facilities clearly comports with notions of due care, again the concern arises that in the quest for patient welfare, regulatory requirements should not be unduly intrusive. Imposing such requirements must be reconciled with the holistic enterprise, in which the patient's total environment becomes part of the healing landscape. Complying with perceived legal requirements thus may require a delicate balance, as the institution will need to monitor quality while protecting the therapeutic encounter and the notion of sacred healing space.

Competent Providers

The second requirement, which relates to competent providers, ideally can be met if the institution selects providers with the highest level of professional training and accreditation legally recognizable and available. Other obvious credentialing concerns should be observed as well:

for example, checking whether the provider comes with a history of malpractice litigation or professional discipline.

From the institution's perspective, credentialing provides comfort, yet professional competency as defined by state licensing boards does not necessarily guarantee sensitivity and care on the part of licensed providers, and lack of licensure similarly may not indicate lack of contribution or skill in realms that have not yet found their way into licensing schemes (for example, shamanic journeying techniques to facilitate psychospiritual healing in the dying process).

Moreover, credentialing mechanisms for complementary and alternative medicine providers will vary by state and raise complications as different modalities are expressly included, excluded, or not mentioned in the licensing statute. For example, in some states, the practice of massage therapy will require licensure, while in others, credentialing may be a matter of local ordinance. In some states, reflexology may come within the purview of massage therapy, requiring reflexologists to obtain a massage license, while in other states, reflexologists lacking a massage therapy license may be permitted to practice. In some states, chiropractors are permitted to offer nutritional care, while other states expressly forbid such practices. In some states, only licensed psychologists may engage in "counseling," whereas other states do not require a psychology license for counseling adjunctive to other services within the provider's scope of practice. Similarly, acupuncturists may be authorized to recommend herbs within traditional oriental medicine but not Western dietary supplements.

The rules governing scope of practice are frequently ambiguous. Licensing statutes may define professional practice with open-ended language (for example, defining chiropractic in terms of alignment of "nerve energy" and using such terms as "acupuncture diagnosis and treatment"). Interpretation will require sensitivity to context and review of any applicable judicial decisions. There may be applicable rules and interpretations by professional boards as well. Finally, institutions will have to develop their own assessment as to whether there is a sufficient level of professional organization—for example, the development of strong internal ethical codes and professional self-regulation—to justify utilizing nonlicensed professionals.

These and other institutional concerns again suggest the need to continually reconsider the parameters of legal authority as integrative practices evolve. For instance, on the one hand, scope-of-practice boundaries create organizing principles for institutions seeking to integrate complementary and alternative medicine; each provider within the network is legally authorized to provide services within a certain scope, or range. On the other hand, these rules restrict providers in ways that may seem artificial or antithetical to addressing the whole person in the pursuit of health. More specifically, scope-of-practice rules carve the body into blocks (for example, nerves, muscles, emotions, physiology), which theoretically are addressed separately by different professions. These limitations reflect the law as it is and not as it should be. The evolution of law will correspond to developments in integrative practice.

Quality Care

The third requirement from *Thompson* asks what kinds of rules and policies should be articulated and implemented to ensure that patients receive quality care in the area of complementary and alternative medicine. Health care institutions thus have a duty to protect the best interest of the patient by ensuring that risk management does not unduly compromise principles of holistic health care practice. As studies accumulate and protocols develop, institutions will have greater experience with the kinds of combinations of therapies—and practitioners—that are most successful in different kinds or phases of patient care.

Ideally, institutions will foster vision, compassion, and innovation in the evolution of medicine toward a more integrative system of care. An overly conservative set of policies may prematurely curtail possible services and deprive patients of needed treatments. This is particularly undesirable when conventional medicine has failed to provide satisfactory results for the patient. Yet an overly liberal policy expands risks of patient injury and malpractice liability.

The problem is complicated by the fact that it may be difficult to predict future responses of a judge or jury when the standards for integrative practice have not yet been developed by the numerous and often competing groups of health care providers. While hospitals, in setting rules for medical staff, have the benefit of existing licensing regulations, accreditation standards, common bylaw provisions, and rules developed by long-standing professional organizations, they face a relative void in applying these to integrative practice, and even such matters as granting staff privileges to chiropractors can provide thorny internal disputes. Many national professional organizations are only beginning to develop significant practice parameters and ethical standards for their own practitioners.

The questions facing health care institutions are national and regional, as well as local, and may require collaborative problem solving. For example, many hospitals are beginning to grapple with the implications of widespread patient use of herbal remedies. Legal risks inhere both in denying patients use of such remedies and in prescribing such remedies. The issue is particularly acute given most physicians' lack of education and training concerning such remedies and their use in other systems of medicine.

Recently, staff members at a nongovernmental regulating and accrediting agency suggested that herbal remedies are being used as therapeutic agents and have pharmacological actions in patients and therefore fall within the broad definition of a medication or drug. Such an opinion creates jurisdiction over such remedies but does not resolve clinical and legal issues when herbal remedies are not used for specific pharmacological effects (for example, certain herbs in Chinese medicine). Further, such a conclusion gives little guidance to the clinician contemplating not only potential adverse-drug interactions but also the range of collaborative possibilities involved in teaming up with complementary and alternative providers and therapies, particularly when the patient already has placed reliance or found relief in such resources. As a starting point, institutions should at least begin to develop guidelines determining the level of credentialing and due diligence required to protect against claims of direct negligence in hiring or utilizing complementary and alternative providers.

Vicarious Liability

Courts have found a variety of scenarios in which to impose vicarious liability. Most of the principles applying vicarious liability to physicians referring to complementary and alternative medicine providers (chap. 4) will apply to institutions utilizing such providers within their walls or possibly referral networks. Thus, if a referring physician employed by the hospital is directly or vicariously liable for a negligent referral to an acupuncturist, the hospital will face liability, because an employer is vicariously liable for the acts of its employee committed within the course and scope of employment.

Agency in vicarious liability may be not only express (that is, directly authorized) but also "apparent" or "ostensible," which occurs when the patient could reasonably infer that the employee has the given authority from the health care institution.[6] An example would be a patient's assumption that his or her oncologist has the authority to recommend or deliver injectable nutritional therapies in lieu of chemotherapy. The patient would argue that he or she reasonably could have expected such a protocol to have been approved by the institution; the institution then would be vicariously liable for any negligence attributed to the oncologist.[7]

While some health care institutions successfully have argued that negligent providers were independent contractors for whose acts vicarious liability does not attach,[8] the likely trend is toward broader imposition of liability as greater integration of services, providers, and financing organizations enhances the possibility of actual or ostensible agency.[9] Thus, it is difficult to imagine that attempts to keep an arm's-length relationship with complementary and alternative medicine providers will succeed in insulating health care institutions from vicarious liability or that a court might treat access to a discounted network of complementary and alternative medicine providers, for example, significantly differently than inclusion of complementary and alternative medicine providers as part of a benefits package.

If health and insurance organizations have not done due diligence in credentialing providers to whom their patients have access, courts more than likely will pierce such veils and allow injured patients to reach the deeper corporate pocket. Again, though, rigorous credentialing efforts alone guarantee neither immunity from malpractice liability nor the satisfaction that patients have received all the benefits of a safe, effective, and appropriate integration of biomedicine with complementary and alternative medicine. Further, credentialing schemes fail to account for the many nonlicensed providers (such as the pastoral counselor) who work in modalities whose therapeutic value may be only partially understood through the concept of the placebo effect.[10]

The law leaves many additional unresolved issues in the area of institutional liability for integration of complementary and alternative medicine services and providers. One area of interest is employer liability for negligent acts of complementary and alternative medicine providers who see patients pursuant to health plans covered by the employer. The Employment Retirement Income Security Act of 1974 (ERISA), the federal statute that regulates employer-sponsored pension plans and fringe benefits, such as health insurance, allows only injunctive and direct contract damages (value of the promised benefits) but provides no remedies for personal injuries or pain and suffering that result from breach of promised benefits.[11]

ERISA preemption of state malpractice law is determined by the interaction of three statutory clauses: (1) ERISA broadly preempts any state law that "relates to" an employer-sponsored health plan;[12] (2) state authority is restored where states regulate the business of insurance (the "savings clause");[13] and (3) states may not deem employers who self-fund rather than purchase insurance benefits to be engaged in the business of insurance (the "deemer clause").[14] The deemer clause exempts self-insured plans from state regulation.[15]

A number of courts have held that direct liability malpractice suits against HMOs that administer employer-funded plans, claiming they made negligent coverage decisions or were negligent in supervising and selecting their physicians, "relate to" employer-sponsored insurance and are therefore preempted.[16] While other courts have found that ERISA does not preempt such claims against HMOs, the Supreme Court has not had the opportunity to rule conclusively on this issue. It remains to be seen whether Congress will mandate specified benefits for employer-sponsored health plans in the area of complementary and alternative medicine.

Conclusion

Developing appropriate institutional protocols relating to complementary and alternative medicine and developing rules and policies governing such protocols will be a creative, visionary, and interdisciplinary enterprise. It may take time to develop nationally uniform rules and policies on which health care institutions can rely to minimize liability exposure and serve patient needs.

While protecting institutions from liability and arguably enhancing patient safety, premature development of national standards could stifle a more organic and intuitive development of integrative care, a care consistent with holistic principles and respect for the patient's individuality. For the present, institutions should at least begin to define the clinical parameters of integrative practice and establish the limits of collaborative care they are willing to explore.

PART 2

Ethical Issues

CHAPTER 6

Energy Healing:
An Emerging Enigma

For thousands of years, shamans, medicine men, and healers from many traditions across the world have healed using spiritual energy flowing through sound, ritual, movement, hands, heart, and thought. Spiritual healing, or the power to heal through human touch, intentionality, and consciousness—also known as energy healing, hands-on healing, and laying on of hands—has ancient sacred roots. In biblical Israel, the *cohanim*, or priests, would bless the multitudes by raising their hands over their shoulders, palms facing the people, thumbs outstretched, fingers arranged to channel a specific kind of healing energy. When Moses wished to invest the seventy elders with his ruling power, he did so by laying his hands on their heads and allowing the *ruach ha-kodesh* (sometimes translated as "Holy Spirit") to pass through his hands. In the New Testament, Jesus is reputed to have transmitted healing energy through touch. Jesus apparently was sensitive to "spiritual energy": when he has walking through the marketplace and a woman brushed by his robe, he said he felt the energy drain out of him. In the Christian tradition, many invoke the anointing of the Holy Spirit for healing.

The notion of a universal spiritual energy that permeates all living things and has healing properties is common to many traditions. In Hinduism, there is the creative energy known as the *Shakti;* in oriental medicine, the energy is known as *chi.* The flow of *chi* is fundamental to acupuncture and traditional oriental medicine, practiced in China, India, Japan, Tibet, and other nations for over five thousand years. Other, similar traditions are found in ancient Egypt *(ankh),* South America *(gana),* Japan *(ki),* Polynesia *(mana),* ancient Greece *(pneuma),* and India *(prana),* and in Native American cultures *(ton, wakan).* Today, the institutionalized counterparts of tribal shamans—physicians, surgeons, nurses, psychotherapists, and other conventional health care providers—practice within well-defined regulatory and professional structures, using technologically sophisticated, scientifically validated therapeutic techniques. Many also incorporate Reiki, Polarity Therapy, therapeutic touch, healing touch, *chi gong,* and other forms of energy healing.

The Chantilly Report used the term "biofield therapeutics" to describe energy healing.[1] The term presupposes the existence of a human energy field (or biofield) that surrounds the human organism and whose vitality affects health.[2] I prefer the term "energy healing" because it is more commonly in use by practitioners. Though practitioners of energy healing rely on different healing techniques, most agree that energy healing involves at least three common steps: (1) centering, (2) scanning (or assessing the human energy field), and (3) directing healing energy to benefit a client.[3]

Some preliminary scientific literature has suggested evidence of[4] and explanatory models for[5] the effect of healers' consciousness and intention to heal on patients through the human biofield.[6] While further research is both necessary and desirable, currently at least fifty thousand health professionals provide about 120 million sessions annually.[7] In addition, many consciously apply "'healing energy' through touch" without naming a particular style, school, or technique.[8]

As the study of energy healing continues to evolve, healers and physicians can engage in a variety of collaborative projects. One such collaboration has involved the attempt to correlate medical diagnostic conclusions with intuitive diagnosis, which involves scanning the human biofield for blockages or congestion. The physician, a Harvard-trained neurosurgeon, reported that the healer was 93 percent accurate in her intuitive scans and diagnoses of patients.[9] Other research could involve the use of healers in wound healing,[10] healing from burns, and reducing postsurgical trauma.[11]

Numerous legal questions arise in connection with energy healing. First, to what extent is the practice of energy healing legal? Second, does credentialing as a minister provide appropriate legal protection? The latter question provides opportunity to reflect on the commonalities and distinctions between energy healing and prayer; the difference, if any, between the "scientific" and "religious" views of healing; the law's placement of energy healing in the category of religious, or "faith," healing; and the interrelationship between law, healing, faith, and medicine. This chapter initially focuses on whether energy healing has an appropriate legal foundation irrespective of issues connected with religious freedom.[12]

Legal Barriers to Energy Healing

One could argue that medicine and energy healing are distinct fields with overlapping professional boundaries. More specifically, medicine involves assessing and treating disease using primarily (but not exclusively) technological methods and procedures based on physiology, biochemistry, and other sciences; energy healing involves scanning the biofield by means of intuitive methods[13] and directing spiritual energy toward the patient, either by laying hands on the patient's body or from a distance.

Until practitioners of a complementary or alternative therapy develop into a politically organized, coherent profession (such as acupuncture, chiropractic, or massage therapy) and receive separate statutory authorization, they are subject to medical practice acts, which, as noted, make the unlicensed practice of medicine a crime.[14] As discussed in chapter 1, any individual who "diagnoses," "treats," or purports to "prevent" or "cure" disease practices "medicine" and is subject to criminal sanction unless he or she is a licensed physician or other provider acting under specific authorization and within the scope of practice. The statute reads "diagnosis," not "medical diagnosis." The statute does not provide, "an assessment of the biofield by an individual trained in therapeutic touch, healing touch, Reiki, or other school of energy healing shall not be considered a 'diagnosis' within the meaning of this medical practice act." These would be useful modifications to medical practice acts, but for the present, courts interpret existing language and do so broadly.

One New York case, decided prior to licensure of acupuncturists, suggests the way courts might interpret such statutes in situations involving energy healers. In *People v. Amber,* the court held that when an acupuncturist determined "the existence of a disharmony brought about by the disequilibrium of Yin and Yang," he had "diagnosed" a patient and thus had practiced "medicine" unlawfully.[15] The court rejected the defendant's argument that Chinese acupuncture differs in "philosophy, practice and technique" from "Western allopathic medicine," and the court held that any "'sizing up' or a comprehending of the physical or mental status of a patient" constituted a "diagnosis" subject to the medical practice act.[16]

The decision suggests the extent to which some courts are willing to view alternative providers as practicing "medicine," even if the practitioner merely is assessing and addressing the patient's condition using so-called subtle energies (such as *chi*). In fact, in many courts' view, the legislative intent behind the medical practice acts supports broad readings that favor providers' conviction. Legislatures passed these statutes to protect the public from unskilled practitioners and unsound treatment or advice, as well as from overreliance on nonmedical practitioners.[17]

Medical practice acts have remained largely intact since enacted and could be enforced even against healers who merely claim to intuitively scan a patient's biofield. Moreover, physicians who collaborate with energy healers conceivably risk disciplinary sanction for "unprofessional conduct" in aiding and abetting an individual who is illegally practicing medicine.[18] Legal models require reexamination to accommodate changing medical models.

Energy Healing as an Independent Profession

As long as medical practice acts remain broadly drafted and interpreted, practitioners of energy healing can run afoul of these statutes. The risk is particularly acute when clients see healers for serious or chronic diseases. Prosecutors could argue that in such cases, conviction is especially appropriate as a means of protecting the public against dangerous and unscrupulous practitioners. Yet the Chantilly Report shows the extent to which energy healing has begun to pervade U.S. health care. Energy healing is practiced by many licensed massage therapists under the guise of massage, by nurses under the guise of nursing, by chiropractors (especially in such forms as network chiropractic)[19] as within chiropractic, by practitioners of traditional oriental medicine as within acupuncture, and even by physicians and surgeons, psychologists, and psychiatrists as within their own professional practices.

A psychiatrist recently sought advice concerning legal and clinical parameters for use of energy healing with psychiatric patients. The psychiatrist believed that patient mood, affect, and stability could be improved by a simple scan of the biofield and removal of stagnation or blockages. Such releases of bioenergy are common to therapeutic touch and *chi gong,* as well as to disciplines involving physical movement, such as various forms of yoga and the martial arts.[20] Indeed, the Chantilly Report notes that energy healing is widely used to affect emotional states.[21]

A major concern in psychology and psychiatry, however, is the use of "touch," even above the surface of the body. Fear of malpractice liability, of professional discipline, and of inappropriate relationships with patients all inhibit experimentation with altering the conventionally accepted boundaries of the therapeutic process.

One of the major gifts (and challenges) presented by energy healing is the way it changes notions of personal space, privacy, and intimacy. Reaching into someone's biofield with intentionality and consciousness is intimate for both sender and receiver. Each can become aware of subtle cues in the other's physical body and of subtle material embedded in the emotional body and at spiritual levels. This concentrated attention also can stimulate altered states of consciousness, a unique experience of spaciousness or Presence, and can unlock doors that unleash powerful emotions in the psyche and soul.[22] This aspect of energy healing is challenging enough to the psychiatric profession, which prides itself on defining and understanding the ego structure as well as being able to handle its diffuse manifestations. Upheaval of these parameters sufficiently stretches psychiatrists' comfort level, without the additional questions of professional sanction and legal liability.

Psychiatric use of energy healing could go even further, however, than the analytical investigation of the meaning of "boundaries" in the context of the biofield. For example, it could explore to what extent disturbing "energies" in the patient's biofield are the same as "entities." To the extent that the phenomenon is an external one—that is, not just internal to the patient's mind but present in the biofield—psychiatry crosses into religion and even exorcism.

Potentially, there is an opportunity here to help heal a split in the West between science and religion. Western culture dismisses the latter as "irrational," "unprovable," or (at worst) "fraudulent." Introducing such activities as "scanning a patient's biofield" could cause difficulties at the level of the state medical board. Curiously, the psychiatrist might be on safer professional ground with a pharmacological intervention, which, on the physical level, is more invasive than a bioenergetic scan, and with "talk therapy," which, at present, has greater documentation of safety and efficacy. Yet consider how integrating intuitive insights and phenomena into psychiatry might profoundly impact the Western social vision.

Western culture has had a long history of persecuting or shutting away people who "see things" and "hear voices." The DSM-IV has numerous sections describing such experiences as pathological; yet in every culture, these clairvoyant, clairaudient, and clairsentient phenomena have been experienced by human beings who have been recognized as great spiritual leaders, initiators of social change, and unconventional thinkers.[23] Saints and psychotics share the encounter with the numinous and/or "paranormal."[24] Central figures in Judaism, Islam, and Christianity—Moses, Mohammed, and Mary—each claimed to hear divine voices, whether emanating from a pillar of fire or from an angel; yet when Joan of Arc claimed to hear divine voices, she was brought to trial and burned as a witch. Today, she might be institutionalized instead.

I do not mean to suggest that all saints are psychotic or that all psychotics are saints. The saint's erratic tendency to get swept up in voices and visions generally lacks the destructive potential of the psychotic's. Most saints seem to function in consensus reality, whereas the psychotic generally cannot tell the difference. Yet both saints and psychotics are absorbed in other realities, and the saint's ability to move into these different realms and return resembles that of the shaman, medicine man, or energy healer operating in the biofield. However, the shaman, like the psychotic, claims that the other reality has validity at least equal to or greater than consensus reality.

Language becomes significant, as connotations change depending on whether one uses such words as *psychic* and *clairaudient* or the more acceptable *intuitive*. Certainly, intuitive diagnosis is one of the skills that practitioners of energy healing can bring to mainstream health care, including to medical students.[25] Intuitive diagnosis potentially could contribute to lowering overall health care costs and to reducing invasive diagnostic procedures, such as exploratory surgery. Practitioners of energy healing have served in operating rooms and might facilitate organ transplantation and other procedures involving biofield considerations.[26]

Once energy healing receives sufficient entrée into the medical and allied health professions and recognition as containing viable diagnostic and therapeutic adjuncts to mainstream health care, it can take its place as a profession, like acupuncture and traditional oriental medicine. Such recognition is not merely a matter of seeking legal protection against overbroad medical practice acts or even massage laws. Practitioners arguably would have a distinctive contribution that does not depend on spinal manipulation, massage, medical care, psychology, or other disciplines; practitioners might affect different stages of health education, prevention, promotion, and recovery. For example, practitioners might meaningfully participate in reduction of acute and chronic pain and of medication and anesthesia, in management of postoperative complications, and in dealing with bereavement and the dying process.[27]

Yet another area of potential contribution—or stimulus and provocation—from practitioners of energy healing involves medical ethics, particularly at the boundaries of birth and death. Whereas Western medicine, and thus bioethics, tends to split science and religion, energy healing regards sentient beings, from animals to patients in a "persistent vegetative state," as having consciousness on some level—irrespective of whether such consciousness can be measured through prevailing medical concepts and instruments. Secular humanism regards attempts to describe consciousness outside of medical measurement as speculative and futile. Biomedicine and medical ethics frequently strive to perpetuate biological existence at all costs; to draw artificial boundaries between life and death; and to assume that animals, pre-embryos (who can be "selectively terminated"), anencephalic infants (who are born without a brain stem and thus presumed to have only a reflexive response to painful stimuli), and other life forms lack consciousness—or do not deserve our respect in the form of freedom from undue or undignified invasion. As illustrated in chapters 10 through 12, perspectives from energy healing can enrich and inform such topics as multifetal pregnancy reduction, decisions regarding termination of life support, and considerations surrounding organ donation.[28]

Credentialing Energy Healers

To make potentially vital, vibrant contributions, the emerging profession of energy healing needs greater coherence, organization, and focus. It must move from metaphysics into medicine, through conciliation with conventional therapists and therapies. Many benefits would accrue from a recognized professional body, providing quality assurance, established disciplinary procedures, a code of ethics, and legal recognition through an appropriate state credentialing process. Yet the dangers of excessive intrusion by the regulatory scheme into the therapeutic encounter are especially noteworthy where the modality in question relies on emotionally and spiritually potentiated transfers of bioenergy between practitioner and patient.

One possible response is to consider a range of less restrictive credentialing alternatives, such as registration and permissive certification of providers. Permissive certification requires a demonstrable level of skill or training to claim a particular occupational title. Uncertified providers may continue to offer services without risking prosecution for "unauthorized practice," provided they do not use the statutorily defined title. A statute certifying practitioners of energy healing, for example, might require a certain level of training or demonstrated level of competence to use a title such as "certified energy healer."[29]

Mandatory registration requires that providers register their name, address, training, and practice with the state; a state agency receives and investigates complaints against those registered and provides appropriate disciplinary measures. Nonregistered providers are prohibited from practicing; however, registration imposes few, if any, requirements relating to training, knowledge, and skill. Under mandatory registration, an energy healer would be required to register with the state, be statutorily prohibited from diagnosis and treatment of disease in the medical sense, and have a minimum level of training and skill. The statute also could, if appropriate, clarify that practitioners of energy healing may provide their services outside clinical settings and need not practice under physician supervision.

One issue that arises is how the law should differentiate healers required to register from those practicing in a religious context as part of a recognized spiritual tradition and practice and who neither wish nor should be required to be part of the registration process.[30] Although the distinction raises the question as to whether or in what contexts it is appropriate to separate energy healing—which potentially *bridges* science and spirituality—from religion, presumably a statutory exemption could be crafted similar to the exemption offered to religious practitioners under medical practice acts. Native American medicine people and Christian faith healers are two categories of healers that probably would fit the exemption or could be specifically designated as exempt.

Some energy healers may object that any form of government control over their practice violates the soul of the profession by subjecting its parameters to bureaucratic leverage. Moreover, the use of legal authority to define professional practice boundaries can lead to internecine warfare, as different groups within professions compete to preserve professional hegemonies (an example would be efforts by some massage therapy associations to force the requirement of a massage therapy license on those who wish to offer energy healing or Feldenkrais). Many legal problems faced by complementary and alternative medicine providers—for example, in the area of professional discipline—stem from overreaching by such providers' own regulatory boards.[31] The tendency of those in power to define professional and legal parameters for the practice of healing and to exclude, suppress, or condemn others outside the narrow paradigm runs through the history of professional health care regulation. There is no reason to believe that abuse of power will be confined to biomedicine.

A further challenge energy healers confront is finding sufficient bridges to create a professional body of knowledge. Much of energy healing depends on subjective scanning or intuitive experience, and healers differ in their perceptual abilities. By attempting to formulate an examining process of their own, practitioners of energy healing will be forced to explore whether there are observable measurements of professional proficiency that can be used to certify their competency. Practitioners arguably have entered the thicket by offering techniques that diagnose and treat illness, by bringing energy healing into nursing and related disciplines, and by proposing explanations for health and disease that defy conventional science (for example, the notion that disease originates in the energy field and precipitates down through into the physical body and the contention that high blood pressure partly is a result of misdirected anger that displaces too much "red energy").[32] Further, practitioners, having synthesized the art of energy healing from bioenergetics, transpersonal psychology, religious healing, and other sources (including, perhaps, personal revelation), now must build bridges to scientific research, medicine, and government. On a practical level, practitioners doubtless will confront numerous legal and ethical questions as they consolidate professional status and enter into arrangements with physicians, chiropractors, acupuncturists, and other professionals or seek to receive third-party reimbursement for their services.

Many of the statutes licensing massage therapists, naturopaths, practitioners of traditional oriental medicine, and other providers make reference to the fact that such practices are, in part, based on the notion of an energy flow that can scarcely be quantified (for example, notions that chiropractors treat "nerve energy," acupuncturists "vital energy").[33] Thus, it does not stretch current law or imagination to conceive of some regulatory framework governing energy healing. The licensing process has given each group of providers not only a good measure of legal acceptance and recognition within the health care system but also concomitant ethical and legal limitations, such as the requirement of providing services within the statutorily authorized scope of authorized practice.[34] Energy healers, like their predecessors, will face the challenge of crafting legal definitions that provide legal protection, capture the essence of their professional intentions, and promote the public good.

The Biofield as a Unifying Concept for Energy Medicine

Energy healing based on the biofield is not only an emerging health care profession deserving regulatory acknowledgment but also a new emerging scientific understanding on which many health care practices are based. Energy healing thus can move health care as a whole into the new era of energy medicine.

Assumptions of Energy Medicine

The biofield serves as a unifying concept for the notion of energy medicine, a collection of health care modalities within complementary and alternative medicine, which are grounded in vitalistic or "subtle" energies, such as the therapeutic transmission of healing intentionality and consciousness. Energy medicine increasingly is becoming an important part of complementary and alternative medicine and a counterpoint to the tendency to narrow access to and practice of such modalities— through research, credentialing, and reimbursement structures—into biomedical structures of thought and care.

The dominant assumption of energy healing is that disease originates in the biofield and precipitates into the physical body. This assumption correlates with the notions in holistic health that much of physical disease stems from emotional and spiritual imbalance, that illness is a message from the body, and that healing involves not only eradicating physiological symptoms and curing disease but also leading the person on an inner journey.

One understanding of the biofield is as a living informational system through which thoughts, emotions, and access to different levels of universal consciousness are transmitted and filtered through human consciousness.[35] Thus, the ideas of yin and yang in traditional oriental medicine, the "innate" in chiropractic, the "spiritual vital essence" in homeopathy, and the *prana* in Ayurvedic medicine all reflect the unifying notion of vital energy embedded in consciousness.[36] Loss of vital energy leads to disease, while conservation and cultivation of such energy leads to deeper access into personal wholeness and human essence.

Such thinking is directly at odds with the reductionistic and mechanistic biomedical model and therefore may, as a result, provide a different lens on the question of integrating biomedical practices and complementary and alternative medicine than presumed in medical circles. Rather than fitting therapies based on biofield phenomena into a medical and regulatory system based on a mechanistic, reductionistic science, perhaps integration requires expanding the parameters of old structures to accommodate a new understanding of the human being, as existing beyond the confines of the body.[37] Rather than viewing energy medicine as a suspect class outside the purview of provable biomedicine,[38] one could view biomedicine as a subset of biofield phenomena. This tantalizing suggestion is hinted at in the work of physicist David Bohm, among others. In fashioning a model remarkably analogous to Kabbalistic and Eastern esoteric thought, Bohm has proposed the concept of successive enfolded realities, of which the physical level is merely the grossest emanation.[39]

Alternatively, biomedical and biofield phenomena may occupy different territories on the map of healing, each influencing the other. Thus, the classifications of the Chantilly Report might be regrouped according to whether they fall within energy medicine, lie outside the field, or straddle both energy medicine and biomedicine.

For example, the second, fifth, and seventh major fields of practice (bioelectromagnetics applications in medicine, pharmacological and biological treatments not yet accepted by mainstream medicine, and treatments focusing on diet and nutrition in the prevention and treatment of chronic disease, respectively) are biomedical therapies in that they operate primarily on biochemical and physiological levels. In contrast, the first major field of practice, mind-body interventions, involves energy medicine (for example, healing by projection of mental energy).[40]

Some of the subfields of practice identified in the Chantilly Report also may be characterized as either biomedical or bioenergetic systems of healing, and the new classification could have major research and social implications. For example, some of the subfields in the third category, alternative systems of medical practice, incorporate energy medicine (consider traditional oriental medicine, Ayurvedic medicine, homeopathic medicine, anthroposophically extended medicine, and Native American medicine, all of which purport to operate on subtle levels of reality that are not readily testable). Other subfields within alternative systems of medical care are based on assumptions in the physical and chemical sciences (for example, home health care, environmental medicine, and aspects of naturopathic medicine).

The sixth major field, herbal medicine, contains subfields that draw on either biomedicine or energy medicine. For instance, some claim that herbal medicine operates solely on pharmacological levels, although the synergistic effect of multiple active ingredients has not yet been fully researched. Others claim the herbs have an energetic effect (stimulating, nurturing, or counteracting certain aspects of the individual's vital energy) and thus operate on the level of the biofield. Many believe, for example, that when they ingest hallucinogenic plants and go into altered states of consciousness as part of a healing ritual, the consciousness of the plant directly reveals its teachings to them. Both the biomedical and bioenergetic may in fact be true, although current scientific method can only test the former.

The fourth field of practice—manual healing—likewise may be viewed as embracing both biomedicine and energy medicine, and in fact, which classification and explanatory model one chooses may depend on the extent to which one wants the field of practice to be acceptable to the biomedical community or outside its purview. For example, both osteopathy and chiropractic had their roots in mesmerism and spiritual healing, focusing on spinal manipulation as a means to help the patient's "innate intelligence" flow more freely. Credentialing battles led to osteopathy largely merging into biomedicine, while chiropractors divided into the more vitalistic "straight" group, who insisted on the original view of subluxation as the origin of disease, and the "mixed" chiropractors, who incorporated biomedical techniques into their therapeutic armamentarium. The many camps within chiropractic today can be viewed as a split between those more inclined toward a bioenergetic or subtle energies approach to healing and those more inclined to give patients chiropractic in a mechanistic and reductionistic fashion, along the medical model. The drive for greater acceptance and inclusion in the professions of law, medicine, and insurance has led many within the profession toward the latter camp, while concerns for doctrinal purity and truth (or possibly sheer rebellion against their longtime rivals and suppressors) has led many toward the former. The same phenomenon has affected other complementary and alternative medicine providers, pitting proponents of biofield theories within the profession against those desiring greater inclusion in current Western, scientific medicine.[41]

Western Prayer and Eastern Wisdom

Within the fields of practice previously discussed, a closer look at Western notions of prayer, traditional oriental medicine, and Tibetan medicine advances the notion of the biofield as a unifying concept among many of the complementary and alternative medicine modalities and a possible template for future developments in medicine.[42]

Prayer as a Biofield Phenomenon

The unifying concept of the biofield may provide some ways to bridge the "objective," neutral worldview of science and the subjective, intuitive world of mystical religion or personal revelation. For example, studies have been conducted to determine prayer's "effectiveness."[43] As it is "proved" through Western scientific method that prayer works, prayer then can become acceptable to biomedicine and can join the group of complementary and alternative medicine modalities that physicians can administer from a safe, detached, neutral, and scientifically verified zone. In this process, the centrality of prayer, its personal meaning, and its resonance on the soul level are neutralized or at least shielded from the purview of sanctity. Prayer is relegated to a subgroup within a systematic catalog of nonconventional medical practices.

If we proceed from the metaphysical to the physical, though, rather than the reverse, prayer takes on an added dimension. If prayer operates, in part, as a nonlocal application of energy healing, then its "efficacy" is simply a manifestation of the real and tangible power of intentionality and consciousness. Perhaps when one prays for a loved one, the prayer transmits some form of vital energy, which is healing, through the prayer's biofield to the biofield of the prayee.[44] Interestingly, the point has been made that prayer seems to affect lower organisms, which presumably are not subject to suggestion and placebo effects.[45]

The Chantilly Report acknowledges that "nonlocal manifestations of consciousness are not limited to prayer" but include "secular laboratory settings as freely as in a church, implying that prayer is only one of the possible avenues for the expression of these events."[46] The report even suggests that "nonlocal mental events . . . may pervade all healing endeavors to some degree, even those that appear overwhelmingly mechanical, such as pharmacological and surgical therapies."[47] The suggestion lends support to the proposition that biomedicine is a subset of energy medicine. It also subverts the notion that complementary and alternative medicine in general, and energy medicine in particular, should be judged by the structures of biomedicine.

Traditional Oriental Medicine as a Biofield Modality

Traditional oriental medicine is making increasing inroads into integrative health care practice. For example, clinicians are beginning to recognize the beneficial effects of acupuncture on such conditions as pain, chemical dependency, and nausea following chemotherapy. There is much debate about whether acupuncture does what it purports to do—stimulate and affect *chi*—or operates on levels known to Western science, such as the anatomical, physiological, or even bioelectromagnetic.[48] It remains to be seen whether acupuncture, among other traditional oriental modalities, will be understood as strictly energetic (potentially ushering in a new paradigm of medicine and science), strictly biochemical (potentially demystifying Chinese medicine or reducing it to a set of Western algorithms) and physiological, or both.

The *chi gong* longevity exercises within traditional oriental medicine likewise challenge biomedicine to investigate whether the health benefits of working with *chi* operate solely on the physiological level or suggest the existence of subtle energies moving through the biofield.[49] Millions of Chinese practice these exercises each day, and the small measure of Western interest in this phenomenon suggests the ethnocentrism of a health care system that has certain requirements before therapies can enter mainstream care.

Above all, therapies within traditional oriental medicine raise medical, ethical, and legal issues when used to simultaneously treat disease and imbalance or spiritual development. While statutes licensing practitioners of traditional oriental medicine differ in language and scope, by and large these statutes authorize the practitioner to engage in diagnosis and treatment within the parameters of traditional oriental medicine.[50] Some statutes refer to "flow and balance of energy."[51] The statutes do not clarify the clinical distinction between a traditional oriental medicine diagnosis and treatment and a medical diagnosis and treatment.

Theoretically, nonmedical complementary and alternative medicine providers, such as traditional oriental medicine providers, do something *other* than diagnose and treat disease, since they otherwise run afoul of medical licensing laws. But given that such therapies are premised on holism, it is difficult to imagine that any given intervention by a complementary and alternative medicine provider will *not*, in some fashion, touch on diagnosis and treatment of the patient's condition. Thus, the distinction between treating disease (legally questionable) and treating imbalance or spiritual development (legally permissible) may be clinically problematic, if not indefensible—a distinction without a difference.

Tibetan Medicine and the Biofield

Tibetan medicine does not purport to treat the biofield; rather, it addresses the roots of suffering, which are viewed as causing human disease. Tibetan medicine derives from the teachings of the Medicine Buddha, the realized, enlightened being who has transcended the sources of suffering in body and mind. Tibetan medicine understands the outer manifestations of illness as including "physical illness, psychological illness, mental illness, planetary and psychic illness, demonic illness, spiritual illness, illness of unvirtuous actions, karmic illness, or illness produced immediately by wrong negative actions, environmental imbalances, and/or wrong nutrition."[52] The tradition also recognizes illnesses "caused by 'negatively motivated' magic such as possession of life force, or control of vital fluids and essence."[53]

The eighty-four thousand teachings of the Buddha are divided into twenty-eight thousand teachings on each of the three humors (wind, bile, and phlegm).[54] Imbalances of the humors represent basic psychological, emotional, and spiritual imbalances in the areas of ignorance/confusion, hatred/aversion, and desire/attraction.[55] At its most fundamental level, therefore, illness from the perspective of Tibetan medicine results from distortions of the mind.[56] This teaching bears some resemblance to the basic assumption in energy medicine that disease ultimately emanates from distortions in mental concepts and belief systems that resonate through the biofield.[57]

In 1998, the Dalai Lama gave the opening address at the First International Congress on Tibetan Medicine in Washington, D.C. The Dalai Lama gently reminded the audience that the *first* international congress on Tibetan medicine was actually held in the eighth century. Tibetan medicine existed as an authentic healing tradition, internationally recognized for its effectiveness, more than a millennium before the U.S. conference. In this present culture and century, though, Tibetan medicine finds itself on the precarious ground between science and religion; its practitioners in the United States lack independent licensure; and its esoteric formulas, secret doctrines, paths of illumination, and streams of truth may or may not mesh with contemporary scientific notions of safety, effectiveness, or even the real. Many Tibetan herbal formulas are so rich and complex—there are no Latin names for many of the ingredients—as to defy any conceivable efforts at Food and Drug Administration approval under prevailing legal rules.[58]

In attempting to find an appropriate venue for the world revitalization of an ancient medical tradition, the Dalai Lama was challenged as to whether Tibetan medicine could be divorced from its religious roots. The very question suggests the bias (and, some would argue, the genius) of Western scientific method—seeking to make the indivisible, divisible; clawing duality from unity; removing something from the realm of paradox and trying to classify it as either one thing or another.

A related question arose as to whether Tibetan medicine would be utilized primarily to treat disease or to treat spiritual development. These questions obviously created a dilemma: if Tibetan medicine is religion, then it may not be acceptable to Western science; if Tibetan medicine must fit Western science to gain acceptance and usage, then our culture is reducing a greater and perhaps ungraspable whole and reconstituting a sacred tradition as a mechanistic series of parts. Either way has implications for licensure or other credentialing mechanisms of Tibetan medicine practitioners. The challenge for Tibetan medicine, like energy medicine, is to retain its integrity, authenticity, and attunement to subtle energies in a medical culture that only accepts what can be proven on *its* terms.

Conclusion

Energy healing and therapies based on the biofield could change the way medical professionals view health care. Such skills as intuitive diagnosis and perspectives from energy healing on psychological and spiritual dimensions of health and the disease process can deeply affect mainstream care. The more controversial insights of energy healing potentially could transform social as well as clinical models of well-being. Such insights also may find common ground with such disciplines as psychology, psychiatry, philosophy, sociology, and religion. They can form bridges between these disciplines, the medical profession, and professions within complementary and alternative medicine that rely on so-called subtle energies, such as *chi.*

The National Center for Complementary and Alternative Medicine at the National Institutes of Health and other government and private research institutions are well poised to investigate such implications. The full clinical, legal, ethical, and social dimensions of these studies await further exploration.

CHAPTER 7

Encountering the Medicine Man

Within the field of alternative systems of medical practice, the Chantilly Report lists the subfield of community-based health care practices. These practices emphasize the following belief: "when one person becomes sick, the whole community is in danger. Therefore, the treatment must address the whole community rather than just the patient."[1] Within its understanding of "community," the Chantilly Report includes "the whole network of existence, the natural world, and the spiritual world."[2] The community-based health practitioner often mediates between the patient and the spirit world, and he or she delivers health care in public, with members of the community present.[3] Practitioners include the medicine man, or shaman, a spiritual healer "distinguished by the practice of *journeying* to nonordinary reality to make contact with the world of spirits, to ask their direction in bringing healing back to people and the community."[4]

At some point, each individual makes a personal journey through the landscape of health. Indeed, it often is the personal journey that brings a legislator, judge, or physician to try to understand complementary and alternative medicine on its own terms and within its own structure. A personal journey may include folk practices, spiritual healing, and traditional and herbal medicine as part of community-based health practices. This chapter describes an encounter with Don Mistral, an indigenous Mexican healer.

About Don Mistral

I learned of Don Mistral through my friend Shanel, who had discovered this eighty-three-year-old man's unusual healing abilities while unable to recover from pneumonia on a trip to Mexico. Through herbal preparations made from various plants, bone-setting, and certain manipulative techniques unknown to Western medicine, Don Mistral reportedly had cured Shanel of bronchial pneumonia.

Don Mistral was a *bruja,* a sorcerer (Shanel claimed to have seen some matches move when Don Mistral pointed at them, although the phenomenon never was corroborated). His persona was humble: he presented himself as a simple, self-taught man who had accumulated some skill in the healing arts. His background was simple. Don Mistral spent several decades studying animal and human anatomy (often through autopsies), figuring out how bones and muscles worked. Over time, he began helping people. Locals preferred him to doctors and hospitals. He had a steady stream of daily visitors; among his visitors were a child with a broken ankle, a woman thrown from a bus, and a visitor from France, seeking relief from abdominal pains. I decided to visit him in Mexico.

"Clinic"

Shanel and I arrived in a lush, tropical, mountainous region by the ocean. Don Mistral's place was hidden behind a green, iron gate, which was sandwiched between modern, air-conditioned condos and a bank. As we turned through the gate and onto the dirt road behind it, a new-born, feral cat darted in front of us. A rooster and his mate responded to the honk of our car horn and moved to allow us to park underneath a tree. As we exited, a mango fell and clanged against the car roof.

Don Mistral greeted us warmly. His smile showed evidence of considerable dental work, but otherwise his face and body were sturdy and strong. He had a full head of salt-and-pepper hair, bright eyes, and large, leathered hands, which hung loosely from his relaxed shoulders.

"I'm sorry I don't speak Spanish," I said, shaking his hand, while Shanel translated.

Don Mistral, immediately putting me at ease, replied that it was not necessary to say much.

He introduced us to his two sons. Immediately they tried to make us welcome: Gabriel began hacking coconuts and inserting straws into them so we could suck out the milk, while Rafael sang a love song. Sisters appeared, and with them came a half-dozen grandchildren, ranging from age six to a newborn who continually cried. To honor the arrival of guests, the six-year-old stood and recited a poem about the apparition of the Virgin of Guadaloupe.

Soon, people began arriving for healing. They parked their bicycles, mopeds, and cars outside the gate, beside the woman selling roadside tamales, and entered cautiously.

The healing room was an outdoor, concrete area beneath an oblong hut made of dried palm leaves. The leaves were woven to make the area waterproof. There were rotting benches and unvarnished wood chairs in bad need of repair. Abundant clumps of bananas hung from the hut's wooden beams, and chickens and roosters ran through freely.

"Eso va con esa" [this one's dating that one], Don Mistral explained, laughing, as various pairs did the equivalent of a two-step across the concrete floor.

There was a sacred feeling about this open-air space that had seen patients for decades. The area felt magically sheltered from the rest of the world, and even though the noise and fumes of buses from the road outside intruded, the dirt, the trees, and the plants exuded peace.

A mother arrived with her three year old, who had just twisted his wrist.

Don Mistral worked the bones while distracting the child with pleasant conversation. His sure hands traced the injury from the wrist up to the shoulder. When finished, he wrapped a cloth bandage around the wrist, telling the child: "I am putting a pretty watch on your arm. When you wake up tomorrow, you'll see this pretty watch and be happy." This stopped the child's tears.

Shanel explained, "If they go to the hospital, the doctors will just put a cast on it; later, the boy will grow up with this injury set in place." She watched Don Mistral work, adding, "When something has just happened, he can work in a matter of minutes."

When Don Mistral finished, the mother, slipping a ten-peso bill into Don Mistral's pocket, said: "Usted es el maestro" [you're a Master (of this knowledge)].

"Yo no sabe nada" [I don't know anything], Don Mistral replied. He pointed to the sky, saying, "El Alto sabe todo" [God (who dwells in the highest) knows everything].

Treatment

After a recent car accident, in which I was a passenger, conventional medicine had said there was nothing to be done: I was discharged from the emergency room only hours after the accident, with an X ray revealing no broken bones, no fractures. The attending physician did not alert me to the residual stiffness that would remain in my neck after the accident, nor did he suggest adjunctive forms of health care that might provide some further relief. There was also a growing pit in my stomach—some dread, perhaps leftover trauma; it seemed that sometimes food went in and accumulated like compost.

Now Don Mistral showed me a plant. "Good for digestion," Shanel translated. "I boil it up and you drink it before each meal."

Somewhere in the back of my mind a thought registered about the ongoing debates across the globe surrounding access to herbs, dietary supplements, and other medicinal substances, about the controversies surrounding Food and Drug Administration approval of such substances and related health claims. The FDA never approved this herb and most likely had never heard of the plant (Shanel did not even recognize the Spanish name), and any physician would question simply boiling something off the road and putting it in the body. Yet, intuitively, I felt Don Mistral was a man who knew what I needed, who could help my body find the healing it needed.

The purple color that emanated from this boiled green plant was unexpected. But I liked the unusual taste.

After I drank, Don Mistral hoisted me up on his back, to oxygenate the troubled area and "loosen things up." This was done while I stood on the ground and he held himself on a flat rock. He then invited me into the private area—a run-down, two-room building that was musty and filled with dust. A chicken was concentrating in the corner, laying her eggs. Modern sanitation was not observed, and at first, I was shocked; yet the setting addressed Don Mistral's concerns for privacy and comfort. Don Mistral laid some mats down on the floor and invited me to recline.

He began kneading all the way from the solar plexus to the bladder. His hands made quick, pushing strokes. From time to time, his hands worked a particular point—he seemed to know each place where something was stuck. Other times, he was sensing heat above my body, in the energy bodies. His hands felt sure, masterful, firm. He spoke rapidly as he worked.

Shanel translated: "He says you've been taking herbs for several weeks." This was true. "But more is needed to loosen the blockage."

Don Mistral continued working as I made grunting sounds each time he pushed.

"If left untreated, he says, this can be dangerous. But if he moves it out all at once, the treatment will be too strong."

I turned over on my stomach; Don Mistral kneaded the kidney area with his elbows. He pushed several times to adjust my upper back. He addressed specific organs. Then, he asked me to rise, slowly. He asked me how I felt, and I said, "Fine." He took me outside the healing room, to the water faucet where he often cleaned freshly caught fish from the ocean. He slapped my abdomen a half-dozen times with cold water, to improve circulation and increase *fuerze*, "strength" or "force." He explained that the "force" to continue comes from God, that many people are overtaken with malady and cannot continue their tasks on earth, but that I was in good care. He took a leaf from one of his plants—a large, triangular leaf—and stuck it on my abdomen. Then he secured it with a cloth bandage, which he wrapped firmly around my hips.

"Do I look like Adam?" I joked.

Shanel translated as Don Mistral said, "The bandage will give you support today; the leaf helps calm and soothe the digestive system."

I sat down to integrate the healing. I was sitting under a mango tree, in the chair Don Mistral used for meditation and prayer. As I sat, I melted into a slightly altered state of consciousness. I felt the soothing energy from the leaf radiate into my organs. As I closed my eyes, words came. The herb was communicating with me: "I will be a friend to you. My spirit will return to America and assist you, and even though my physical body remains here, I will heal."

As I continued sitting, feeling quiet inside, my mind began asking why I had come, what I had expected to receive. Intuitively, the answers came from within. It was as if a wiser part of myself was addressing the mind. Words formed: "The journey is completing something on a soul level. Your initiation includes an indigenous healer putting his hands on your physical body in the digestive area. This is grounding. You have been a scholar, a writer, a lawyer; you have learned so much about air, water, and fire; now, learn from a man of earth."

Conclusion

As I prepared to leave Don Mistral's compound and return to the United States, I began to wonder whether Don Mistral minded living behind his gate. Around him was this sprawling city; many decades earlier, he had been one of its founders. Recently, he had been offered two million dollars for his land so someone could build a hotel. He had summarily refused, saying, "Soy le suficientemente rico" [I'm rich enough].

An objective observer would have seen poverty and squalor there, several families living on a small plot of dirt, with tiny, concrete homes, bare floors, makeshift plumbing (a toilet that could not handle toilet paper—you had to throw the paper in the trash basket), rudimentary appliances (an aging refrigerator, a gas stove, no air conditioning), some naked bulbs for lighting, and a frequent smell of rotting mangoes and chicken excrement. Yet among the flies, sitting in a maroon leather chair, which was torn in dozens of places, Don Mistral exuded the majesty and confidence of a king.

And Don Mistral never faced malpractice liability or had to pay for liability insurance, never had to satisfy managed care organizations or medical staff bylaws.[5] Those whom he had helped remained grateful; no one was turned away for lack of money or insurance. How can Don Mistral's work be evaluated, and on whose terms?[6]

The Chantilly Report states that research on such practices as those of indigenous healers should be both "culturally sensitive and scientifically grounded," with cultural sensitivity requiring that "issues of conflicts between basic paradigms, worldviews, or belief systems are recognized and openly dealt with when a dominant culture tries to study, influence, or assist a different culture or subculture."[7] William James, quoting the Bible, has argued that in evaluating such explorations, one's perspective should be pragmatic: " 'by their fruits you shall know them.' "[8]

Don Mistral treated patients on a dirt mat, sharing a healing room with some streetwise chickens. In this way, he pursued the wisdom of the body, of plants, of nature. Yet, the "maestro" also had a disclaimer— "Yo no sabe nada; El Alto sabe todo." Such a disclaimer may provide the note of humanity—and humility—to approach the subject of integrative care and energy medicine, as the blending of modern technologies and ancient wisdom creates more and more glimpses of a truth involving the total human being.

Postscript

Whether one in three Americans use complementary and alternative medicine or two in three or some other statistic, the individuals who

become passionately involved in pursuing integration of these different systems of care frequently have some life-changing experience,
either firsthand or through family members, that makes them comfortable with entrusting their bodies to streams of healing traditions outside the narrow confines of present scientific understanding. For others, use of "traditional" medicine, including community-based
practices, is a way of life.

While Don Mistral lives in Mexico and therefore is not subject to
the jurisdiction of U.S. courts for treatments delivered abroad, he is
emblematic of the shaman, *curanderismo*, medicine man, or traditional
healer, which account for a large percentage of U.S. health care, particularly among Native American, Hispanic American, and other minority U.S. populations. The Chantilly Report notes that such healers "are
specialists of symbology who have a good deal in common with priests
and psychotherapists" and who emphasize "naturalistic, personalistic,
or energetic explanatory models."[9] The report further maintains that
community-based practices (such as seeing the indigenous healer) are
prevalent throughout the United States, "although many people would
not consider that they were participating in such a system when they
attend a healing service at a local church or go to a meeting of Weight
Watchers" (or Alcoholics Anonymous or other such groups).[10]

The interest in community-based practices for health care and
healing reveals the interplay between biomedicine and care based on
beliefs, attitudes, values, and spirituality. The biofield grouping, broad
enough to encompass such therapies as acupuncture and homeopathy,
embraces community-based practices that touch on shamanism, "journeying," and interaction with the spirit world, as, for example, when
the plant "spoke" to me after I was treated by Don Mistral; the connection I had made with the plant was more than pharmacological.

When turning from the spirit world to the spirit of law, several
issues arise in connection with the indigenous healer and other
shamans. One is the role of licensure and accreditation: the rigorous
credentialing requirements imposed on various complementary and
alternative medicine practitioners are absent when it comes to community-based practices. Don Mistral and his U.S. counterparts are not
expected to take a multiple-choice exam and satisfy a regulatory board
of their competence in order to practice.

As noted in chapter 6, current medical practice acts contain exemptions for prayer and mental healing offered in the context of an established religion. Yet it is not clear that the shaman's work would be con-

sidered practice within "the religious tenets of any church."[11] Even if it would be, such constructs, while perhaps appropriate to "shape-shifting, voodoo, or animal sacrifice," are inappropriate if the shaman's work purports not only to operate on spiritual levels but also to affect the patient's physiological processes.[12] Arguably, the therapeutic significance of shamanistic practices will be even more fully honored when such practices are appropriately integrated in critical care units, in operating rooms, in hospice care, and elsewhere within the biomedical world.

Another concern is the interplay between the First Amendment and community-based practices. The First Amendment prohibits Congress from making any law "prohibiting the free exercise" of "religion." The U.S. Supreme Court has had difficulty defining what constitutes "religion" and has resisted any underinclusive definition. In *Thomas v. Review Board*, the Court held that Thomas, a Jehovah's Witness, could not be denied benefits on the basis that he refused to work in a factory that made components for army tanks.[13] The Court refused to question Thomas's understanding of his religion, stating that courts "are not arbiters of scriptural interpretation."[14]

The Court similarly refused to evaluate the truth of a religious doctrine in deciding whether the doctrine would receive First Amendment protection. In *United States v. Ballard*, members of a religious group called the "I Am" movement were prosecuted under mail-fraud statutes for making assertions, which they allegedly knew to be false, that they were divine messengers of healing.[15] The Court held that whether the assertions were true or false could not be put to the jury, stating: "Heresy trials are foreign to our Constitution. Men may believe what they cannot prove. They may not be put to the proof of their religious doctrines or beliefs."[16]

In its struggle to define or not define religion, the Court has recognized the breadth of individual conceptions of religion, noting that many religions "do not teach what would generally be considered a belief in the existence of God," including "Buddhism, Taosim, Ethical Culture, Secular Humanism."[17] In striking down a state requirement that public officials swear their belief in God, the Court stated that government may not favor "those religions based on a belief in the existence of God as against those religions founded on different beliefs."[18]

In *United States v. Seeger*, the Court analyzed a federal statute exempting from the draft conscientious objectors whose objections were based on "religious training and belief."[19] Seeger was an agnostic who opposed war based on a "belief in and devotion to goodness and virtue for their own sakes, and a religious faith in a purely ethical creed."[20] The Court gave a broad definition of religion, sufficient to include a "sincere and meaningful belief which occupies in the life of its possessor a place parallel to that filled by the God of those admittedly qualifying for the exemption."[21]

Turning to an Establishment Clause case, the Supreme Court held in *Wallace v. Jaffree* that an Alabama statute authorizing a moment of silence in public schools for "meditation or voluntary prayer" violated the "wall of separation" between church and state, since it had the purpose and effect of favoring prayer.[22] The Court was particularly troubled that the Alabama statute had been amended, from authorizing only a moment of silence for meditation, to add the words "or voluntary prayer," since the addition suggested a legislative decision to return voluntary prayer to the public schools.

One wonders whether the three steps in energy healing—(1) centering, (2) scanning (or assessing the human energy field), and (3) directing healing energy to benefit a client—would be considered religious or not. If the biofield is an indispensable part of the legacy of being human, then its form, nature, and use should be taught in secondary schools; one should not have to wait for the hospital bed to learn about Reiki, Polarity Therapy, and other such modalities. Similarly, if shamanistic practices, which include guided imagery, mental journeys to different regions of psyche and spirit, encounters with different forms of consciousness (including those of plants and nature), and other biofield activities within the medicine man's ken, are viable means of health prevention and promotion, such practices should be accessible to public school students and others, without being placed in the category of Bible study, posting of the Ten Commandments on school walls, and other such patently "religious" activities.[23]

The Supreme Court's struggles with the definition of religion resemble the difficulties encountered in the Chantilly Report in distinguishing prayer from nonlocal mental healing and from energy healing.[24] The shaman's therapeutic devices in any given context may or may not raise First Amendment claims,[25] but they do trigger the discussion of what constitutes religion.[26] This discussion, in turn, raises the question of whether old dichotomies—such as the distinction between religion and medicine, between subjective belief structures and "objectively" validated truth, between the realm of the mind/emotion/spirit/biofield and the realm of mechanistic reality—continue to have enduring significance and validity.

CHAPTER 8

Sex, Scandal, and Spirituality

During debates surrounding the enactment of a federal law governing health insurance portability, complementary and alternative medicine providers expressed concern about language that made it a federal crime to engage in health care fraud. Congress then included language in an accompanying report to clarify that alternative medicine would not, per se, be equated with health care fraud.[1]

Fraud has been a pervasive concern in health care regulation. On the state level, the common-law tort of fraud, which pervades state law actions for fraud, requires not only deception of a consumer or patient but also a mental state of intent to deceive.[2] Thus, theoretically, providers who in good faith offer therapies resulting in less efficacious results than either provider or patient would wish may be liable for other claims but not for common-law fraud.

A recent federal court decision, applying Massachusetts law,[3] sheds light on the way state law claims for health care fraud may affect complementary and alternative medicine providers who offer holistic health care services within a psychospiritual framework. Like the mental health professional or pastoral counselor, the spiritual healer crosses the boundary between mind and body, between spiritual development and physical health, between legally permissible activities affecting the cultivation and expression of human essence, on the one hand, and legally impermissible activities constituting the practice of "medicine," on the other.

The spiritual healer's power has potentially salutary as well as dangerous aspects. The healer's ability to connect with the patient at deep emotional and spiritual levels shares ground with the placebo effect, which is defined as the power of the physician-patient relationship to stimulate healing irrespective of any pharmacological power in the drug. Thus, a healer's violation of the power entrusted can become especially toxic. Spiritual healers, like physicians, are fiduciaries; their own development and level of evolution are part of the healing; and their behavior may play a role in health and wellness as important as the physician's conduct and expectations of the patient's response to treatment. The spiritual healer who has exceeded the boundaries of ethical behavior further provides an archetype or example for behavior that law and biomedicine seek to avoid and have traditionally ascribed to (or projected on) their shadow cousins in complementary and alternative medicine.

The case of *Dushkin v. Desai*[4] involved fourteen former "disciples" and residents of the Kripalu Ashram in Lenox, Massachusetts, who sued their "self-proclaimed yoga guru" Amrit Desai. While this chapter makes no judgment or conclusion regarding the merits of their claims, it highlights aspects of the court's opinion concerning ashram life and the judge's determination to give little legal weight to ashram members' disillusionment with their former spiritual teacher. The chapter also highlights the extent to which disillusionment with spiritual leaders, teachings, and practices touching on the broad field of health can, if insufficiently attended, leave providers open to legal action.

The Allegations

The fourteen plaintiffs in *Dushkin* brought suit in the United States District Court for the District of Massachusetts, seeking damages for emotional distress, mental anguish, and other losses when Desai allegedly was exposed as a fraud. They alleged that Desai, as "resident guru," professed celibacy and "commitment to a non-material, physically and financially simple lifestyle." Desai conducted "life spiritual leadership, and health and educational services."

According to the plaintiffs, Desai cultivated an "intense emotional dependence" in his followers; his photograph and video image were displayed throughout public areas, and he offered books and tapes for sale as part of his ministry. Allegedly, Desai urged followers to donate all their possessions to the ashram and thus received hundreds of thousands of dollars in payments and benefits.

But according to the plaintiffs, Desai was a false guru or fraud: he did not live up to his teachings and in fact manipulated followers for his own profit. Further, the plaintiffs alleged that Desai engaged in illicit and abusive sexual liaisons with various female disciples in the community. Desai ultimately broadcast a public apology for his behavior and then moved to Florida. Neither action, however, protected him from forthcoming litigation.

The plaintiffs brought five claims: (1) intentional infliction of emotional distress, (2) breach of fiduciary duty, (3) breach of contract, (4) fraud and misrepresentation, and (5) unfair or deceptive trade practices in violation of Massachusetts law. Desai moved to dismiss the complaint.

Intentional Infliction of Emotional Distress

First, the court addressed the claim that the plaintiffs suffered emotional distress by virtue of Desai's representing himself as an authentic guru while lying about his celibacy and engaging in clandestine and abusive sexual relationships. The court noted that to succeed in such a claim under Massachusetts law, plaintiffs must show, among other things, that the conduct alleged is "extreme and outrageous, beyond all bounds of decency and utterly intolerable in a civilized community." The court noted that "promiscuity and brazen lies about one's chastity" may not necessarily amount to "extreme and outrageous conduct" in a particular setting.

The plaintiffs, in emphasizing Desai's spiritual influence over the group, compared Desai's alleged behavior with that of a therapist who has sexual intercourse with a patient. In assessing this aspect of the claim, however, the court observed that the plaintiffs were not themselves victims of Desai's alleged sexual encounters; rather, their claims stemmed from the shock and disillusionment from seeing their leader fall from grace. This shock and disillusionment, according to the court, was once-removed from the conduct and thus insufficient to sustain the emotional distress claim.

Breach of Fiduciary Duty

The plaintiffs next alleged that Desai tortiously breached the faith, confidence, and trust reposed in him by virtue of his position; however, they cited no Massachusetts case establishing a fiduciary duty arising from a relationship of spiritual guidance. Thus, the court declined to find such a duty. The court further noted that although some jurisdictions have recognized such a duty (for example, where parishioners had been sexually violated by members of the clergy), the court would decline to "blaze new and unprecedented jurisprudential trails" and expand existing Massachusetts law in this case.

Breach of Contract

The third claim alleged that the ashram contracted with Desai for certain services and that the plaintiffs were deprived of benefits as third-party beneficiaries of those services. The court noted that to succeed in this claim, the plaintiffs would have to show that they were the intended (as opposed to incidental) beneficiaries of a contract between Desai and the ashram.

Even if they could show that they were the intended beneficiaries of such a contract, however, the court stated that the plaintiffs' "disappointment" with Desai's behavior did not amount to a cognizable claim for breach of contract. The court noted further that no contractual provision specifically required Desai to maintain celibacy or refrain from any particular behavior in his role as spiritual head. Therefore, the contract claim could not possibly succeed.

Fraud and Misrepresentation

The plaintiffs also alleged that Desai knowingly misrepresented his celibacy, honesty, and status as an authentic guru and that they detrimentally relied on these misrepresentations, devoting many years and savings to the ashram. The plaintiffs further alleged that Desai lived off their almost free labor and monetary contributions.

The court noted that at this stage of the litigation, it need not inquire into whether Desai actually intended to deceive the plaintiffs. The court further stated that it could "readily infer" from the plaintiffs' allegations that Desai had made false representations to retain the plaintiffs' devotion and labor. Accepting the plaintiffs' allegations as true, therefore, the court held that the fraud and misrepresentation claim could not be dismissed.

Unfair or Deceptive Trade Practices

Finally, the plaintiffs alleged that Desai knowingly deceived them in a commercial or business context. The court stated that although at first blush, the "guru/disciple relationship" appears "so far from the world of business" as to fall outside the statute, the allegation that Desai used his "public image as an authentic guru" to attract residents to the ashram in order to profit financially sufficed for purposes of surviving Desai's motion to dismiss.

Further, the court found that Desai's teachings and counseling constituted commercial services within the Massachusetts statute. The court looked to Desai's twenty-year relationship with the plaintiffs as demonstrating that this was "more than just a personal hobby," particularly since Desai allegedly was motivated, at least in part, by profit. Thus, the court held that the unfair or deceptive practices claim could be sustained.

Implications

To summarize the disposition, the court granted Desai's motion to dismiss the first three claims but denied his motion with respect to the fourth and fifth claims. Thus, the court's decision allowed the claims for fraud and misrepresentation and for unfair and deceptive trade practices to continue to the next phase of litigation (discovery).

The court accepts as true the allegations of the complaint for purposes of deciding a motion to dismiss the complaint. In other words, the court does not decide what is true and what is false; it simply decides whether the plaintiffs, if they proved the facts alleged, would have a legal claim. Thus, the court's disposition does not establish whether Desai did, in fact, do any of the things alleged in the complaint. Indeed, the court noted that it remains to be seen "whether plaintiffs were victims of their own unreflective yearning, or of the deliberate manipulations of a clever swindler." The court indicated doubt, for example, that claims for damages flowing from such matters as "disillusionment," "dislocation," and "bewildering and persistent turmoil" would succeed.

The claims are representative of theories of liability that could conceivably be applied against a variety of health providers engaged in activities similar to Desai's—for example, spiritual and life counseling and health and educational services within a broader spiritual context. While providers might not be held by their patients to the same kind of expectations projected onto Desai (for example, strict celibacy and complete aversion to monetary attachment), such claims as intentional infliction of emotional distress, breach of fiduciary duty, and fraud and misrepresentation could be brought when patients similarly experience disappointment, deflation, or even betrayal following results of some forms of complementary care that are lower than anticipated or desired.

Patients could allege, for example, that the provider intentionally represented being able to do more for the patient than was possible or that the provider breached a fiduciary duty by acting in ways contrary to therapeutic ideals presented in the healing relationship. Similarly, patients could allege that the provider engaged in deception, misrepresentation, or breach of promise in using an esoteric, unconventional modality (such as bioenergetics or energy healing) to address a chronic or terminal physiological condition.

Particularly when caregivers are magnetic or charismatic, brimming with spiritual insight or spiritual energy, or able to cross into therapies beyond the boundaries of conventional science (for example, using certain hands-on or shamanistic therapies), providers may be open to inflated expectations and demands, positive and negative projections (transference), and "unreflective yearning" by patients, leading to later legal imbroglio. Fantasies, longings, and idealizations are a natural outgrowth of matching a vulnerable patient who needs care with a powerful healer offering spiritual strength and access to higher dimensions of consciousness and realization.

Since facts alleged in a complaint are taken as true for purposes of a motion to dismiss, defendant providers may find it difficult to extricate themselves from claims prior to extensive discovery. Even then, summary judgment cannot be granted if there are genuine, disputed issues of material fact requiring jury determination.

The very fact that legal claims plagued Desai following his unsuccessful bid for lifelong status as a guru suggests that providers should exercise caution in making claims or therapeutic promises, ensure that clear documentation records therapeutic protocols and recommendations, and have conversations with patients that not only meet informed consent but also ensure that patients have realistic ideas about the respective roles of provider and patient in the healing process. Further, while encouraging a positive attitude and visualizations that promote health, providers should act to curb patient fantasies about providers' access to extraordinary realms, powers, and sources of information that exceed patients' grasp. In other words, providers should empower patients, not themselves.

The court in *Dushkin* repeatedly refers to the intimate role Desai played in the plaintiffs' spiritual and corporeal lives. One wonders whether Desai would have been as vulnerable to these claims had his influence and advice been more limited, or his personal boundaries clearer, than those the plaintiffs represented. One also wonders about the role financial lures played in the tragedy. One wonders whether Desai, as a model or archetype of the healer/shaman, could have left less room for the plaintiffs to see him as a demigod or a potential bridge to "the Source" on one day and as a fallen master or even a con artist the next.

On a different note, the opinion describes the potential responsibilities of individuals seeking Desai's expertise. While the notion of medical paternalism expresses courts' traditional concern for protecting patients from their own ill-advised choices, this court returns responsibility for such choices to the patients themselves. Among other things, the opinion expresses one court's reluctance to permit mere disappointment with a spiritual leader to suffice as a basis for legal claims predicated on emotional distress, fiduciary duty, and contract. The court's opinion also expresses some reluctance to entertain the fraud and unfair practices claims. Certainly, the court has something to say about the way clients or devotees of Desai hoisted themselves on the petard of their own expectations, demands, and unconscious projections.

Conclusion

Although couched in legal language, the *Dushkin* opinion ultimately is about something more than immediate legal rules. It concerns a higher law, also known as dharma—a relationship between healer/spiritual leader and followers.[5] The Desai case is a moral tale on many levels.[6]

As noted, the court's opinion is somewhat balanced in its implicit critique of both the would-be guru and his followers. According to the court's analysis, neither guru nor disciple, doctor nor patient, healer nor client is totally responsible for the debacle. Perhaps it is fair to suggest that Desai may have promised too much and that his followers may have expected too much. The paradox of the exquisitely refined human being who is said to be established in God-consciousness is that the being possessed of such consciousness is simultaneously divine *and* human.

Ultimately, then, any healer or spiritual leader owns and offers his or her own humanity as well as divinity. One can only offer what one has attained. It is the sobering task of legal rules to mediate and harmonize when conflicts arise. Law thus streams, when leaders and followers move out of balance, and into the land of dreamy dreams.

CHAPTER 9

Beliefs, Values, and Dietary Supplements Regulation

Herbal medicine is perhaps the fastest growing category of complementary and alternative medicine. Most patients do not tell their physicians about use of dietary supplements, and relatively few physicians presently inquire about such use or are versed in herbal medicine. A few herbs have become more popular and/or proved more effective than their synthetic counterparts, while others have raised concerns about potential adverse herb-drug interactions.

Regulation of dietary supplements presents perhaps the greatest area of regulatory controversy in complementary and alternative medicine regulation today. Ongoing efforts by the Food and Drug Administration to increase enforcement efforts have generated intense debates among lawmakers, consumers, providers, and supplement manufacturers.

In addition, the complementary and alternative medicine practices involving dietary supplements illustrate the clash in paradigms alluded to earlier: while herbal medicine is being widely researched and efforts are being made to understand herbs from a strictly pharmacological perspective, many complementary and alternative medicine practitioners regard herbs as sacred, having properties beyond the pharmacological. In Native American traditions, for example, the relationship between humans and herbs involves profound relationship exchange; in traditional oriental medicine, herbs are chosen to influence *chi*, the Chinese notion of vital energy, rather than produce specific pharmacological responses. Even researchers recognize that many herbs, particularly in Chinese and Tibetan medicine, have multiple active ingredients that may have a synergistic effect on the body. And some herbal formulas have effects that are not understood—for example, research has shown *that* but not *why* St. John's wort elevates mood. Whether herbs have a biofield effect—for example, the consciousness of the herb (such as a property relating to happiness) interacting with the consciousness of the human being—has not been extensively considered.

The starting point for current debate regarding regulation of dietary supplements in the United States is the federal Dietary Supplements Health and Education Act (DSHEA), enacted in 1994. One of the major justifications the statute provides for its enactment is the need to "protect the right of access of consumers to safe dietary supplements . . . in order to promote wellness."[1] This justification is amplified in the report of the Senate Committee on Labor and Human Resources on the DSHEA. The committee specifically found that the FDA had "pursued a regulatory agenda which discourages . . . citizens seeking to improve their health through dietary supplementation" and that "[i]n fact, the FDA has had a long history of bias against dietary supplements . . . [and] pursued a heavy-handed enforcement agenda against dietary supplements for over 30 years."[2]

In light of these findings and comments, the DSHEA has had enormous popular appeal yet has generated controversy among regulatory authorities. Since the statute's enactment, various regulatory proposals have circulated to further restrict consumer access to dietary supplements. Rather than devoting detailed analysis to one or more such specific proposals, I will address a broader and more pervasive question—namely, ideally, how should the government regulate dietary supplements? In setting controls on the dietary supplement market, should regulation tip toward restriction or freedom? How do underlying beliefs about consumer health and intelligence shape regulatory values, policies, and rules? In what ways do the paradigmatic differences between conventional medicine, on the one hand, and complementary and alternative medicine, on the other, suggest the way that underlying belief systems ultimately influence the regulatory stance and resulting legal rules?

Key Provisions

Key provisions of the DSHEA follow.

1. Definition of Dietary Supplements: The statute defines "dietary supplements" to include products that contain, either individually or in combination, vitamins, minerals, herbs, or other botanicals; amino acids; or other products for use to supple-

ment the diet by increasing total dietary intake.[3] The dietary supplement must be available for consumption as a tablet, capsule, powder, softgel, gelcap, or liquid or, if not intended to be taken in such form, must not be represented as conventional food or for use as the sole item of a meal or diet.[4] All dietary supplements must be so labeled.[5] Dietary supplements are not classified as "food additives."[6]

2. Regulatory Status of Dietary Supplements: The DSHEA reaffirms that dietary supplements are "foods" and not "drugs,"[7] thus exempting dietary supplements from the requirement of new drug approval under the federal Food, Drug, and Cosmetic Act (FDCA). "Drugs" include, among other things, "articles intended for use in the diagnosis, cure, mitigation, treatment, or prevention of disease."[8]

3. Status of "New" Dietary Ingredients: Dietary ingredients present in the food supply before passage of the DSHEA (October 15, 1994) are presumed safe. "New" dietary ingredients are held to be adulterated unless (1) the ingredient has been present in the food supply as an article used for food in a form in which the food has not been chemically altered; or (2) the dietary ingredient has a history of use or other evidence of safety establishing that the ingredient, when used under the conditions recommended in the labeling, will be reasonably expected to be safe, and such information regarding safety is submitted to the Secretary of the Department of Health at least seventy-five days prior to the release of the dietary supplement.[9] The safety of a dietary supplement is to be judged only under its labeled conditions of use or, in the absence of such labeling, under the supplement's ordinary conditions of use.[10]

4. "Adulterated" Supplements: The Secretary of Health and Human Services may employ emergency authority to declare a supplement adulterated and immediately remove the supplement from the market if the supplement poses an imminent hazard to public health or safety.[11] The government, however, has the burden of proving that the dietary supplement is adulterated.[12] The FDA must notify an alleged offender at least ten days prior to filing a formal complaint with the U.S. Attorney, to allow the alleged offender to present evidence in defense.[13]

5. "Misbranded" Supplements: The FDA may remove misbranded dietary supplements from the market. Misbranding

occurs where the manufacturer fails to list the name of each dietary ingredient of the supplement and the quantity of each ingredient.[14] Misbranding also occurs where the dietary ingredient's nutritional information, if any, is not contained on the product label.[15] The DSHEA also provides for regulations prescribing good manufacturing practices for the production of dietary supplements.[16]

6. Use of Literature in Connection with Sale: The DSHEA authorizes the use of literature in connection with the sale of dietary supplements by modifying the definition of "labeling." Specifically, a publication used in conjunction with sale is not "labeling" under the FDCA if the publication (1) is not false or misleading; (2) does not promote a particular manufacturer or brand of dietary supplement; (3) presents a balanced view of the available scientific information; (4) if displayed in a store also selling dietary supplements, is displayed separate and apart from the dietary supplements; and (5) does not have appended to it any information by sticker or any other method.[17] Thus, dietary supplement retailers may sell books, reprints of articles, abstracts, bibliographies, and other publications as part of their business under the above conditions; and again, the government bears the burden of proof to establish that a book or article is false or misleading.[18]

7. Statements of Nutritional Value: The DSHEA allows manufacturers to include a statement of the supplement's nutritional value provided that (1) the statement claims a benefit related to a classic nutrient deficiency disease and discloses the prevalence of such disease in the United States, describes the role of a nutrient or dietary ingredient intended to affect the structure and function in humans, characterizes the documented mechanism by which a nutrient or dietary ingredient acts to maintain such structure or function, or describes general well-being from consumption of a nutrient or dietary ingredient; (2) the manufacture of the dietary supplement has substantiation that such statement is truthful and not misleading; and (3) the statement contains a disclaimer that the statement has not been evaluated by the FDA.[19]

The statement may not claim that the product will diagnose, mitigate, treat, cure, or prevent a specific disease or class of diseases.[20] For example, without FDA approval, a manufacturer may not make the following health claim for a calcium supplement: "Calcium will prevent osteoporosis." However, the manufacturer, without FDA approval, may make a "structure/function" claim, such as, "calcium helps build healthy bones."[21] The disclaimer must include a statement that the product is not intended to diagnose, treat, cure, or prevent any disease.[22]

8. Health Claims: A "health claim" is a "claim made on the label or in labeling of . . . a dietary supplement that expressly or by implication . . . characterizes the relationship of any substance to a disease or health-related condition."[23] The Nutrition Labeling and Education Act of 1990 (NLEA) provided that health claims for foods must be based on well-designed studies and "significant agreement among qualified scientists that the claimed link between a nutrient and disease is valid, taking into account the totality of publicly available scientific evidence."[24] Thereafter, the Dietary Supplement Act[25] imposed a one-year moratorium on implementation of the NLEA with respect to dietary supplements.

The DSHEA did not define what standard would be applied to health claims for dietary supplements[26] but instead created an independent Commission on Dietary Supplements Label to provide recommendations on the issue.[27] The mandate of the commission was to study and make recommendations concerning the regulation of label claims and statements for dietary supplements and, in so doing, "evaluate how best to provide truthful, scientifically valid, and not misleading information to consumers so that such consumers may make informed and appropriate health care choices for themselves and their families."[28] The FDA subsequently promulgated a rule providing that the "significant scientific agreement" standard would be applied to evaluating the validity of health claims on dietary supplements.[29]

Pandora's Box

From Extreme Paternalism to Radical Autonomy

Politically, the DSHEA marked a victory for advocates of increased access to vitamins, minerals, herbs, amino acids, and other dietary supplements, while it marked a defeat for those who believed in strict regulatory controls on dietary supplements. Philosophically, the DSHEA represented a compromise between two poles: extreme medical paternalism, on the one hand, and radical patient autonomy, on the other.

Paternalism involves interference with autonomous choices. Medical paternalism refers to the notion of the physician as a benevolent parent making decisions for dependent, ignorant children.[30] By extreme medical paternalism, I refer to the notion that patients' choices should be overridden despite their making voluntary and autonomous choices based on information available to them from a variety of sources, including but not limited to information printed on the labels of goods. Extreme medical paternalism holds that majoritarian medical consensus, based on existing medical orthodoxy or the views of a government agency, such as the FDA, should dictate consumer access to products and substances. At the other extreme, radical consumer autonomy means that patients should have unlimited access to goods whether or not their decisions are informed or even volitional.[31]

Traditionally, health care regulation in general and food and drug law in particular have tilted the balance toward extreme medical paternalism.[32] In food and drug law, the FDCA provides that no new drug may be introduced into interstate commerce until the manufacturer has proven, to the FDA's satisfaction, that the drug is "safe and effective" for its intended use. Today it is almost unthinkable that the law would change to allow manufacturers to introduce drugs into interstate commerce without proving effectiveness as well as safety.

The policy is justified from a paternalistic perspective of patient protection. Yet safety and effectiveness are judged by the FDA; the focus is on FDA approval rather than consumer access. Thus, even if the patient wants to use the drug, understands that it has not been proven safe and effective to the FDA's satisfaction, and makes a knowing, intelligent, and voluntary choice to assume all known and disclosed risks of the product, as well as those that cannot be disclosed because they are unknown, the patient still cannot have access to the drug.

In recent years, the policy has been softened in certain situations—for example, there have been some cases of expedited approval of and expanded access to potentially promising new drugs for life-threatening diseases. Still, some patients may not fit the required parameters for such approval, and their receipt of the drug still is contingent on FDA procedures and approval. When patients testified before Congress on the issue of access to treatments,[33] one testified that her son, Dustin, was two and a half years old when he was diagnosed with a brain tumor. The oncologists gave him a few months to live and offered radiation treatment, which would have left him "a vegetable."[34] His mother described his condition on unapproved treatments: "Dustin . . . is a happy, healthy four-year-old who has outlived his prognosis—there is no [FDA-approved] treatment that would have kept him alive with such good quality of life."[35] This provides a concrete, human example of the effect of defining patient protection from a paternalistic vantage.

Another example comes from litigation in the late 1970s during which patients sought to establish a constitutional right to freedom of access to medical treatments—a right to select the treatment of choice, whether or not such treatments have been approved by the FDA. In *United States v. Rutherford*,[36] the U.S. Supreme Court rejected efforts by terminally ill cancer patients to obtain laetrile. The Court concluded that Congress reasonably could have intended to protect terminal patients from such drugs as laetrile, which had not been proven safe and effective, and that it was not the court's function to overturn a "longstanding administrative policy [by the FDA] that comports with the plain language, history, and prophylactic purpose" of the FDCA .[37]

On remand, the Tenth Circuit held that a patient's decision to have treatment or not is a constitutionally protected right but that the patient's "selection of a particular treatment, or at least a medication, is within the area of governmental interest in protecting public health" and is not encompassed by the constitutional right to privacy.[38] Thus, *Rutherford* rejected the claim patients made, based on a constitutional right to privacy, to greater autonomous decision making; the courts instead rested on the medical paternalism inherent in the FDCA and the statutory grant of authority to the FDA.[39]

Both sides probably would agree that the DSHEA represented a marked departure from historical legal strictures on patient access to nontraditional treatments and remedies. Reasonable minds have differed and will continue to differ on whether this departure constituted an evolutionary leap in federal health care regulation or a reckless unlocking of a Pandora's box. At the very least, the DSHEA raises several unresolved regulatory problems.

Key Problems Raised by the DSHEA

Major areas of difficulty raised by the DSHEA follow.

1. Safety of Dietary Supplements Generally: The statutory presumption of safety for dietary supplements in the food supply prior to October 15, 1994, troubles some, as the manufacturer is not required to substantiate safety, even if it later increases the dosage or adds a new statement of nutritional support.[40]

2. Regulation of Potent Supplements Posing Risks of Harm: Because of the potential risk to consumers, one question that has arisen is whether highly potent supplements should be governed by stricter regulation, such as new drug approval procedures, rather than being allowed the easier access provided by the DSHEA.

3. Distinguishing (Permissible) Nutritional Support Claims from (Impermissible, Unapproved) Health Claims: Since passage of the DSHEA, debate has arisen about whether specific statements made by manufacturers constitute the kind of claims prohibited without FDA approval (for example, claims impermissibly linking the dietary supplement to the diagnosis, mitigation, cure, or treatment of a disease) or statements of nutritional value permitted under the DSHEA (for example, descriptions of the role of a nutrient or dietary ingredient intended to affect structure and function in human beings).

   In practice, it is difficult to distinguish structure/function claims from health claims. This difficulty can be seen, for example, in claims that ginkgo biloba "improves memory and concentration," that saw palmetto can "maintain prostate health and well-being," and that echinacea "supports healthy immune function."[41] The various analytical models proposed for making distinctions may be unworkable in practice.[42]

   In addition, even, if no formal claims are made linking a specific supplement to a particular disease, patients and health care professionals regularly are turning to dietary supplements as instruments of healing specifically targeted toward resolving particular conditions. Since passage of the DSHEA, the increasing role of dietary supplements in health promotion and protection has led to a blurring of the conceptual lines between foods and drugs. The situation is reminiscent of Hippocrates' aphorism "Let your medicine be your food, and your food be your medicine."

4. Inappropriate Claims through the Publication Exemption: The publication exemption allows consumers to receive promotional statements that could not independently be made by manufacturers for their products. The concern is that consumers will remain unprotected from claims made by manufacturers, which have relatively few restrictions in publications so long as they are marketed as part of dietary supplements sales.

Framing the Debate

The Effect of Belief Systems on Legal Rules

When evaluating whether the DSHEA has gone too far in moving from extreme medical paternalism toward radical consumer autonomy and opening the door to unbridled consumer access to dietary supplements, it is useful to frame the debate in terms of the core values involved in the degree of control proposed. Four separate levels of discussion arise: regulatory proposal, policy, values, and belief system. Each level generates the succeeding one (see chart 2).

1. Regulatory Proposal: This level of the debate asks what legal rule is the most appropriate. For example, should dietary supplements continue to be classified as "foods," provided no impermissible health claims are made; should they be considered "drugs"; or should some intermediate category be created in which access is more or less carefully controlled by federal officials?

2. Policy: The second level asks what overall stance legislation or regulation should adopt toward complementary and alternative medicine generally and dietary supplements specifically. What attitude should govern rule making? How should lawmakers, FDA officials, and others regard these products and the inclusion of dietary supplements in health care? Should the pos-

---

CHART 2. Generation of Regulatory Proposal from Core
Belief System

4. One's core **belief system** generates → 3. operative **values,** which
generate → 2. **policy** choices, which generate → 1. the **regulatory
proposal** and arguments for such a proposal.

---

   ture be favorable or unfavorable; are supplements generally to
   be regarded as helpful or dangerous, as integral to a health care
   regime or as deviant?
3. Values: The third level asks who or what the rules and policies
   are attempting to protect. Is it the individual, the wealth of an
   industry, or the power of a government institution? What is at
   stake—consumer autonomy, medical authority, or regulatory
   control? What are the ultimate values guiding any balancing of
   these interests? Further, what kind of world do we hope will
   emerge from the regulatory proposal and policy we set? What
   kind of legacy will we leave?
4. Belief System: The fourth level addresses what we ultimately
   believe about such large topics as truth, human existence, and
   the nature and purpose of the body. Do we ultimately believe
   that science has the best answers? Or do we believe that there is
   a role for intuition—for personal revelation—in our health care
   choices, irrespective of whether that intuitive choice is validated
   by existing scientific methodologies (for example, the decision
   to integrate certain minerals)? Do we feel that the body is inert,
   mechanical, and insentient? Or do we believe that, within a
   larger biofield, it is alive with conscious, intelligent energy, a
   responsive repository of personal wisdom, to which we can
   attune in moments of misalignment?

The link between rules, policies, and values is summarized in chart 3.
The generator of values, policies, and legal rules is one's personal belief
system. Chart 4 describes the different belief systems generating
assumptions in conventional medicine and in complementary and
alternative medicine. Chart 5 suggests ways in which such belief systems ultimately influence the side of the debate one takes in dietary
supplements regulation.

CHART 3. Values, Policies, and Legal Rules

	Strong Controls (FDA Position)	**Weak Controls (Industry position)**
Proposed rule	Require physician recommendation for potent supplements.	Allow complete consumer access unless the FDA proves the product dangerous.
Policy	Protect consumers (who are gullible).	Protect autonomous choices of consumers (who are informed).
	Prevent ignorant choices based on inadequate or faulty evidence or based on stupidity.	Protect intelligent decisions based on sufficient disclosures.
Values	Protect regulatory authority. Prevent public deception.	Protect industry. Prevent bureaucratic encroachment on individual liberty.

As the charts suggest, conventional medicine generally adopts a mechanistic and reductionistic view of the human organism and disease. This view derives from Newtonian physics and Cartesian dualism, two paradigms that dominated intellectual thought during the late nineteenth and early twentieth centuries. Briefly, Newtonian physics views the universe as a gigantic machine, whose whirring parts function according to predetermined laws; Cartesian dualism splits body and mind and regards the two as separate and independent. Conventional medicine thus views the body as a series of parts (much like a clock), which are amenable to pharmacological interventions whose effect can be precisely measured and which operate in isolation from emotional, social, psychological, and other factors.[43] The focus of conventional medicine is on curing the body; disease is viewed as caused by germs, genes, and biochemically- and pharmacologically-controlled phenomena; healing is viewed as coming from drugs, surgery, and

CHART 4. Mechanistic versus Holistic Healing Models

	Conventional (Mechanistic)	Complementary and Alternative (Holistic)
Focus	Cure; the body	Care; the Self; grace
Cause of disease	Germs; genes; biochemical, pharmacological phenomena	Imbalance of energies; stress; weakening of life force
Source of healing	Drugs; surgery; technology; the doctor; placebo effect	Within; internal self-healing; resolution of emotional and spiritual dimensions as well as physical manifestations of illness
Opinion on altered states of consciousness	Delusional; nonscientific; abnormal or meaningless	Central to healing; potential sources of information regarding disease and transformation; part of the journey to wellness

technological interventions, as well as from the knowing doctor and the placebo effect; altered states of consciousness—such as (1) a moment of personal insight into underlying emotional and spiritual issues behind the physical symptoms or (2) experiences of visits from departed relatives (in the case of dying patients, for example)—are viewed as abnormal, nonscientific, or meaningless at best and as dangerously delusional at worst.

Since complementary and alternative therapies generally adopt a holistic, biopsychosocial view of health and disease and interpret health and disease as products of dynamically interrelating physical, emotional, mental, and even spiritual factors,[44] the ultimate focus transcends relief of symptoms and eradication of physical illness and moves into the notion of self-care, reverence for one's own

CHART 5. Influence of Belief System

Belief System	Strong Regulatory Controls	Weak Regulatory Controls
Who determines what is "healthy"/ dangerous	Scientific authority as filtered through the FDA	The individual, operating on truthful, nonmisleading information from a variety of sources
What authority is ultimate in health care choices	Scientific principles	Personal intuition; personal revelation; personal choice
How should consumer choices be understood	Irrational and hence unworthy of credence or authority	Worthy of respect irrespective of FDA or majoritarian medical views
What is the nature of the body	Mechanistic and subject to reductionistic interpretation	Holographic, alive, and filled with conscious, intelligent energy, or "body wisdom"

being, and grace. Disease is seen as having origins in an imbalance of energies, in stress, or in a weakening of the life force. Healing comes from within a Supreme Being. It involves a resolution of emotional and spiritual dimensions of illness as well as of physical issues. Altered states of consciousness are frequently seen as central to healing or as potential sources of information regarding the disease and one's healing journey.[45]

Application: Health Claims

The FDA standard for health claims on dietary supplements has been "significant scientific agreement." From the standpoint of the need to protect patients and prevent consumer fraud, it is defensible to require that health claims have a certain level of generally agreed scientific validity. However, the underlying belief system is that scientific authority—as filtered through the FDA—should be the arbiter of what is healthy or dangerous for the human body. This assumption is so ingrained in the regulatory system that it hardly makes sense to question it.

Yet, returning to the hierarchy of values described in chapter 1, one could adopt other positions—for example, the belief that the individual, operating on nonmisleading information from a variety of sources, should determine for himself or herself what is healthy, safe, or dangerous. This belief accords greater respect to personal authority for decision making regarding one's own health care choices. It asserts that the individual, not scientific authority, ultimately determines what is "healthy" or "dangerous."

Thus, the other five regulatory values, such as creating health care freedom and the ability to make autonomous health care choices, are goals as important as controlling fraud. Yet another value described in this fivefold taxonomy is transformation. Facilitating personal transformation through an individual's choice of herbs could become an important regulatory objective. This has particular appeal if herbs are viewed, from the perspective of energy medicine, as conceivably having properties beyond the pharmacological level.

Yet again, one could argue that the above analysis begs the question of what information is misleading. Are health claims misleading when they are not backed by "significant scientific agreement"? This kind of reasoning, though, is circular; it assumes that the only way consumers will have valid information is when a certain level of scientific authority states that such information is valid. Again, the underlying belief is that consumers lack the ability to discern what is healthy and nondangerous; rather, the god of science must determine their choices.

Many consumers walk into a health food store and select certain vitamins, minerals, or other supplements merely because they feel this is good for them. They have some intuitive sense that some substance on that particular day will have a medicinal effect. Maybe their grandmother or a friend recommended zinc or echinacea to help fight off a cold; maybe they had a dream in which some spirit spoke to them and told them to get the zinc; or maybe it was simply a "gut feeling." We can call this phenomenon personal intuition; we can call it personal revelation, body wisdom, or the revelation of the body; or we can simply call it personal choice. Whatever name we use, by recognizing a valid force in consumer health care choices other than government or biomedicine, we are lending authenticity to a nonscientific process—one that is ultimately personal.

Invoking the irrational, the emotional, the intuitive—and suggesting that it has validity, that it deserves respect—subverts accepted notions of medical orthodoxy. But this subversion is, in fact, what complementary and alternative medicine does. It challenges accepted structures of thinking. Complementary and alternative therapies—such as acupuncture and traditional oriental medicine, Ayurvedic medicine, folk medicine, energy healing, and even some forms of chiropractic and massage therapy—signal a potential revolution in thinking about disease and health. These therapies propose explanatory models that have not been and in many cases cannot possibly be measured in Western science. The reference to supposedly scientific phenomena (such as dietary needs) in terms that sound mystical is particularly offensive to the medical model yet important to acknowledge and emblematic of many modalities within complementary and alternative medicine.

A Judicial Response

Recently, in *Pearson et al. v. Shalala*, manufacturers and advocates challenged the FDA standard of "significant scientific agreement" for health claims on dietary supplements, in the U.S. Court of Appeals for the District of Columbia. Specifically, the appellants (plaintiffs) challenged the FDA's rejection of four health claims: (1) that consumption of antioxidant vitamins may reduce the risk of certain kinds of cancer; (2) that consumption of fiber may reduce the risk of colorectal cancer; (3) that consumption of omega fatty acids may reduce the risk of coronary heart disease; and (4) that .8 milligrams of folic acid in a dietary supplement is more effective in reducing the risk of neural tube defects than is a lower amount of foods in common form.[46]

The appellants claimed, among other things, that the standard of "significant scientific agreement" had violated the First Amendment by failing to employ "a less draconian method"—the use of disclaimers—to serve the government's interest in consumer protection. The government's response to this challenge was that even with disclaimers, consumers still could be confused about which claims were preliminary and which were supported by significant scientific agreement.

The D.C. Circuit rejected this argument and characterized it as stating "that health claims lacking 'significant scientific agreement' are inherently misleading because they have such an awesome impact on consumers as to make it virtually impossible for them to exercise any judgment *at the point of sale.*"[47] The court added, "*It would be as if the consumers were asked to buy something while hypnotized, and therefore they are bound to be misled.*" The court then characterized this perspective as "almost frivolous" and analogized this to a case in which the Supreme Court rejected the "paternalistic assumption that the recipients . . . are 'no more discriminating than the audience for children's television.'"[48]

The court thus called the FDA's position paternalistic and chastised the FDA for treating dietary supplements consumers like an "audience for children's television." The court further pointed to the underlying assumption that consumer choices should be understood as irrational and hence unworthy of credence or authority, as if consumers were "hypnotized, and therefore . . . bound to be misled" when they purchase dietary supplements. It criticized the notion that it is "virtually impossible" for consumers "to exercise any judgment" when it comes to buying dietary supplements. In this sense, the court respected consumers' own determination of what is healthy or dangerous, with the individual operating on nonmisleading information from a variety of sources, including the label.

The court characterized as "more substantial" the government's argument that health claims on dietary supplements could be potentially misleading because the consumer would have difficulty independently verifying these claims. However, the court suggested that such a concern might be addressed by disclaimers informing consumers that the evidence for the claims made is "inconclusive." As to the government's concern that consumers might assume the FDA had approved the claims, the court suggested a disclaimer stating, "The FDA does not approve this claim." The court further suggested that the FDA could require a prominent disclaimer setting forth adverse effects of the dietary supplement. The court concluded that the government had not met its burden in showing that suppression, as opposed to disclosure through disclaimers, was justified as a sufficiently tailored restriction on speech to achieve the government interest in consumer protection. The court thus endorsed the notion of increasing the amount of information available to the consumer on the label, as opposed to limiting the kind of statement the manufacturer could make.[49]

The court's decision does not, of course, adopt or endorse a holistic view of wellness and illness, suggest that the body has its own intelligence or consciousness, or in any way delve into some of the propositions advanced earlier in this chapter. It does, however, rebuff a regulatory perspective that robs the individual of freedom to make decisions that deeply affect one's own self-care. Though based on First Amendment grounds, the freedom the opinion articulates is broader than freedom of expression through labeling on a dietary supplement container; in respecting freedom of choice in health care, the opinion revivifies the notion that even though the FDA has decided that the consumers will be inherently misled and confused, the consumers are legally empowered to make certain health care decisions, at least in purchasing dietary supplements.

DSHEA Revisited

As noted, continuing debate surrounds both the question of safety of dietary supplements and the question of regulation of claims on dietary supplements. The second question—determining the proper boundaries for approval of health claims—remains unanswered and complex.[50] Yet the D.C. Circuit's recommendation of use of disclaimers shows greater acceptance of consumer power of intelligence and autonomy in making health care choices surrounding dietary supplements. Such a movement toward greater autonomy in turn suggests a growing belief, as regards the first issue, that with some exceptions, consumers should have the freedom to make their own choices regarding dietary supplements and that safety issues can be addressed by a regulatory system that encourages information rather than restricting access.

Ideally, one would hope that the shift toward a more open and accessible market for medicinal substances, represented by the DSHEA, would expand rather than contract; that the new millennium would bring a greater awareness, on the part of legal and medical communities, of the role of personal responsibility in individual health care choices; that the notion of health care freedom would generate greater emphasis on, rather than more fears about, consumer self-abuse and misuse; and that the body politic would be seen as a holographic collection of autonomous, responsible beings, intelligently engaged in the individual pursuit of well-being, rather than as a ravenous, gullible, and unpredictable horde prey to mesmerizing, holistic pill-pushers.

Integrative and energy medicine potentially offer new under-standings of what it means to be a human being, making conscious choices to nourish and sanctify the human body. The diverse beliefs and values underlying these different world healing systems also offer new understanding of what it means for consciousness to reside in a human body, and how that consciousness interacts with substances and therapeutic interventions that affect the body and the intelligence within it.

If anything, the blurring of conceptual lines around "drugs," which are subject to extensive regulation, and around "foods" and other substances may be the DSHEA's gift and legacy toward the development of new thinking about medicine. Lawmakers have tended to interpret notions of "medicine" and "drug" broadly, expand-ing state medical boards' authority in the first instance,[51] and expand-ing medical board authority as well as FDA jurisdiction in the second instance.[52] Yet, the continuing controversy surrounding food and drug law involving dietary supplements suggests the need to draw limits around government intervention and to honor greater individual con-trol of the choices involved in caring for the body.

Framing the debate in terms of belief systems helps open the levels of structure—the complexes of thought and emotion—that generate the assumptions underlying the various regulatory proposals and the pol-icy arguments behind each proposal. By creatively examining the core values underlying the positions on health care—and by challenging regulators to do the same—the debate may be clarified, the doors of perception may be opened, and, ideally, the laws that govern self-care more faithfully track the core of human aspirations toward health.

PART 3

Bioethical Issues

CHAPTER 10

Toward a Bioethics
of Compassion

Traditionally bioethics, the study of legal and ethical issues arising in health care, has centered on four essential values: respect for patient autonomy, nonmaleficence, beneficence, and justice.[1] Although some commentators have criticized overreliance on such broad principles for ethical decision making,[2] others believe that the four principles describe common, core values.[3] Autonomy refers to the patient's self-rule and the opportunity to make meaningful choices;[4] nonmaleficence, to the physician's obligation to do no harm;[5] beneficence, to contributing to patient welfare;[6] and justice, to fairness and equity.[7]

These moral principles establish ideals for relationships between physicians and their patients.[8] In addition, emotional responsiveness— the caregiver's feeling response to the patient—enhances the moral quality of the relationship in a way that transcends ethical principles and rules.[9]

A Medical Institute for Law Faculty provided an opportunity to evaluate these values in clinical settings at a prestigious medical institution. I was one of nine law professors who participated in the program and accompanied the physicians on rounds as an observer.

The first section of the chapter distinguishes two models of physician-patient relations, caregiving and curegiving. The second section describes these models through a narrative impression of the rounds. This in turn provides a backdrop for the evaluation of bioethical values in the third section. The fourth section extends the model of caregiving by describing its application in an interdisciplinary framework for health care. Such a framework will integrate insights of complementary and alternative medicine professionals, who view interactions with patients from a variety of perspectives that challenge accepted models of health, disease, and transitions between death and life.

Caregiving and Curegiving

A preliminary disclaimer is helpful. The following stories are impressions and recollections, not verbatim transcripts of conversations or actual events. Ten days at the clinic produced a multitude of impressions. While many healthcare professionals were caring, sensitive, and emotionally responsive to patients, others followed a more detached, objective, institutional model.

The first model might be described as caregiving—employing personal powers in the "art" of medicine.[10] Caregiving might include, for example, asking questions about the body that take into account the patient's meanings[11] or promoting the expression of feeling by patients to enhance psychological well-being.[12] The second model might be described as curegiving. This is the historical model, in which "the doctor knows best," the patient follows "doctors' orders," and the physician-patient relationship follows the physician's historical role as omniscient, authoritative dispenser of healing.[13] Curegiving occurs when physicians reinforce patient feelings of dependence and personal estrangement, "as they exchange the status of person for that of patient."[14]

Health care providers' tendency to adopt the curegiving model in some situations is not so much a moral failure on the part of the profession but rather a series of unconscious individual choices, reflecting a larger societal failure to honor patients' feeling states and responses. Conventional medical care is dominated by technology;[15] many new technologies, touted merely for their innovation, actually harm or even kill patients.[16] Conventional care tends to hide the experience of suffering, perhaps in the attempt to disguise human vulnerability.[17] Even with the hospice movement, which seeks to provide a humane, caring environment for the dying, our culture engages in a kind of "pornography of death—the thing without the appropriate human emotions."[18] Many physicians keep demented elderly patients alive by feeding tubes, not because they believe it is right, but because of the legal consequences of allowing the patients to die.[19] The result is widespread estrangement between physicians and patients, evoking feelings of abandonment in patients and retreat by patients into silence.[20] Consequently, patients bring their own self-estrangement to doctors, along with unconscious idealizations and transferences, as well as disempowerment.[21]

Thus, despite the variety of metaphors available for the physician-patient relationship,[22] the one most frequently used identifies the physician as "benevolent parent"—hence the term *medical paternalism.*[23] However, whether supported by silent codes within the profession or by such codes within culture, the paternalistic, curegiving model frequently denies patients dignity and contradicts such core values as autonomy, nonmaleficence, beneficence, and justice. Such a model counters notions of care for the whole person. The following narratives illustrate an experience of that proposition.

Rounds: Impressions, Aspirations

Mattie: Intensive Care

Mattie, a ninety-four-year-old patient, lies openmouthed, her chin hanging down in a grotesque, silent moan. Her eyes stare, without blinking, at the ceiling. Her breath is faint, almost inaudible, drowned out by the steady blip of the video monitor over her head. Her gray hair is thinned, her face withered.

"She is completely passive, totally tuned out," says Dr. S. "She's what you call a 'bad patient,'" he jokes. "She went home from surgery, fell and broke her hip. Complications developed, and she ended up here."

The words echo in my mind. She's what you call a bad patient. My grandmother, a sweet and loving woman, also fell and broke her hip. In the nursing home, her appetite dissipated; the nurses assailed her for having a "bad attitude."

A nurse lifts Mattie's arm as if it were a shopping bag. She pokes it with a series of needles. Mattie does not register the piercing of her skin. She does not speak—has not spoken in weeks, we are told. Her son, an executive, visits her once in a while. More injections.

Dr. S reminds us that Mattie is feeling no pain. "She's really out of it," he says, throwing his head back and rolling open his mouth in an O shape to mimic Mattie's cadaverous stare. "A classic case of incompetence."

The law professors are happy now. At last, they have something they can discuss: decision making for an incompetent patient. The debate begins: Who should decide when to terminate Mattie's life support? Her son? The physician? We have shifted from a real encounter with Mattie's pain to an esoteric discussion of legal standards. This is clearly more comfortable.

From the back of the group, I ask Dr. S: "How do you know what Mattie wants? Have you asked her?"

"Of course not."

"Then, have you asked her whether she would like to see a member of the clergy, to talk about end of life?"

He dismisses the question and takes another: what is the son's position? Mattie's own choice in the matter is not terribly interesting. Or perhaps it is too immediate. And the attending physician has not even bothered to ask about spiritual needs. Mattie's death, like her life now, is medicalized. And the discussion swirls around patient decision making, ignoring the fact that the patient has not been consulted and is lying in bed—awake—within earshot. It is as if we were in the midst of a very interesting hypothetical. But we are not in the lecture hall; we are in Mattie's presence. Then again, Mattie is like anesthetized patients who go into surgery—tuned out, vegetative, uncommunicative (after all, she doesn't speak); and Dr. S again reminds us that Mattie feels no pain—in fact, feels nothing at all.

I push my way to the front of the group. "How do you know she's feeling no pain?"

"It's simple." Dr. S nods in Mattie's direction. "Just look at her."

I pause, take in the human being before me. The expression on her face reminds me of Edvard Munch's painting *The Scream*. "Look at her face. How can you claim she experiences no pain?"

Dr. S cannot believe I have challenged his pronouncements. He grabs my elbow and pulls me to the patient's bedside. He is going to prove his point. The tubes connected to Mattie's arms flap like seaweed as more medicine is pumped in. I hear the video screen beep.

"Mattie," the doctor intones, leaning in toward her ear. "ARE YOU IN PAIN?"

"No," she groans, turning her head the other way. I am surprised; Dr. S had given the impression that she was incapable of communicating.

Now he reiterates: "ARE YOU SUFFERING?"

"No," she moans feebly.

"ARE YOU SURE?" he insists.

"Yes." She turns away, closes her eyes.

Dr. S flashes a triumphant smile. "See? See?" He shakes his head and jabs his thumb toward the patient. "You ask her!"

"No . . . I don't want . . ."

"Go ahead!" His flushed face leans in toward mine. "See for yourself."

Instinctively, my hand reaches for Mattie's. We connect. Something flashes—a shared sense of inner life; scenes from the past; memories of family; a mutual recognition of the moment's physical reality; a shared awareness of Mattie's awareness of her experience in this bed. I am breathing, I am feeling the ground under my feet, and I am feeling this connection with this person. The emotions rise, subside. I do not know whether emotions are safe. There are the machines. There are the injections. The doctors. The rising and falling of Mattie's breath. The snaking tubes. The video bleeps.

Dr. S storms off. I am left alone with Mattie. And the nurse, and the bewildering technology.

"It's okay," I say. "We care about you."

The emotions rise, refuse to subside. Two tears slip from Mattie's left eye. Her face contracts. "I want to cry," she says softly.

"It's okay, Mattie. It's okay to have feelings." I think about all the pent-up grief; the denial of Mattie's inner world; the beauty of her heart.

A colleague comes up behind me and gently pulls on my arm. "We need to complete the tour."

I release Mattie.

Our group has a coffee break. I am quiet. The others critique the program: the communication with physicians is one-way; we pay them deference, and they have no interest in our ideas.

Later, when pressed, one professor—a former nurse—admits what she felt when she saw me confront Dr. S about Mattie's pain. She asks what Mattie whispered.

I tell her, "Mattie said she wanted to cry."

But otherwise, Mattie is forgotten. Nobody wants to talk about it.

Teddy: Pediatrics

"And this is our pediatric ward," says Dr. T, a tall, gaunt man in his early thirties. He leads three of us into a clean, narrow corridor, where medical personnel in scrub uniforms are gazing quizzically at our name tags. He takes us to the children's playroom; shows off the art on the wall, done by children; describes awards. The cartoon drawings tell all: they hate injections, like the nurses, want to go home as soon possible.

A four year old, wearing an eye patch, is playing ball with her mother, who sits cross-legged on the floor. I kneel down to say hello. The ball rolls toward me.

"It's a tough place, pediatrics," Dr. T says. "Extra training. Credentials."

Our next stop is an operating room at the end of the hall. The operating table is child-sized. A handwritten sign above the table reads:

REMEMBER PERSON AWARENESS.
There is A *Person* Under
Those Jabbing Needles.
Talk to Me.
Comfort Me.
I could be *your* child.

In the next room, a child is undergoing a heart procedure. We are told his name is Teddy. He is completely covered with a green blanket. The only thing showing is the offending organ.

"Why do they need to cover him up?" someone asks. You can't even tell there's a person under there."

Dr. T shrugs. "Best medical care," he says. The tone in his voice suggests he means, "leave the doctoring to the doctors." It reminds me of something a student told me concerning the time he asked his wife's physician what drugs were safest during her pregnancy. The doctor replied, "*We* know what to give her and when."

Dr. T introduces the parent room. There are sofas, books, a sturdy table; a great view out the window. A couple is sitting at the table; the wife is putting together the largest jigsaw puzzle I have ever seen. There must be over three hundred pieces.

"How is the puzzle coming?" I ask.

The woman lowers her eyes. "The doctors kicked us out."

Dr. T, ushering us out and closing the door behind him, editorializes: "That tells the whole story, doesn't it?"

Sylvia: Surgery

"If anything happens, you'd better have an anesthesiologist around," says Dr. P. "He knows pathology; the surgeon's just a pair of hands."

Dr. P is an old-timer. He calls each of the male surgeons "boy." They call him "sir."

Dr. P "puts people to sleep." Some years earlier I had studied hypnotherapy. Our group had delved into techniques for age regression, catalepsy, amnesia, time distortion—even so-called past life memories. I was impressed with the power of the unconscious mind, with the notion that the body has memory, absorbs impressions even while the conscious mind is somewhere else. Dr. Milton Erickson used to tell his patients, "Your conscious mind is very smart; your unconscious mind is smarter—so why not let *it* do the work for a change?" Apparently Erickson used to put his class to sleep—literally; boredom was a favorite technique for inducing trance.[24]

Now we watch brain surgery: in a delicate maneuver, a man's ear and the right side of his head have been sliced off, to allow access to a particular part of the brain. The surgeons are playful, as they scoop out some muck.

In the next room, rock music blares while the surgeons excise the cancer from an old man's liver.

A green curtain separates the patient's face from his body; all the surgeons see is the slit-open skin and the underlying organs. This is somebody's grandfather; under the plastic bag that covers the patient's face, I see a gray mustache. Dr. P explains that for years, they tried to find a way to keep the patient's body warm during surgery. Finally, they made a breakthrough discovery: the plastic bag over the face.

The chief surgeon is young, handsome. "We can cut it up and take it out," he says. "No more cancer." He smiles, clearly impressed with the technology and with his skill. "Couldn't do this a few years ago." The radio announces a baseball game. Now there's a commercial for facial cream. This torrent of verbiage, electric guitars, sales pitches: is this mustached older man really not "there"? What does it mean to say he's "asleep"? Isn't he aware, on some level, of everything around him—commercials, bad jokes, electric guitars, braggadocio, and all?[25] If he dies, will the last thing he hears before leaving this world be the ad for facial cream? Would the surgeon be this cavalier with his own grandfather? Or would someone be praying—perhaps someone is praying, in stillness, upstairs in the chapel, just now.

The attending nurse smiles at us, makes chitchat. "You're law professors?"

Another surgeon, from the last operation, enters. "Did anyone see my keys?" They shake their heads. The operation continues.

Now Dr. P jokes: "Are you guys okay? Nobody's nauseous, are they?" He rolls his eyes. "Okay, let's get some excitement."

We rendezvous with our colleagues. One has seen a penile implant. It's the joke of the day ("How about that penile implant in OR 23?"). We split up again. A woman is lying nude on the operating table, legs splayed like a chicken. We enter; the surgeon flashes an angry look at Dr. P.

"Do you have a problem, *boy*?" Dr. P says.

The surgeon pauses, then says, "No problem, sir." He looks us over, continues. "Sylvia's doing fine," he says. We watch, huddled in the corner of the room. We can see the patient's innards on a giant computer screen over her head. We watch the surgical instruments proceed through her body.

"Why don't they cover up her breasts?" one of the professors whispers to me. Another answers her: "Must be standard medical procedure."

Dr. P, ushering us out, informs us that earlier this patient stopped breathing for ten seconds. He asks us whether, after the operation, the patient should be informed of this development. He argues that the information is of "no medical value." I suggest that it might be of psychological or religious significance to the patient. He dismisses the suggestion. "If it's of no *medical* value, what's the point?"

Our next patient is a black woman, thirty years old. Cancer. She lies, anesthetized, in limbo; the surgeons around her have opened her up, found that the tumor has spread much further than anticipated. Now they wait for the pathologist's report. They are expectant, impatient; there is nothing to do but wait. It is as if we are waiting at the bus station. The patient lies before us, anesthetized, opened up.

Finally, the head surgeon breaks the silence. "So where you guys from?"

Somebody answers, awkwardly. "We're law professors—not

lawyers, professors. From different parts of the country." He describes the program. There's commentary; response. We wait for the pathologist. It is awkward, this conversation. The silence that ensues is equally awkward; we are not used to being present in the face of the moment; something must fill the space. More science, perhaps. Unprompted, the surgeon decides to use the time instructively.

"See, her cancer's worse than we thought. It's spread all over the place. It started here . . ." She lifts the patient's liver with the tongs. She lifts it up, way up, out of the body. "See? Her diet's awful. It spread to the stomach." The tongs drop the liver, seize the stomach and yank it up. Finally, the pathologist arrives, says the magic words to the surgeon. "Yeaah!" she shouts. "Just as I thought." She is happy, because she won a bet with the resident as to what kind of cancer it was.

The pathologist, perhaps aware that he has an audience, reprimands her. "What're you cheering for? This means she's going to die."

The surgeon lets a flap of skin fall toward the patient's organs. "Then we'll sew her up. There's nothing more *we* can do."

The night after the surgery, at the hotel, we reflect on our experiences. Cigarette smoke fills the space between the dark-paneled walls, as we sip our gin-and-tonics.

"That's so sad," someone says. "That woman, thirty-three. What will they tell the family?"

"The question is, *who*'s going to tell the family. That surgeon?"[26]

"To think she was operated on for nothing."

"Did they sew her up because it was futile to operate or because the surgeon was defensive?"

"Who knows—there's no accountability in the operating room."

"Maybe it was because she was black."

"I doubt it."

"I know one thing," I say. "The next time someone I love goes in for surgery, I'm going to insist on being in the operating room."

"You can't do that!"

"Why not? We were in there today. There's nothing magical about the OR that requires excluding loved ones."

"What would you do in there?"

"Just . . . be . . . present. That way the doctors will remember there's a human being on the table, not just a body."

Suddenly the others defend the physicians, arguing that they *need* to be desensitized in order to do what they do.

But, I argue, every patient *is*, first and foremost, a person. This is debated at great length, the conclusion being that once the individual enters the hospital, the person is, first and foremost, a patient. Once disease enters the body, the best attitude is to be, simply, patient.[27]

Toward a Bioethics of Compassion

The three sets of patients described in this chapter—Mattie, the child, and the anesthetized patients—have several features in common. First, they are dominated by invasive technology and live in a precarious position of extreme dependency and vulnerability. Mattie lives by the grace of constant injections delivered by a nurse; above her, the video screens feed back continuous information as to her physiological state. The child is unconscious as the surgeons perform a lifesaving operation. The other patients undergoing surgery similarly depend on their caregivers, as the anesthesiologist behind the screen constantly monitors vital signs. If the heart stops or a reaction occurs, these patients depend on instantaneous, competent decision making and care.

Second, these patients are silent. Mattie cannot, or does not, disclose her wishes and feelings. Although the attending physician presumes to know Mattie's state of mind (by interpreting her brief, emotionless responses to his impersonal and businesslike questions), in actuality we have no idea how she is reacting—other than physiologically—to the steady stream of injections. We do not know how she regards the dying process and decisions related to her dying. In fact, caught up in the swell of medical, legal, and ethical decision making—all of which proceeds independent of the patient's psyche—no one has thought it important to ask.

Similarly, the child has no say about anything, since he is "under." And the parents have lapsed into paralysis: they are putting together a puzzle, as the surgeons put their child together; they can only hope, or possibly pray—but only from a distance.[28] The anesthetized patients likewise have no voice once the anesthesia takes over; it is as if they are "not there."

Third, these patients exist at the gray edge of law and bioethics, where legal rules and ethical principles do not necessarily apply and, indeed, where the caregiver's "emotional responsiveness" may be of greater importance. For example, it is unclear whether, as a legal matter, Mattie is "competent" or "incompetent."[29] The physician says she is "incompetent," but that is a personal judgment more than a medical one, with some vague reference to legal standards. Clearly, Mattie can speak; but, like Herman Melville's protagonist in "Bartleby the Scrivener," she would prefer not to. Her "care"—whether she perceives it thus or not, that is the term—proceeds as if on its own volition: bleeps, injections, even the dragging of a law professor to her bedside to test his estimation of her suffering.

Likewise, children in general—as evidenced by the sign in the pediatrics operating room—are particularly unaware of legal rights and ethical choices; they exist in the unregulated, undefined world of emotional nuance. Here, the child probably cannot imagine that he will have his entire being covered, save the wretched organ, for several hours. The parents cannot know; nor, according to advocates of paternalism, should they be allowed to see. They must bide their time in the duly designated space.

Finally, these different patients lack full awareness and choice relative to decision making about their bodies. For instance, the patients undergoing surgery probably do not know about the plastic bags over their faces or about the crude jokes or operating-room banter. The law of informed consent does not require such disclosure;[30] and despite the individual's Fourteenth Amendment "liberty interest," which includes the right to make a "voluntary and informed choice" regarding treatment,[31] the patient has no opportunity to decline, or even discover, the more tasteless aspects of the experience of surgery. Rights of dignity are important when the individual is competent, or even incompetent, but less attended to when patients are "etherized upon a table."[32] As Mattie is screened off from her neighbors, her muffled moans hidden behind the tubes, so the patients in surgery are screened off, masked—literally—from others. The patients do not operate as autonomous agents; they are literally operated on. Here the physician-patient relationship is particularly vulnerable, existing as it does beyond legal and ethical norms, behind the scenes, and with patients who are, above all, silent and powerless.

A court conceivably could decide that the right of informed consent requires doctors to make available to patients videotapes of patients' surgeries. That way, a patient could witness whether liberty and dignity were unfairly and needlessly assaulted during medical procedures. Similarly, a legislature could decide that medical practitioners must show, by "clear and convincing evidence," elderly patients' assent to any medical care and to continued medical care (with assent, say, every two months).[33] The law's further intrusion, however, would raise additional problems. For instance, surgeons might be intimidated by videotaping or might raise privacy objections. Similarly, evidence of a patient's continued wishes might be difficult to extract. The law cannot force Dr. S to ask Mattie what she wants, anymore than it can force Mattie's son to visit her more frequently, or anymore than it can force Mattie to speak or to respond honestly to Dr. S's questions.[34]

In these situations, the patients cannot rely on either legal or ethical norms; nor do the physicians have rules to guide them. The situations are shaped by individual power, a personal sense of responsibility, and larger cultural expectations. If surgeons can lift organs up for show and if patients can be shut away from their loved ones, then perhaps we expect, and accept, to give up power—and even dignity—in the operating room and to be shunted from our children in our hour of crisis. Perhaps we expect physicians to be curegivers and they step into the role to fulfill the unconscious bargain. Or perhaps fear and denial of suffering distort the experience of health "care" and transform it into one of health dependency.[35] Or perhaps the culture remains enmeshed in outmoded notions of physician dominance.[36]

The model of caregiving recognizes that patient well-being entails not only cure but also care.[37] It acknowledges compassion, fidelity, and humanity as common denominators, across time and cultures, in the ethical aspirations of healing professionals.[38] Ideally, this is one of the premises behind holistic health care: attention to the unified human being, whose physical, mental, emotional, and spiritual dimensions each deserve respect and care. A beautiful prayer encapsulates these values: "May the pain of every living creature / be completely cleared away. / May I be the doctor and the medicine / And may I be the nurse / For all sick beings in the world / Until everyone is healed."[39] Respect for the patient, as person, though embodied in legal rules, transcends them.

In any event, if medicine heals, it also creates a circle of interaction where, in one physician's words, "the physical does not always have the last word."[40] My impressions of rounds highlight, in part, both our culture's overemphasis of the logical and physiological and its denial of the analogical and psychological.[41] If patients were no more than magnificent machines, rather than whole persons, then a technocratic approach to health and bioethics would be called for and any additional sensitivity would be wasted.

The stories presented will not solve ethical conflicts according to rigorous, theoretical criteria. They are not criticisms of the institution or its staff but rather a commentary on a collective consciousness that medicalizes life and death and denies the language of the body, the wisdom of feeling, the truth of inner experience. I engage in storytelling more than rule making, for in storytelling, we reclaim the parts of ourselves that have been fragmented or denied.[42]

The tales suggest that persons do not begin and end at the level of skin.[43] Persons, as patients, experience physical, emotional, and psychological realities.[44] These realities must be recognized in all phases of health care. Although anesthesia and so-called incompetence describe physiological and legal states, they also may be states of being that test our respect for personhood. Ideals are tested not in litigation but in the warp and woof of human conduct. Whether medicine and law ultimately can affirm caregiving over curegiving and can truly embody respect for persons is the ongoing, silent task of a bioethics of compassion.

Toward Integration: Some Keys to Compassion

Postmodern scholarship has shown that different aspects of reality can be illumined by different perspectives.[45] Such different perspectives are the hallmark of complementary and alternative health care—they include viewing the organism through the lens of *chi*, for example, or understanding medicinal substances in terms other than their pharmacologically active ingredients.

As Michael Polanyi observes, one "lives in the meanings he is able to discern."[46] Previously, this chapter has examined caregiving and curegiving from analytic and narrative perspectives. This section extends the metaphor of caregiving, by exploring its meaning through vision, dream, myth, and archetype.[47] Exploding ruling metaphors through such "alternative, even conflicting," perspectives can inform, enrich, and challenge unconscious legal paradigms.[48]

For example, my encounter with Mattie exploded the legal dichotomy between "competent" and "incompetent" patient that informs much of bioethics. While described by the attending physician as "incompetent," Mattie was in fact quite capable of communicating.[49]

The night after meeting Mattie, I saw a magnificent lady, wearing a brilliant white gown with a blue sash, who proclaimed: "I am the Mother of all beings. It was I, standing behind Mattie, whom you recognized, as you felt the energy circuits connect between your hand and hers; it was my hand you were holding, as I am holding yours always, until the end of time."[50] Should such an experience change the dreamer's notions of appropriate clinical care or ethical questions concerning Mattie's end-of-life decisions?

The following morning, at a neighboring hospital, an obstetrician described to our group a new medical technology known as multiple fetal pregnancy reduction (MFPR). The technology arises from the woman's capacity to bear more than one fertilized egg through pregnancy at a given time.[51] Essentially, MFPR assists such patients to bear healthy babies, by "reducing" the number of embryos—that is, arranging for destruction of excess embryos.[52] Ethical issues raised by MFPR have only begun to enter the literature.[53]

In assessing MFPR, our group analyzed the "maternal-fetal conflict," in which the mother's right to choose or refuse recommended treatment may conflict with the physician's obligation to promote her well-being as well as that of the fetus.[54] The discussion plied abstraction; though the organism concerns itself with nourishment, the law addresses "rights."[55]

In meditation, I entered the feeling state of those semideveloped, discarded units of consciousness. I felt the joy of physical embodiment, the ecstasy of incarnation. In the next moment, I suffered overwhelming, indescribable grief, as the embryos experienced themselves discarded, emptied of life like trash tossed from a car window. In my sense impression, the embryos mourned the casual, technocratic disposal process[56]—essentially being treated as objects.[57]

Again, do symbols, metaphors, and mythmaking matter? Should a trance vision shift analytical frameworks?[58] Does an embryo, terminated like a line of products, suffer?[59] Does a fly suffer as, having escaped the deadly blow of a swatter, it is being crushed by someone's heel? Does an ant experience pain when it is smushed by a child's thumb? Does an "incompetent" patient like Mattie, who admits to her doctor that she is feeling no pain, suffer? Do patients undergoing surgery suffer from ironic barbs about their organs? Does suffering require its articulation through language? Is consciousness limited to persons and only to persons declared legally competent?[60] Is the negation of suffering merely denial,[61] or is it, at times, a lie?[62]

In this exploration, I do not profess to know, and take no position on, whether abortion is a good thing or a bad thing, a moral procedure or an immoral one, a right essential to a woman's control of her body or an evil.[63] I make no moral judgment on MFPR or selective termination.[64] I do not draw rational principles from accepted philosophical premises. Similarly, I do not judge whether Mattie's care was "reasonable under the circumstances."[65] Rather, I proceed from a place that is deeply uncomfortable in Western medical, as in religious, orthodoxy: the interpersonal, the spiritual, the emotional, the mythic, and the archetypical. This place is uncomfortable because it is subjective and fraught with potential tyranny and distortion. Yet, for most humans, this place is real; it touches the core.[66]

All beings experience trauma, whether their pain is intelligible to their human caretakers or not,[67] and although legal rules circumscribe choices, humans choose how to act in a realm infinitely larger than rules can dictate. What links the excess embryos to Mattie, the children, and the surgery patients is that their experience of care occurs in a consensus reality that denies their capacity to feel and suffer. The embryos are simply "multifetal gestations"; Mattie, the children, and the surgery patients are "tuned out." Their objectification results from a reduction of "care," as a ruling metaphor, to "medical care";[68] from an overly mechanistic view of their condition; from the denial that they have, at the moment of care, a consciousness of that care. Their dignity, if you will, is impinged, because in treating them as objects of technological intervention, their aliveness is ignored—for example, by use of the euphemism "reduction" as a substitute for "destruction"; by use of the terms "incompetent" and "noncommunicative" as medical pronouncements rather than functional realities; by reference to a body part or procedure rather than the person (the "penile implant in OR 23").[69]

Moral progress, it has been argued, "often depends as much on finding (or fashioning) the right words as on applying the right principles."[70] In many cases, the human touch may be as important to the patient's progress as the medical intervention; the rule may matter less than one's behavior within the boundaries of the rule; and decision making may be less important than simply communicating.[71] Debates on rights and decision-making power often obscure intersubjective realities, whether the subject is an elderly woman, a patient prepared and naked before surgery, or an embryo.

If myth, archetype, and metaphor matter, then the regulatory perspective shifts from rights and power to embrace perceptual realities.[72] For instance, asserting the state's so-called interest in prolonging life shifts to enhancing the quality or radiance of one's final moments;[73] and concern about altering the "natural course" of illness yields to furnishing dignity, comfort, and peace.[74]

These propositions undermine the conventional view of the physician's role as "healer" in denying patients the right to a peaceful death,[75] and they underscore the notion that mythical, archetypical, and intersubjective realities can and should play a role in medical care and bioethical decision making.[76] One could argue that the personal sphere must reclaim part of the power ceded to the medical; that MFPR is more than is implied by the euphemistic term "intervention";[77] that the decision to end one's life is not necessarily "suicide," the decision to guide the dying process is not necessarily "killing,"[78] and the notion of death as either nothingness or heaven is limiting and reflective of cultural taboos and Western belief systems.[79] Language, again, is critical to one's belief system and ultimately to what will be considered ethical and legal, as well as clinically appropriate.

In a larger sense, "healing" refers not to a particular technology, medication, or procedure but rather to a process of moving toward wholeness at all levels of being.[80] Such movement can and should force Western culture to reexamine its assumptions[81] about life and consciousness.[82]

The conventional wisdom is dualistic: one is either for something or against it.[83] Humans have slaughtered each other for millennia for such differences in belief.[84] Being for or against something never gave rise to compassion, which is supposed to be a fountainhead of religious feeling[85] and bioethics.[86] The embryos suffered, Mattie suffered, and the woman whose organs were yanked up into the air by the surgeon— whether or not she was consciously aware—suffered. Awareness of suffering cannot be evoked by legal rules, cannot be circumscribed by bioethics, cannot be taught at the blackboard. The placard in the pediatrics operating room expressed it well: "Talk to Me. Comfort Me. I could be *your* child." In short, caregiving—through the lens of dream and myth—includes transcending hierarchical relations and dependencies through the immediate, body- and feeling-centered awareness of our shared vulnerability.

Conclusion

Whether motivated by external rules or inner guidelines, the principles of autonomy, nonmaleficence, beneficence, and justice do express a quest to encourage compassionate caregiving. But emotional responsiveness transcends principles.[87] To unite principles with responsiveness suggests being willing to acknowledge both parts of one's being: the professional and the shaman, at once institutional and healing.[88] The professional helps individuals surmount problems by manipulating technological or institutional know-how;[89] the shaman (the "medicine man" or "witch doctor"), by moving easily between ordinary and nonordinary states of consciousness, helps individuals transcend their normal, ordinary definition of reality.[90]

> When shamans enter nonordinary reality, the rules of the outer world are suspended. Horses fly, plants talk, fairies and leprechauns abound. Time as we know it is suspended. . . . Outer rules of space are equally voided in these nonordinary worlds.[91]

The shaman is a healer.[92] Shamanic cultures existed long before written history and believed all things to be permeated by spirit.[93] Physicians, as healers, are their modern counterparts.[94] So are psychotherapists[95] and even lawyers.[96]

In each case, the dual identity—professional and shaman—has an overt side and a covert side. The professional (overt) side publishes in respectable journals, articulates ideas in neat intellectual packages, impresses with credentials and a detached, neutral language. The shamanistic (covert) side delves into dream, myth, fantasy, and archetype; plunges into metaphor; nurtures the inner landscape; and allows the "inexhaustible energies of the cosmos"[97] to pour through his or her being.

This duality expressed itself at the clinic, where the professional-shaman identity was split between husband and wife or between physician-professional and physician-private citizen. Although the senior physician expressed little interest in holistic medicine, his wife, a cancer survivor, practiced yoga and wore an angel on her necklace. Another physician, a cardiologist, was fascinated by "the possibility that something beyond, that we cannot prove, exists"; he had me speak to his wife, who has had premonitory dreams on a regular basis. A third physician, who was born in India, quoted the Vedas to me and privately observed: "The universe gives you a little bit of knowledge to play with and watches what you do with it." Quietly, covertly, behind the machinery and the titles, far from the gaze of committees and the Annual Physician Review (which rewarded, among other things, efficiency in handling patient volume),[98] lurked the specter of the inner, the hidden, the whole being behind the instrumentation.

It is true that "cultural models that are adopted, consciously or otherwise," affect one's views in bioethics.[99] I share the mythmaking to honor the shaman in self and others; to bring the covert into the overt; to validate subjectivity, intuition, and mystery in equipoise to science and law. By acknowledging these other dimensions of caregiving, the field of knowing may be broadened and enriched.[100]

Dr. S's insensitivity to Mattie's suffering and Dr. P's insistence that only things of medical relevance have significance reflect our culture's reliance on outer pronouncements rather than inner truths.[101] The children's crayon drawings provide as much a representation of their medical care as would an article in a peer-reviewed medical journal or a law review. East has met West—contrary to Rudyard Kipling's famous claim that "never the twain shall meet"—and if we consider East and West to be metaphors for the journey within, our age will acknowledge a greater integration between left and right brain, science and intuition, intellect and feeling.[102] Declaring whether a fetus is "alive" for the purpose of a legal rule, such as on abortion,[103] is quite different from relating to the fetus as one form of consciousness to another—albeit dimly understood—form (see chap. 12).[104]

The insights of such therapies as acupuncture and energy healing resonate with the notion that the patient is more than the physical body,[105] that medical materialism[106] leaves U.S. health care inadequately equipped to handle the full range of human experience, that disease is complex and susceptible to multiple levels of interpretation, and that beyond scientifically acceptable proof is the proof of the heart.[107] Expressing such notions challenges a health care system that views pathology largely in material terms, that defines scientific truth in biophysical realities, that dismisses the "irrational" and the "mystical." William James writes:

> We are surely all familiar in a general way with this method of discrediting states of mind for which we have an antipathy. We all use it to some degree in criticizing persons whose states of mind we regard as overstrained. But when other people criticize our own more exalted soul-flights by calling them "nothing but" expressions of our organic disposition, we feel outraged and hurt, for we know that, whatever be our organism's peculiarities, our mental states have their substantive value as revelations of the living truth; and we wish that all this medical materialism could be made to hold its tongue.[108]

As Franz Kafka noted, before the law stands a doorkeeper.[109] The doorkeeper is human experience, filtering unconscious impressions and condensing experience into appropriate phrases and rules; and beyond a bioethics of compassion is compassion itself.

CHAPTER 11

From "Flatland" to "Spaceland" and Beyond

This chapter concerns Flatland, a mythical place that is undergoing a transformation as lawmakers struggle to integrate "conventional" and "complementary and alternative" ideas about medicine, philosophy, social structure, and policy. It is a tale of two (or more) dimensions, a parable for our times.

The Man with the Withered Arm

Recently, a friend named Dr. Valerie Hunt told me the following story.

> I was asked to help a man who has a withered arm. I went into meditation and asked to see the origin of the trauma. I saw the man's soul floating above his fetal body, waiting to enter. His mother already had nine children and was going to a clinic to have an abortion. This was about the first week of the second trimester. However, she was a good Catholic and felt torn about the abortion. And so she turned around and went home to have her pregnancy. Still she felt conflicted about her choice to have the child. And so the embryonic form reflected the split in her consciousness.[1]

Dr. Hunt told me she came out of her trance and asked the client about his birth. He replied that his mother had told him on her deathbed that after he had been conceived, she had decided to have an abortion. She had told him that this had occurred the first week of the second trimester but that she had passed a church along the way and decided to have the child.

I asked Dr. Hunt, "Can the arm be healed?"

She replied, "I asked the man to go into meditation every day and visualize himself, as an embryo, developing the arm along the line of its

147

normal growth. I have asked the man's physician to measure changes. So far the arm is growing; and I believe that in the end, he will have a normal limb."

I asked, "Is he just meditating and visualizing, or is something else occurring? For example, is he going back in space-time and altering reality?"

She said, "It is the present."

About Flatland

When I first taught a seminar on the legal ramifications of complementary and alternative medicine, I put Edwin Abbot's novel *Flatland* on the syllabus.[2] The students wondered why a satirical science-fiction piece was required reading in addition to the usual repertoire of statutes and cases. They initially were puzzled as well by the appearance of a poem, written by the then-current director of the Office of Alternative Medicine, entitled "Unpaid Shaman" and by the suggestion that they get together in groups to assess Ayurvedic tongue diagnosis—imagine a bunch of law students sticking their tongues out to search for hidden cues to emotional or spiritual deficiencies.

Flatland is written in a humorous, satirical vein intended to expose the limitations of a conventional worldview. In the novel, Flatland is a world inhabited by two-dimensional creatures. Men come in various two-dimensional shapes, from triangular to circular; women are straight lines. Because a woman can inadvertently puncture a man with her backside (Abbot's characterization is obviously tongue-in-cheek here), various regulations have been designed to allow the peaceful coexistence of women and men. The regulations invariably give men the "edge," so to speak.

While the linearity of the women lends itself to a relative social equality among them, the men have social rankings according to their angles. Circles are at the top of the hierarchy, since their three-hundred-and-sixty-degree circumference expresses perfection; Octagons, Hexagons, and other multisided beings come next; and at the bottom are Isoceles Triangulars, whose unaesthetic angles suggest true social inferiority.

Flatland, thus, is a world like our own. The social order has hierarchy, privilege, class structure, and distinct lines of status. In this sense,

Flatland resembles our culture—at least prior to *Brown v. Board of Education* (the U.S. Supreme Court's desegregation decision) and related civil rights legislation. Flatland also can be seen as a metaphor for the quest for health and the cult of the body. Those whose physical form expresses perfection (Circles) are at the top of the pyramid, while those with irregular shapes have lesser status. In our society, certain ideals of physical beauty often are worshiped, while lesser adulation typically accrues to the physically irregular. The Circle is the *Übermensch*[3] of Flatland, with no particular qualifications except the genetic endowment of flawlessly embodied form.

The Miraculous Apparition

One day, the narrator of Abbot's novel, who has angles of noble birth, experiences a miraculous apparition: a Sphere descends into Flatland.

At first, the narrator is dumbfounded; from his two-dimensional perspective, he sees only a curve, growing alternately larger and smaller. Because his sensory apparatus is limited, he cannot even conceive of an object existing in more than two dimensions. He cannot grasp the very concept of a Sphere. Initially, therefore, the apparition terrifies him. Later, though, the Sphere convinces the narrator that he is real and even manages to engage the narrator in conversation.

The narrator's experience parallels that of many prophets in Western religious tradition. When first encountering a mystical apparition, the prophet, saint, or holy person is frightened. For example, Moses fell to his face when the Lord appeared to him; Mary trembled at the sight of the archangel Gabriel until he comforted her; on the appearance of another angel, Hermas, a brother to Bishop Pius of Rome, was "astonished" and seized by "horror" until the angel comforted him and provided a vision.[4] Once the numinous encounter becomes more familiar, though, it yields the blessings of communication from higher realms. The aforementioned visionaries received angelic or divine messages that could be transmuted into evolutionary actions and vehicles appropriate to their cultures. They acted as mediums, in their attempt to receive messages by developing clairaudient abilities and "tuning in" to deities and guides in different realms and levels of reality. These messages and experiences are as inconceivable and incredible to us, in our ordinary state, as they were to the narrator who experienced the penetration of a Sphere from the ethers to his world. We either accept (on faith) or dismiss (on another kind of faith), but we rarely understand, from a place that represents neither acceptance nor dismissal, neither belief nor disbelief, neither faith nor doubt.

The Out-of-Body Journey

In *Flatland,* the Sphere lifts the narrator out of Flatland and gives him a three-dimensional perspective of his city. The narrator is astonished to see Flatland from the perspective of a three-dimensional being. His journey violates the laws of space and time as he has known them (and as the most eminent scientist-Circles have no doubt described them). He sees the conventional worldview as illusory. Eastern traditions refer to the conventional world perspective as *maya,* complete illusion, and assert that only through meditation can the seeker attain the vision of ultimate reality. Aldous Huxley once wrote that when the doors of perception are cleansed, things appear luminously clear. The journey of the narrator in *Flatland* propels him out of ordinary body consciousness and into a world that makes his prior understanding seem highly limited and even counterevolutionary.

In Western mystical tradition, the seer is frequently transported beyond this world and into other dimensions. For instance, the prophet Ezekiel traveled in his *merkabah,* or chariot, to the heavens and other worlds.[5] Similar journeys were taken by the prophet Isaiah, who saw the Lord on a throne, surrounded by celestial hosts. More recently, Robert Monroe, a businessman, described out-of-body journeys to specific realms. Monroe even established an institute dedicated to facilitating such experiences and showing that they do not solely depend on grace but can be stimulated through specific mind-body technologies. Carlos Castaneda similarly has written:

> Don Juan contended that our world, which we believe to be unique and absolute, is only one in a cluster of consecutive worlds, arranged like the layers of an onion. He asserted that even though we have been energetically conditioned to perceive solely our world, we have the capability of entering into those other realms, which are as real, unique, absolute, and engulfing as our own world is. . . . Their existence is constant and independent of our

awareness, he said, but their inaccessibility is entirely a consequence of our energetic conditioning. In other words, simply and solely because of that conditioning, we are compelled to assume that the world of daily life is the one and only possible world.[6]

The Regulatory Response

Thomas Kuhn suggested in *The Structure of Scientific Revolutions* that scientific paradigms are not toppled without revolutionary consequences. Whether the revolution the narrator of *Flatland* initiates is truly Kuhnian or not, existing paradigms in the narrator's social order are threatened. Because the narrator's experience defies the prevailing worldview and might, if believed, create anarchy among the lower classes—and even revolution—the Circles suppress the new gospel of the Sphere's existence.

This suppression, too, is familiar to Western religious tradition; prophets often have been rejected, if not outright persecuted, in their own towns. Their own followers flee in terror. For example, we have the story of Peter denying Christ three times before the cock crows. In *Flatland,* the narrator's own brother, who himself witnessed the appearance of the Sphere, denies having seen anything when interrogated by Flatland's Council of Elders. Yet despite his attempt to acquiesce in the belief system of the prevailing scientific hierarchy, the brother is thrown in jail with the narrator.

This punishment seems unjustified. The narrator has not diagnosed or treated any disease or human condition; he has not prescribed any medication or operated on any person;[7] and he has not introduced into Flatland commerce any drug not approved by Flatland's Food and Drug Administration. His brother has not aided or abetted any crime. If Flatland has a First Amendment guaranteeing religious freedom, the narrator's incarceration probably is violative of that right.

Fortunately, the United States is a democratic society with certain laws and freedoms and a bill of rights; and we are not controlled by a priesthood of Circles. Imagine, though, the narrator's identity in terms of U.S. culture. He could be a physician whose license has been stripped because he has advocated a different view of medicine than approved by the Flatland Medical Association or the Flatland Federation of Medical Boards;[8] a nonlicensed healer, jailed for advocating his mystical insights as a healing balm adjunctive to Flatland's system of conventional care; a practitioner whose therapeutic practices differ from conventional Flatland models of care; or a patient accused of evading the Flatland Food and Drug Administration and then haled into court for defrauding the insurer in submitting reimbursement claims for an unconventional therapy.[9]

Medical Models in Flatland

The book *Flatland* is written in terms of the narrator's testament to the existence of the Sphere and his appeal to the denizens of Flatland to adopt a less limited perspective on their reality. We can let the imagination wander and wonder what medical care consists of in Flatland. Although a complete imaginary taxonomy of disease theory in Flatland is beyond the scope of this chapter, I would imagine that Octagons, Hexagons, and other multisided beings, including the unfortunate Isoceles Triangulars, suffer from degenerative diseases in which their angles become deformed or even multiply (in advanced cases) due to genetic and environmental factors (pollutants and so on) as well as the stresses of Flatland society. Even the Circles may be subject to occasional deformities in their perfect circularity due to interactions with non-Circles (Flatland germ theory is relevant here). Women in Flatland would be especially prone to lower-back injuries, as relevant law requires them to exercise extreme caution in approaching men with their pointy backsides. (Flatland in fact doubtless has a government-funded center dedicated to the study of women's health issues.)

Conventional medical theory in Flatland would adopt a mechanistic and reductionistic approach to health and disease, asserting that the previously described dysfunctions are caused, as mentioned, either by environmental or genetic (in Flatland lingo, geometric) factors. Pharmaceuticals, surgery, and gene therapy would be treated identically in Flatland, as all three would involve making an incision in the patient's circumference or triangular or irregular physical boundaries, as the case may be; inserting the appropriate remedy; and sewing up the incision so as not to leave the geometric form open to invasive influences. Flatland would also have a technology that involves soothing the geometrical shape, whereby the patient is numbed or anesthetized. (Flatland proponents of "therapeutic slouch" would assert that such a calming effect can be achieved by relaxing the patient's geometric structure; softening the rigid, obtuse angles and protruding points; and creating better bodily *feng shui* through a noncontact therapy involving the projection of mental energy.)

In my imagination, the narrator's vision of the Sphere would lead to a manifesto for a new medicine.[10] The outline of this system, which might be scrawled on the walls of the jail cell of the narrator (or his brother), would assert as follows:

> Flatlanders are souls embodied in physical (geometric) form. Health consists of a state in which mind, body, and spirit are unified in alignment with the individual's divine purpose and experience of a sacred existence.
>
> The glorious Circle suggests physical perfection, but such perfection must be matched with emotional and spiritual perfection as well in a unified whole. Perfection can be found even in the form of the irregular Isoceles Triangular or in the delicate straight line of the feminine, when the person expresses emotional and spiritual wholeness within that form. Each form is subject to potential degeneration whenever the being adopts a belief that he or she is less than whole, is less than a perfect image of the One Sphere, whose absolute reality is perhaps even beyond contemplation. Sometimes genetic deficiencies are inherent in the physical form, but this is to teach the being and others around certain lessons, which can only be understood from the vantage point of the Sphere, lifting one above ordinary understanding. . . .
>
> This and many other mysteries were revealed to me, from a higher holographic order, during my journeys with the Sphere. However, they are not religious but practical and scientific and intended to be used to treat disease and heal suffering.[11]

The manifesto would conclude:

> I am aware that these views defy conventional paradigms, subject us to ridicule, and perhaps land us in jail; yet we have glimpsed truth, as revealed to us by Spheres in a land of Circles, Squares, and Triangles.

This manifesto is reminiscent of the time in the United States, within the past century, when "Go to jail for chiropractic!" was a professional slogan because *being* a chiropractor was a status offense.

From Flatland to Pointland

The narrator of *Flatland* gives an analogy to an even more limited world than his—Pointland. In Pointland, the reigning monarch, a mere Point, experiences himself as encompassing the entire universe of being. Even when the narrator addresses him, essentially saying, "I am from Flatland and you are nothing but a puny Point," the monarch experiences the voice as coming from within him; he cannot acknowledge the existence of a being from more than one dimension. This can be analogized to those who dismiss auditory perception of other realms as delusional, fantastic, or coming from "within" the mind.

Thus, Pointland, Flatland, and Spaceland (the Sphere's home) are metaphors for our own limited perspective of reality. In our normal state of awareness, we experience reality as composed of three dimensions. If a fourth-dimensional being were to enter our world as the Sphere descended into Flatland or as the Flatlander intruded into Pointland, we would be dumbfounded. If a fourth-dimensional being spoke to us, we would take the voice to be our own, as did the monarch in Pointland. It would be useless to argue; we would call this an "inner voice" or perhaps a "hallucination." We might even diagnose ourselves as schizophrenic or as delusional. By definition, having failed to attain sainthood or be recognized as avatars, we would have to be declared psychotic. Certainly, our meditative encounters would be explained away through some reductionistic understanding.

From Spaceland to Multidimensional Reality

In very general terms, the legal issues that the *Flatland* narrator's experience implies for our social order include the overbroad definitions of "practicing medicine" in medical licensing laws, which threaten such nonlicensed providers as practitioners of biofield therapeutics and lay homeopaths with criminal liability; the balkanization of licensed healing along professional scope-of-practice lines; the failure to define mal-

practice liability and professional discipline rules with sufficient preci-
sion to provide a safe legal haven for responsible medical innovation
and visionary development of nontraditional therapies; the restrictive
effect of specific legislation (such as California's historic cancer-care
laws) on use of therapies disfavored by an established orthodoxy; the
lack of meaningful integration of therapies outside the conventional
order into reimbursement structures; and the failure of existing legal
rules to account for therapies based on intuition, vision, or other natural
aspects of human experience relegated to religion or mystical practice.

Above all, the narrator's experience raises questions about regulating healers, whose experiences transcend normal legal and medical
boundaries. What regulation is appropriate if we take their experiences
not as mystical aberrations but as part of the wealth and wisdom of
medical and scientific lore? The narrator of *Flatland* might assert that
spiritual forms of healing based on the Sphere's teachings potentially
offer doorways into multidimensional reality, one that may steadily
become accessible not only to scientists, researchers, and meditative
travelers but also to health care professionals in the course of Flatland's
ordinary and mainstream care.

Yet these queries also create qualms. One could imagine, for example, that the narrator has been released from jail and has formed a professional association, complete with credentialing, state-accredited
educational institutions, a code of ethics, and a state-of-the-art research
center. Consider this perspective:

> All religions, like all philosophies, are ultimately lies; the very act
> of formalizing betrays the spontaneity of the experience. Is it for
> nothing that the words *tradition* and *betrayal* are derived from the
> same root . . . [and] cannot perform the task of *re-integration* or *unit-
> ing* with higher reality—the root meanings of the words *yoga* as
> well as *religion*.[12]

An orthodoxy by any other name is still an orthodoxy. We
embrace the scientific method as a bulwark against religious orthodoxy
and intolerance—yet, some would argue, our culture turns to holistic
health care and individual, mystical experience as a bulwark against a
scientific priesthood or medical orthodoxy. There are dangers in creating an institutionalized religion out of the narrator's experiences with
the Sphere. There are perhaps still greater dangers in "conventionaliz-

ing" an experience.[13] If Genesis were written to conform to conventional models, the first verse might be revised to use the passive voice and delete the reference to God: "In the beginning, the atmosphere and the earth were created. . . ." Certainly this reductionistic approach would remove the perplexing use of the Hebrew word *Elohim*—which is translated as "God" but plural.

Conclusion

Flatland could be a description of the U.S. medical system. None of the terms used to date to describe health care systems parallel to biomedicine ("holistic," "alternative," "complementary") adequately describe the kind of experience contemplated in *Flatland*. If modalities within the realm of spiritual healing truly encompass information being downloaded from higher realities (a term from religious life might be "personal revelation"),[14] then even the term "integrated" barely begins to describe the task of bringing together medicine, law, ethics, and spirituality.[15] Certainly it is an interdisciplinary project, in which the rational and the "irrational" will be bridged and in which aspects of the mind other than the intellectual will find use. Neither blanket dismissal nor blind acceptance of the findings of "unconventional" medicine will serve the higher purpose of truly understanding human experience— the meaning of, and means of alleviating, suffering. If the biofield provides a working map of human health and illness, the answer may lie not so much in the body as in these other dimensions of human experience. Of course, the question arises as to whether these "higher" (and "lower") realities are ones we want or need or rather portend enormous error and evil. Humanity's encounter with the spirit world largely has been relegated to religion, with little recognition in this culture of its potential importance to preventative medicine, care, and cure.

In turn, this leads to a larger contemplation of the proper role of spirituality in everyday clinical practice. Few would question the importance of the connection between the material and the spiritual at the end of life; serious contemplation of spiritual realities is viewed as entirely appropriate and a valued addition to modern medicine's technological armamentarium. The patient who prays before death or prior to surgery doubtless would argue that "higher realities" are ones we want or need. Further, when medicine denies such realities at death, medicine, by attempting to perpetuate biological existence at all costs, engages in a "pornography of death"[16]—and arguably of sickness as well. Advances in energy medicine suggest that spiritual realities are part and parcel of ordinary medical care and should be taken into account long before the end of life.

But are we humans, as a species, evolved or mature enough to handle all that this awareness entails? Certainly spirituality has been misused throughout human history; one cannot discuss Christianity in its historical context, for example, without considering the Inquisition. The excesses and abuses of the spiritual healer discussed in chapter 8 fuel this debate. Perhaps the fear of misuse of spiritual power is one reason for the historical split between biomedicine and its rivals in the late nineteenth century and for the present split between biomedicine and bioenergy—that is, between health care systems grounded in biochemistry, physics, and other sciences we know, on the one hand, and health care systems based on vital energies, spiritual forces, and phenomena of the biofield, on the other. The split leaves us with highly effective technologies, which seem precise, reliable, and mechanical enough to serve as repositories for a consensus faith in scientific knowledge. Yet, without the beyond, faith that is limited to things tangible becomes a mirage.

The man with the withered arm is an example of a patient whose condition was consciously addressed with an approach beyond the familiar. I asked Dr. Hunt what her purpose was in working with this individual. Was it to help regenerate the arm physiologically, to facilitate an emotional release of old trauma, to create a new awareness on a soul level, or to create some other therapeutic effect?

Dr. Hunt was silent as my questions multiplied. After a few minutes, she said: "This is what consciousness can do. We are realizing our full potential as human beings."

CHAPTER 12

Do Clones Have Souls? and Other
Medicolegal Mysteries

Do clones have souls? Are they more than replications of genetic material? Do they share a soul with the clone donor, the being from whose genetic material they are cloned? Does the answer differ depending on whether the clone is a human, an animal, an insect, or a tree?

The very use of the technology of cloning has met its share of questions. For example, does cloning represent a positive evolutionary development in health care and human history, or is it the "ultimate symbol of commodification" of human essence?[1]

As both conventional and nonconventional medical practitioners struggle to find answers to these questions, complementary and alternative medicine therapies such as energy healing can shed light on cloning and other medicolegal mysteries.

The Origin of the Species

When I studied energy healing, I would receive impressions of a number of issues that my "client," who would be lying on the table, was facing. Some would be unresolved issues from childhood—for example, involving conflicts with father, mother, or siblings. Others would involve events in professional life. Still others involved experiences transcending the normal events of childhood, professional life, and other aspects of physical and emotional life on this plane. In the system we learned, many of these experiences stemmed from other lifehoods—dimensions of psychospiritual life beyond the existence of the person's consciousness in the present physical body.[2]

> During one healing, I had one hand on my client's sacral chakra
> and one on her solar plexus chakra, while searching for astral
> objects embedded on the fourth layer of the energy field. Suddenly

I pulled a fragment of a disembodied child out of the client's energy field. The being immediately started speaking to me: "My name is ———. I was only so many months in the womb when my mother decided to have an abortion. I have remained in her field to remind her of our bond and of the unspoken grief she has to process in order to clear this experience." The child then addressed his mother: "Know that I love, that I have always loved you, and that I forgive you for what you felt was necessary. We will always love each other, we will always be together, and though I cannot come to you now in the physical body, my spirit will always be a part of you."

At that moment, although I said nothing, the client started crying. I encouraged her to release the feelings, as the child's memory pattern of the trauma continued to lift off her field. I could hear her inside, acknowledging her love for the child, initiating a dialogue with him, and releasing what had been frozen for two decades.

When the healing was complete, I gently asked my client what she had experienced on the table. She reported that she had had an abortion some twenty years earlier and that she had, in the healing, experienced this incredible union with her child, which was releasing guilt and healing her frozen sorrow. We shared and then presented this information to classmates and found that many others were having similar experiences.

A Rebel of Love

I attempted to write about the experiences of energy healing within the framework of medical ethics. One paper I wrote involved multifetal pregnancy reduction—the "selective termination" of fetuses after successful use of fertility drugs (see chap. 10). A colleague advised, "Don't write about abortion—*ever*—not if you want to get anywhere in your professional life." So everything I wrote had to be from the perspective of "a shaman or medicine man." By distancing myself and writing in the third person or in the hypothetical—that is, by shrouding my truth in comfortable academic metaphor—I could present material without risking the ire of colleagues.

The teachers in healing school insisted that deeper psychic and spiritual openings only resulted from speaking the truth and from "clearing" issues embedded in the biofield. "Love," one teacher said, "is an act of rebellion; be a rebel for love." Deeper openings raised the potential for intimacy and manifested as increased light, or radiance, in the face; a visible softening of the features; and increased capacity for joyful relationships. Heartful exchanges were possible from a space of personal power and expression of one's core, as individuals reclaimed more of their own essential energies. In shamanism, a similar process is known as *soul retrieval*.[3]

The contrast between the freedom of this environment and the rigidity and essence obscuration of my professional world—which supposedly dealt with health—presented a split. In healing school, classmates writhed on the floor as spears, hooks, astral entities, and other negative energies were removed from their energy fields. In my office, hundreds of articles piled on the floor as I extracted arguments from appropriate citations. I sat with *Roe v. Wade* and other judicial opinions, extracting legal authority for these intractable social issues and wading through a world of mentation, conflicting perspectives, decisions, authoritative statements of law and ethics; pronouncement about good and evil, right and wrong, heaven and hell, the moral and the reprehensible. The heart center spoke to/through the mind.

Franz Kafka once analogized his study of law to "sawdust which, moreover, has already been tasted in other people's mouths." Kafka's statement resonates if law, medicine, and healing are expressed completely on the mental level, where each noble truth is desiccated, robbed of emotional meaning, and reduced to a conceptual abstraction that has no life. Many providers view the task of integrating therapies in terms of appeasing current medical and legal authorities—as legal defense and protection. The alternative, as Flatland suggests, is jail—or its professional equivalent—isolation, marginalization, and ridicule. Beyond this, though, is an evolutionary task: articulating new models of reality that can shift the way we view legal, ethical, and clinical parameters. Until now, many of these issues have divided, rather than unified, the human spirit.

Assuming that a fair amount of "anecdotal" (or sacerdotal) evidence—people's heartfelt stories—can be connected, these experiences might shed light on some aspects of human affairs that we tend to closet after law and/or religious doctrine have had their say. The result might be a truly "integrated" system in that legal and ethical rules will be unified in a larger philosophical, spiritual, and emotionally complete context.

Complementary and alternative medicine provides one haven for practitioners, patients, and thinkers integrating professional interests with personal, radical encounters with the numinous. Nonetheless, attempts to gain social acceptance, to fit into the medical model, to meet "scientific rigor" (for example, trying to explain biofield phenomena in strictly mechanistic or biological terms), and to prevent the dismissal of personal revelation as "anecdotal" evidence challenge the presentation of a worldview that is so radical, so startling, that it suggests revolutionary changes in the medical and social order.

From the Heart of the Dead

Energy healing changes relationships on all orders of existence. The following tale comes from the time after death, rather than before birth.

> Once I was involved with a medical school student. After a time, it became clear that she still had some unfinished emotional business with her former husband, who had died unexpectedly some years earlier. The lack of resolution, completion, or closure in that relationship was interfering with the possibility of a new heart connection.
>
> Psychotherapists normally do not analyze their lovers or spouses, and therefore it is important for healers to know when to "turn off" the gift. Nonetheless, one day we were sitting across from one another on the sofa, sharing our lives, when this golden ball of light appeared beside her. I asked her to tell me the story of her husband's death.
>
> As she spoke, his presence grew brighter and brighter. She was describing a death that was chaotic, medicalized, and, from an emotional and spiritual perspective, mismanaged—in short, the typical hospital death. As a trained healer, my awareness expanded to other levels: to her husband. There were several angels around and above him. Healing words were coming through me. I spoke them as they passed through my consciousness: helping my friend forgive herself for not being able to save her husband from his own death, from the experience of death he had to undergo.
>
> I did not make a big announcement about what I was doing; I simply channeled the information to help her clear her heart cords,

facilitating a dialogue between them that both of them needed but that had never taken place—a conversation about his departure from the body and the completion of their relationship.

I felt his immense love for her. I also felt clear enough about my own separate identity to distinguish my feelings of love for her from his. This rich state of awareness lasted perhaps twenty minutes, punctuated by rounds of grieving, deeper breathing, and stillness. When the conversation was over she audibly said good-bye, let him go, and sighed.

She was surrounded by a sea of gold and purple light. He blessed our involvement, and I in turn thanked him for the gift. And then he left; a block had been cleared.

A classmate in healing school was the chief executive officer of a New York hospital. Following healings, he would "channel" the archangel Raphael. My friend described a situation at work in which a patient requested some assistance from one of the hospital's physicians involving disconnection from life support. The disconnect was at the gray edge of what was legally and ethically permissible at the time. The patient's physician honored the request, the patient died, and the family sued the hospital. My friend was stuck with the lawsuit. As a channel, he perceived the patient hovering around the various family members, trying to communicate to them that he was having a great time in his spirit body and that he regretted seeing them running around trying to aggravate everyone who had been a faithful caretaker in his life.

My friend was longing to remove the hat of the CEO, release the energies of litigation, and offer his perspective as a healer.

"Jack," I said, "that's not the kind of testimony likely to convince a jury. Moreover, there's no legal standard that says you have to take the patient's wishes into account when those wishes are expressed *after* he has left his physical body."

"Michael," he predicted, "this healership will shift the consciousness of the legal system."

Seven Generations

Beyond cloning, much debate has surrounded other issues in bioethics, from abortion to the "right-to-die." Philosophical distinctions may satisfy the mind but not the heart and spirit. If clones have souls, the debate must be framed from the soul level, not only in terms of the individual, but also in terms of the community.

When we talk about integrative medicine and the evolution of legal authority, we are not only speaking about how to practice medicine or any health care modality within existing legal parameters or about changing the law by adding this or that piece of legislation, although these are important tasks. What we know as complementary and alternative medicine augurs such an immense shift in the social order that we can hardly contemplate what our world will look like in five, ten, or fifty years. Anybody who practices *chi gong,* who meditates, or who turns within and has more than intellectual knowledge has experienced in their own being the magnitude of the shift.

A friend's nine-year-old daughter recently witnessed a television interview with a healer. At one point, the reporter challenged the healer, "Is this stuff really real?" The child told her mother that the healer responded from such a place of center that all the beings in the reporter's energy field simply scattered and got out of the way.

The mother did not send her child to the school psychologist. She listened.

The mother told me: "These souls are starting to incarnate, and they are our teachers; in part, our mission is to prepare the world for *them."* These children of the twenty-second century cannot breathe and spread their wings in a world where regulation and policy are based on nineteenth-century notions of struggle, competition, supremacy, and monopolization of the healing arts.

Enlightenment and Health

If the ultimate goal of healing on all levels is enlightenment, then one might infer that enlightenment produces health. Yet, there is no evidence that enlightenment as understood by the mystics correlates with physical health. In fact, on the contrary, many saints in various world traditions have had severe health problems. Whether one cites Ramakrishna from the Hindu tradition or various Catholic saints, health challenges have often served as stimuli to greater faith in transcendent powers as the ultimate source of a saint's attainment.

No randomized, controlled, double-blind studies have been done of enlightened spiritual masters to determine whether their enlightened state could be correlated with superior physical health. Many of them were less concerned with the physical body and more interested in spiritual transcendence. Even those more grounded in worldly affairs regarded the body as an instrument for divine grace, which could be dispensed with in the service of a higher calling. Hence Gandhi participated in hunger fasts in the midst of his national leadership.

In contrast to saints undergoing physical purification, the theory of holistic health assumes that spiritual health can translate into physical health and that there are correlations between mental, emotional, and spiritual clarity, on the one hand, and physical well-being, on the other. These two paradigms themselves await reconciliation in future discussions of the relationship between enlightenment and health.

Conclusion

Living in the biofield will affect each discipline and move law, medicine, ethics, and healing to the soul perspective, whether dealing with human, animal, plant, stem cell, or clone.[4] Consider intuitive scanning rather than exploratory surgery as an initial procedure; conscious relationships with the living consciousness in "inanimate" objects and nonphysical beings; conversations with the living forces in one's food; parents playing with their children before the children are incarnated; conscious births and deaths and greater efforts to map the in-between; perception of violent thoughts and impulses seen in the auric field before they are manifested; clearing of disease in advance as emotional and spiritual realities are handled;[5] true awareness of who we truly are.

How would an enlightened civilization, composed of enlightened citizens, govern its own evolutionary movement toward the highest possible level of healing? What role would law play? Would the absence of regulation, instead of its pervasiveness, bring peace? Would legal structures be able to handle not only the notion that healing involves mind, body, emotions, and spirit but also such other dimensions of the human experience as interspecies communication and a greater sense of earth-consciousness (Gaia)?

How will integrative and energy medicine shape alternative dispute resolution and its relation to the resolution of litigation? In addition to negotiation, arbitration, and meditation, would a legal counselor work on higher planes and levels of the field to clear destructive energies between disputants?

A century ago, people could not imagine today's society in which many are walking the streets, trains, subways, and supermarkets while carrying on conversations with faraway friends by speaking into portable phones. A person in the nineteenth century who witnessed one such person would dismiss the speaker as schizophrenic. Perhaps in the next century, individuals will take a break from conversation to receive a telepathic communication from an extraterrestrial friend. (Who knows that Joan of Arc was not a time traveler who had implanted into her brain a radio chip through which she heard "voices" that dictated battle strategy?)

Perhaps sooner, we may have scientific instrumentation to measure the subtle bodies.[6] Just as biofeedback instruments today can detect the effect of various thoughts on physical health, future instrumentation may be able to measure the effect of thoughts at a distance. With these changes, old legal structures will require transformation. We have laws, for example, to govern physical pollution, but what about mental pollution? Or take the tort concept of nuisance, currently defined as an unreasonable interference with the use and enjoyment of property. Smoke, odors, and even physical vibrations (such as drilling) can constitute an actionable nuisance. If the disturbance is on the subtle planes but can be definitely detected (and potentially measured), will it constitute an actionable nuisance?

Or consider battery, defined as offensive or harmful touching without consent. What constitutes touching in a world where individuals are conscious of not only their physical bodies but also their subtle bodies, the auric fields that extend several feet from the physical body? Will the concept of negligence, used in malpractice, include the provider's mental, emotional, and spiritual effect on the patient? How will we, individually and collectively, escape, defeat, or transcend the matrix?

As health care expands, our way of looking at health care must expand and embrace new levels of being. An order derived from the mind can no longer superimpose its will on a changing reality; rather, that reality must be shaped by a higher purpose and intelligence. Law, like medicine, inevitably will change, and human evolution will move in the balance. If clones have souls, they will respect the balance, and in that balance, legal rule making and medical ethics will honor health from a place of greater purpose, wisdom, and intelligence.

Conclusion

The Yoga of Medicine

In his *Yoga Sutras,* the ancient Indian sage Patanjali begins by stating that yoga is the stilling of the thought-waves of the mind.[1] Once the thought-waves are stilled, Patanjali states, the human being abides in his or her true nature.[2] In other words, when the mind is calm and clear, a person realizes his or her own true and inborn state, which, Pantjali says, is bliss.[3]

Patanjali thus traces all dis-ease to the distortions of the mind. Innumerable thoughts constantly arise, veiling the shimmering luminescence that comprises the divine core of every human being. Yoga, or union (with that divine core), is the process of shedding the veils that keep individuals from the ultimate realization of who they truly are.

Patajanli's ancient definition of yoga correlates with the modern, legal definition of "medicine." In the codification of statutes relating to education, the state of New York defines the practice of "medicine" as "diagnosing, treating, operating, or prescribing for any human disease, pain, injury, deformity or physical condition."[4] Michigan defines the practice of medicine as "diagnosis, treatment, prevention, cure, or relieving of a human disease, ailment, defect, complaint or other physical or mental condition, by attendance, advice, device, diagnostic test, or other means."[5] The statutory definition of practicing "medicine" thus embraces treatment of physical as well as mental conditions. Disease literally means dis-ease, a state in which the individual is no longer at ease with his or her body, mind, or spirit. The word *disease* is put together with words such as "pain, injury, deformity" (New York) or "ailment, defect, complaint" (Michigan). In other words, almost any deviation from a state of complete comfort with one's physical or mental state is included. The practice of "medicine" is defined to include any attempt to influence an individual regarding a response to this state of dis-ease, whether it involves an actual medical diagnosis or, at least in Michigan, mere "advice."

In essence, what Patanjali describes as the universal human dilemma—a state of alienation from our true nature—New York and Michigan describe as the object of the practice of medicine. The law defines the practice of medicine as yoga: clearing the mental and physical distortions that block us from a realization and experience of our healthy core. Yoga, in turn, defines medicine—in its broadest sense—as law, as the highest duty of every human being.[6]

Medicine versus Healing

Current legal rules do not permit yoga to embody its medicinal aspirations. Indeed, the law assumes that yoga is a branch of medicine, whereas yoga views medicine as a branch of a much larger universe of tools for human health and wholeness.

The statutory definitions selected are typical of the ways states generally define the practice of medicine. These definitions would be satisfactory if they referred to *healing* rather than medicine. Healing means treating dis-ease at any or all levels of being—physical, mental, emotional, environmental, spiritual. The statute, though, regulates the practice of medicine and provides that the unlicensed practice of medicine is a crime. This means that if a yoga instructor tells someone, for example, that a certain posture can release toxins from the liver, help someone who has poor circulation, or empower a patient with a compromised immune function, the instructor arguably has crossed the line into practicing medicine. Healing cannot be separated from medicine: the body, mind, spirit, and emotions are interconnected. As noted in earlier chapters, the issue for yoga instructors is typical of legal challenges facing both licensed and nonlicensed complementary and alternative medicine providers.

The claims that a complementary and alternative medicine practitioner, such as a yoga instructor, can make have to be carefully limited to avoid crossing this legal boundary. For example, one can say that yoga has a relaxing effect and can alleviate stress, thus contributing to healthy functioning. But this is so generalized as to lack significance, particularly since many yoga postures are specifically geared toward strengthening certain organs of the body or performing certain functions for healing from particular diseases. Although Patanjali did not describe specific postures, he did lay out a guide to enlightenment, a process by which the mind can be cleared of cobwebs so that the light of one's inner being can shine. Subsequent yogic texts described in precise detail the relation of various asanas, or physical postures, to health and the human body. The same is true for many other disciplines within complementary and alternative medicine: they correlate physical to emotional and spiritual health, even if the practices are styled as strictly energetic or spiritual.

Overcoming Legal Barriers to Healing

From a public policy perspective, patient safety has been used to justify the notion that yoga instructors and other complementary and alternative medicine providers should not practice medicine in the sense of making medical diagnoses (for example, saying, "you have diabetes") or taking responsibility for a patient's medical treatment (for example, saying, "don't worry about prescription medication, just do 111 sun salutations a day"). In practice, however, teaching yoga can cross the line into advising students about specific physical or mental conditions and the way yoga can expand the student's opening to healing, or perhaps softening around, these conditions. This is not only natural but entirely appropriate, since yoga is thousands of years older than modern medicine and since much of the wisdom for healing that it contains is unknown to contemporary physicians or requires body experience as well as mental comprehension.

Combining such modalities as yoga with biomedical wonders to achieve a healing result is an ideal. Rather than assuming that biomedicine occupies the entire field of healing (an assumption that governs the language of the medical licensing laws), the model of integrative health care assumes that biomedicine can be successfully integrated with different therapies in ways that can augment medical diagnosis and treatment with the therapeutic perspectives of these different disciplines.

From a yogic perspective, mental obfuscation, manifesting in body blockages, may be the diagnosis, and a daily practice focusing on subtle movement in mind and body may be the treatment. This perspective is similar to the Boddhitsatva's Vow in Buddhism: "May I be the doctor and the medicine. . . ." The etiology of the disease, its personal meaning, its message, and the therapeutic response all have the same origin—within the person. Yoga and biomedicine carry divergent technologies yet share the goal of healing. Legal rules should acknowledge the overlap.

Conclusion

The function of law is not to draw ironclad boundaries between over-lapping professions but rather to create a structure in which the patient's healing needs can be optimally accommodated. Enacting legislation is part of the process of legal change; so too are shifts in consciousness among those who make, interpret, and enforce the law. The legal system governing complementary and alternative medicine in the United States as elsewhere emerged out of a certain social, political, and cultural milieu. The conditions that led to a closed system of professional healing, to a Darwinian struggle for inclusion in legally sanctioned practice, and to a model of extreme paternalism are changing. In the future, personal transformation and personal revelation will guide and mold the expansion and reformation of legal authority. In this way, the twenty-first-century legal system will keep pace with developments in health care as new understandings of health emerge.

Health care in the next two thousand years should and will address the whole person. Rather than merely treating physical symptoms or attempting to cure disease on the physical level, health care will integrate mental, emotional, and spiritual components. The focus will be not only on alleviating diseases defined within the medical model but also on maintaining wellness in a deeper sense than we ever have known. As individuals, as communities, and as members of a collective whole, we hope to experience greater mind-body-spirit unity and deeper inner happiness as a result of new perspectives on what it means to be healthy, alive, and expressing our spirit within and through a human body.

To the extent that complementary and alternative medicine will bring a greater sense of wonder, unity, and structure to the individual's quest for health on all levels, legal and regulatory structures will reflect and support this shift toward recognizing the many dimensions of the person's search for wholeness. The gifts of the body, of psyche and of soul, fully will unfold, as health care merges into the process of personal and planetary growth, in soil cultivated for spiritual development and human evolution.

Notes

INTRODUCTION

1. See Paul Starr, *The Social Transformation of American Medicine* (New York: Basic Books, 1982).

2. William G. Rothstein, *American Medical Schools and the Practice of Medicine: A History*, 70 (Baltimore: Johns Hopkins University Press, 1987).

3. See Harris L. Coulter, *Divided Legacy: The Conflict between Homeopathy and the American Medical Association* (Berkeley: North Atlantic Books, 1973).

4. See Michael H. Cohen, "A Fixed Star in Health Care Reform: The Emerging Paradigm of Holistic Healing," 1 (27) *Ariz. State. L.J.* 79 (1995).

5. See Michael H. Cohen, *Complementary and Alternative Medicine: Legal Boundaries and Regulatory Perspectives*, 10–12 (Baltimore: Johns Hopkins University Press, 1998) (describing scientific substantiation and methodological challenges underpinning the various therapies).

6. Stefano Maddalena, *The Legal Status of Complementary Medicines in Europe*, 289–92 (Bern: Stämpfli, 1999).

7. See, e.g., David M. Eisenberg, R. B. Davis, S. L. Ettner, S. Appel, S. Wilkey, M. Van Rompay, and R. Kessler, "Trends in Alternative Medicine Use in the United States, 1990–1997: Results of a Follow-Up National Survey," 280 (18) *JAMA* 1569 (1998); N. C. Elder, A. Gillcrist, and R. Minz, "Use of Alternative Health by Family Practice Patients," 6 *Arch. Fam. Med.* 181 (1997).

CHAPTER 1

1. Michael H. Cohen, *Complementary and Alternative Medicine: Legal Boundaries and Regulatory Perspectives*, 17–21 (Baltimore: Johns Hopkins University Press, 1998) (citing cases).

2. Id., 31–32 (citing cases).

3. *People v. Andrews*, 260 Cal. Rptr. 113 (Ct. App. 1989) (the court, noting that the prescribed fasts and other treatments were for therapeutic and not religious purpose, found the defendant minister to have practiced medicine).

4. *Smith v. People*, 117 P. 612 (Colo. 1911).

5. See chapter 6. In complementary and alternative medicine, "the quest for health takes on sacred proportions, allowing the patient to discern ultimate meaning and make profound connections with the universe" (Ted J. Kaptchuk

and David M. Eisenberg, "The Persuasive Appeal of Alternative Medicine," 129 [12] *Ann. Int. Med.* 1061, 1063 [1998]). However, as social support groups, "relaxation response" therapies, lifestyle choices to reduce risk factors, and other therapeutic tools rife with spiritual overtones enter the mainstream, the obverse claim could be made that patients commit to therapeutic regimens as "religious disciplines . . . which are adopted with the aim of somatic perfection" (id.).

6. Cohen 1998, 2–3.

7. Eric J. Cassell, "The Sorcerer's Broom: Medicine's Rampant Technology," 23 (6) *Hastings Center Rep.* 32 (1993); Ivan Illich, *Medical Nemesis: The Expropriation of Health* (New York: Pantheon Books, 1976).

8. Cohen 1998, 3–8; Jan Smuts, *Holism and Evolution* (London: Macmillan, 1926; reprint, Westport, Conn.: Greenwood Press, 1973).

9. David M. Eisenberg et al., "Unconventional Medicine in the United States: Prevalence, Costs, and Patterns of Use," 328 (4) *N. Engl. J. Med.* 256 (1993).

10. Landmark Healthcare, *Landmark Report on Public Perceptions of Alternative Care* (Sacramento: Landmark Healthcare, 1998).

11. David M. Eisenberg, R. B. Davis, S. L. Ettner, S. Appel, S. Wilkey, M. Van Rompay, and R. Kessler, "Trends in Alternative Medicine Use in the United States, 1990–1997: Results of a Follow-Up National Survey," 280 (18) *JAMA* 1569 (1998).

12. Eisenberg et al. 1998.

13. See Michael H. Cohen, "A Fixed Star in Health Care Reform: The Emerging Paradigm of Holistic Healing," 1 (27) *Ariz. State L.J.* 79, 137–41 (1995).

14. *Alternative Medicine: Expanding Medical Horizons (A Report to the National Institutes of Health on Alternative Medical Systems and Practices in the United States)*, NIH Pub. 94–0666 (Dec. 1994).

15. Id., xi–xxiii.

16. Since the Chantilly Report, a number of studies of various modalities have been published in major medical journals, including a study of the effect of Chinese medicine on breech babies in the November 11, 1998, issue of the *Journal of the American Medical Association.*

17. Tibet's medical tradition already is "integrative," in that some 1,100 or more years ago, it absorbed the medical traditions of China, India, and other neighboring countries and held international meetings to discuss its version of integrative medicine.

18. See W. Y. Evan-Wentz, trans., *The Tibetan Book of the Dead* (London: Oxford University Press, 1960).

19. *Cruzan v. Director, Missouri Dept. of Health,* 497 U.S. 261 (1990) (articulating the limits of technology at death).

20. See Sogyal Rinpoche, *The Tibetan Book of Living and Dying,* 185–86 (San Francisco: Harper San Francisco, 1992).

21. See Cohen 1998, 24–26 (citing cases).

22. Id., 26–29 (citing statutes).

23. Id., 29–31 (citing cases); see also chapter 6, infra.

24. An example is *Stetina v. State,* 513 N.E.2d 1234 (Ind. Ct. App. 1987). This case involved a nonmedical provider of health care lacking independent licensure. The defendant, Stetina, was a nutritionist who practiced iridology. When an undercover investigator visited, Stetina prescribed colonic irrigation and various nutritional remedies. On appeal from an injunction barring her from practice, Stetina argued that her conduct, which aimed at helping individuals follow proper nutritional advice, was outside the purview of the medical practice act and that, in any event, most physicians did not address nutrition and thus her practice was complementary. The Indiana Court of Appeals disagreed and held that Stetina was practicing medicine without a license.

25. Cohen 1998, 39–45 (citing statutes); David M. Eisenberg, "Advising Patients Who Seek Alternative Medical Therapies," 127 (1) *Ann. Int. Med.* 61, 64 (1997).

26. Cohen 1998, 87–95 (citing statutes).

27. Complementary and alternative medicine professionals thus are legislatively forbidden from intruding into the practice of medicine unless they have a medical degree and medical licensure. For example, if the nonmedical provider makes an overbroad claim or purports to treat or cure a disease in the medical sense, the provider not only is subject to potential tort-law claims based on fraud and misrepresentation but also risks prosecution for the unlicensed practice of medicine. Such a provider can be subject as well to a disciplinary proceeding. Thus, medical and other licensing laws help ensure that complementary and alternative practices do not make extravagant promises and claims and do not divert patients from necessary, conventional medical care.

It should be noted that some licensing statutes authorize such activities as "chiropractic diagnosis" or "acupuncture diagnosis." This does not, however, authorize the practitioner to engage in diagnosing and treating disease as understood within the medical model. Further, the effect of licensing laws as a control on dangerous providers must be considered together with other regulatory devices, such as common-law malpractice rules.

28. See, e.g., Walter Gelhorn, "The Abuse of Occupational Licensing," 44 *U. Chi. L. Rev.* 6 (1976); Sue A. Blevins, "The Medical Monopoly: Protecting Consumers or Limiting Competition?" *Pol'y Analysis* no. 246 (Washington, D.C.: Cato Institute, 1995); Daniel B. Hogan, "The Effectiveness of Licensing: History, Evidence, and Recommendations," and Elton Rayack, "Medical Licensure: Social Costs and Social Benefits," 7 (2/3) *L. and Hum. Behav.* 117, 147–50 (1983); Edwin A. Locke et al., "The Case against Medical Licensing," 3 *Medicolegal News* (October 1980); Michael Pertschuck, "Professional Licensure," 43 (12) *Conn. Med.* 793 (1993).

29. See Norman Gevitz, "Alternative Medicine and the Orthodox Canon," 62 *Mt. Sinai J. Med.* 127 (1995); Ted J. Kaptchuk, "Intentional Ignorance: A History of Blind Assessment and Placebo Controls," 72 *Bull. Hist. Med.* 389 (1998).

30. See Cohen 1998, 112–14.

31. See, e.g., *Wilk v. American Medical Ass'n*, 895 F.2d 352 (7th Cir.), cert. denied, 496 U.S. 927 (1990).

32. *State Medical Soc'y v. Board of Examiners in Podiatry*, 546 A.2d 830 (Conn. 1988); Cohen 1998, 35; Thomas L. Greaney, "Public Licensure, Private Certification, and Credentialing of Medical Professionals: An Antitrust Perspective," in Timothy S. Jost, ed., *Regulation of the Healthcare Professions*, 158–61 (Chicago: Health Administration Press, 1997) (describing antitrust concerns in certifying, credentialing, and peer-review activities).

33. See Cohen 1998, 45.

34. See, e.g., *U.S. v. Larn*, 824 F.2d 780 (9th Cir. 1987), cert. denied, 484 U.S. 1078 (1988) (allergist convicted on 17 counts of Medicaid fraud for nurse-administered allergy shot; the violation involved using CPT Code 90040, "brief examination, evaluation and/or treatment same or new illness," rather than CPT Code 90030, "minimal service: injections minimal dressings, etc. not necessarily requiring the presence of a physician"); *Anesthesiologists Affiliated v. Sullivan*, 941 F.2d 678 (8th Cir. 1991) (physicians who had described their services "unartfully" in Medicare claims were held to be liable for civil penalties under the Medicare and Medicaid False Claims statute).

35. See *In re Guess*, 393 S.E.2d 833, 841 (N.C. 1990), cert. denied, 498 U.S. 1047 (1991) (J. Frye, dissenting) (a physician being disciplined for using homeopathic medicine is described as "not a case of a quack beguiling the public with snake oil and drums, but a dedicated physician seeking to find new ways to relieve human suffering").

36. See, e.g., Cohen 1998, 22–23 (citing cases), 106–7.

37. 817 F.2d 987, 995, (2d Cir. 1987) (citing *Schloendorff v. Society of New York Hospital*, 105 N.E. 92, 93 [1914]).

38. 371 So.2d 1037 (Fla. Dist. Ct. App. 1979).

39. *Bushman v. State Mutual Life Ass'n Co. of America*, 915 F. Supp. 945, 953 (N.D. Ill. 1996).

40. 1999 HI S.C.R. 50 (April 5, 1999) (proposing a feasibility study on the potential of establishing a medicinal herb industry in Hawaii). See also 1999 HI S.B. 1235 (April 30, 1999) (proposing a governor's task force on alternative medicine); 1999 MA H.B. 3659 (January 6, 1999) (proposing a study of complementary and alternative medicine regulation, education, and reimbursement).

41. *Standards for Physicians Practicing Integrative and Complementary Medicine, Texas Administrative Code*, 22 TAC §§ 200.1–200.3 (1998).

42. Id.

43. Id.

CHAPTER 2

1. Michael H. Cohen, *Complementary and Alternative Medicine: Legal Boundaries and Regulatory Perspectives*, 21–23 (Baltimore: Johns Hopkins University Press, 1998).

2. Id., 1, 13–14 (articulating the paradigmatic shifts).

3. Liability associated with physician referral to complementary and alternative medicine providers and liability arising in the institutional setting are addressed in chapters 4 and 5, respectively. Liability relating to practice by nonphysician complementary and alternative medicine providers (such as chiropractors, massage therapists, and acupuncturists) and liability relating to insurance or managed care are addressed in Cohen 1998, 56–72, 96–108.

4. Barry R. Furrow, Timothy L. Greaney, Sandra H. Johnson, Timothy S. Jost, and Robert L. Schwartz, *Health Law,* 237–41 (Minneapolis: West Publishing, 1995).

5. NIH Consensus Statement 107, 15(5) (Nov. 3–5, 1997).

6. Cohen 1998, 56.

7. See, e.g., Brian M. Berman, R. K. Singh, L. Lao, K. S. Ferentz, and S. M. Hartnoll, *Physicians' Attitudes toward Complementary or Alternative Medicine,* 8 *Am. Board. Fam. Pract.* 361–66 (1995); M. B. Blecher and K. Douglass, *Gold in Goldenseal,* 71 (20) *Health and Hosp. Networks* 50–52 (1997) (58 percent of HMOs surveyed intend to cover alternative therapies); M. S. Wetzel, David M. Eisenberg, and Ted J. Kaptchuk, *Courses Involving Complementary and Alternative Medicine at US Medical Schools,* 280(9) *JAMA* 784 (1998).

8. 660 N.Y.S.2d 665, 668 (S.Ct., N.Y. County, 1997), affirmed and modified to vacate punitive damages award, 673 N.Y.S.2d 685 (App. Div., 1st Dept., 1998), reargument denied, appeal denied, 1998 N.Y. App. Div. LEXIS 10711 (App. Div., 1st Dept., 1998), appeal denied, 706 N.E.2d 1211 (1998).

9. 660 N.Y.S.2d 669. The decision was affirmed but modified on appeal to vacate the punitive damages award.

10. 660 N.Y.S.2d 668. As noted later in text, however, this statement is qualified to the extent that the physician may have available a "respectable minority" defense, which enables utilization of therapies accepted by a "respectable minority" within the profession.

11. See Cohen 1998, 22–23, 112 (citing cases).

12. Ultimately, practice guidelines may reflect the development of sufficient scientific investigation and peer consensus over time so that the therapy in question becomes part of the standard of care. It has been noted that "[u]sing guidelines as evidence of professional custom, however, is problematic if they are ahead of prevailing medical practice." Barry R. Furrow, Timothy L. Greaney, Sandra H. Johnson, Timothy S. Jost, and Robert L. Schwartz, *Liability and Quality Issues in Health Care,* 136 (3d ed., Minneapolis: West Publishing, 1997).

13. *U.S. v. LeBeau,* 1993 U.S. App. LEXIS 1501, at *5–6 (Jan. 28, 1993). See also Lori B. Andrew, "The Shadow Health Care System: Regulation of Alternative Health Care Providers," 32 *Hous. L. Rev.* 1273 (1996).

14. See, e.g., Cohen 1998, 112 (citing cases).

15. Id., 58 (citing cases).

16. 817 F.2d 987 (2d Cir. 1987).

17. Notably, the jury failed to find fraud, a claim the plaintiff had premised on Dr. Revici's alleged promise to cure the patient of breast cancer.

18. The Second Circuit later held that even without a written consent, the jury could determine whether the patient knowingly accepted the risks of the physician's negligence, thus barring recovery; see *Boyle v. Revici*, 961 F.2d 1060, 1063 (2d Cir. 1992). *Schneider* and *Boyle*, together with *Shorter v. Drury*, 695 P.2d 116 (Wash. 1985) (reducing damages for physician negligence by 75 percent because of a finding that a Jehovah's Witness assumed the risk of bleeding to death), "frame the patient's decision to pursue unconventional treatment in terms of [patient choice and] assumption of risk" (Cohen 1998, 64).

19. 817 F.2d 994. In *Charell*, implied assumption of risk arose from the fact that the patient "did a significant amount of investigation" regarding the unconventional therapy "and hence became quite knowledgeable on the subject," as well as from the fact that the patient "sought to avoid the suffering that accompanied the chemotherapy/radiation regimen" (660 N.Y.S.2d 668–69).

20. 817 P.2d 995.

21. Such responsibility lessens patient dependence on the physician's fiduciary obligation. See Michael H. Cohen, "A Fixed Star in Health Care Reform: The Emerging Paradigm of Holistic Healing," 1 (27) *Ariz. State L.J.* 79, 152 (1995) (citing Heidi Rian, "An Alternative Contractual Approach to Holistic Health Care," 44 *Ohio State L.J.* 185, 187 [1993]).

22. *Larsen v. Pacesetter Systems, Inc.*, 837 P.2d 1273, 1290, amended, 843 P.2d 144 (Hawaii 1992) (products liability case). *Larsen* held that express assumption of risk serves as a complete defense to a defendant's liability; the concept of primary implied assumption of risk is thus abolished, and secondary implied assumption of risk triggers comparative negligence (id., 1291).

23. The jury in *Schneider* awarded Edith Schneider $500,000, finding her 50 percent liable for $1 million dollars in damages. The jury in *Charell* found that although the plaintiff was 49 percent responsible for her injuries, she was entitled to damages for pain and suffering in the amount of $4.5 million, to $200,000 for past and future loss of earnings, and to $150,000 in punitive damages. On appeal the punitive damages award was vacated (673 N.Y.S.2d 685 [App Div., 1st Dept., 1998]).

24. 407 A.2d 555, 567–68 (D.C. Cir. 1979). *Morrison* notes that in cases sustaining the defense, "the patient was specifically warned about a risk, and refused to follow the doctor's instructions" (Id., 574 [citing cases]).

25. 873 F.2d 1453, 1457 (D.C. Cir. 1989) (rejecting the defense where the patient merely followed his doctor's orders). Both defenses hold the patient responsible for certain risks of treatment. Contributory negligence is objective (it assumes the patient knew or should have known of the risk), whereas assumption of risk is subjective (it also assumes the patient knew) (id., 1458).

26. 837 P.2d 1277 (quoting F. James, "Assumption of Risk," 61 *Yale L.J.* 141, 169 [1952], and citing sources).

27. *Tunkl v. Regents of the Univ. of Calif.*, 383 P.2d 441 (Cal. 1963); *Illinois v. Jihan*, 519 N.E.2d 22 (Ill. App. Ct. 1988), affirmed, 537 N.E.2d 751 (Ill. 1989).

28. 817 F.2d at 993.

29. 648 N.Y.S.2d 827 (S.Ct., App. Div. 1996), appeal dismissed, 660 N.Y.S.2d 554 (N.Y. Ct. App. 1997).

30. Id., 29 (quoting *Metzler v. New York State Bd. for Prof. Med. Conduct*, 610 N.Y.S.2d 334, appeal dismissed, 616 N.Y.S.2d 479).

31. Such documentation also may be a key factor in any medical board disciplinary proceeding, because in sanctioning physicians, medical boards are legally authorized to rely on grounds unrelated to the use of complementary and alternative medicine. For example, in *Gambee v. Oregon* (923 P.2d 679 [Ore. Ct. App. 1996], review denied, 927 P.2d 6500 [Ore. 1996]), an Oregon statute, prohibiting revocation of license solely on the basis of physician's use of alternative medicine, was held not to preclude the state medical board from imposing professional discipline on the physician, based on a finding that the physician was guilty of aiding and abetting the practice of medicine without a license.

32. It remains to be seen whether M.D.s will be permitted to disclaim liability for conventional care, offer to provide only complementary and alternative therapies, and contractually allocate to the patient responsibility for continuing conventional care with another physician.

33. Nancy Ehrenreich, "The Colonization of the Womb," 43 *Duke L.J.* 492, 565 (1993).

34. 419 P.2d 981 (Wash. 1974), reaffirmed, *Gates v. Jensen*, 595 P.2d 919 (Wash. 1979).

35. See, e.g., *Burton v. Brooklyn Doctors Hosp.*, 452 N.Y.S.2d 875 (1982); *Toth v. Community Hosp. at Glen Cove*, 239 N.E.2d 368 (1968).

36. Dean Ornish, L. W. Scherwitz, R. S. Doody, D. Kesten, S. M. McLanahan, S. E. Brown, et al., "Effects of Stress Management Training and Dietary Changes in Treating Ischemic Heart Disease," 24 (1) *JAMA* 54 (1983). In malpractice cases as in institutional peer review and medical board disciplinary cases, deviation from accepted standards in and of itself should not be equated with professional negligence. Rather, such deviation should be evaluated with respect to its ultimate effect on patient well-being. One could argue that the history of medicine provides numerous examples of physicians (for example, Pasteur and Semmelweis) whose courageous and innovative departures from medical norms, while initially condemned and even ridiculed by peers, ultimately resulted in significant and paradigmatic shifts in health care.

37. S. Bigos, *Acute Low Back Problems in Adults: Clinical Practice Guidelines*, AHCPR Pub. 96–0643 (Rockville, Md.: U.S. Dept. of Health and Human Services, Public Health Service, Agency for Health Care Policy and Research, 1994).

38. By way of contrast, for an osteopathic physician to rely *solely* on spinal manipulation to treat diabetes probably would constitute a lack of due care, as would treating a cancerous tumor solely with homeopathy and hypnosis. These may be situations in which a layperson could understand the lack of due care without assistance from experts. See, e.g., *Gannon v. Elliot*, 23 Cal. Rptr. 2d 86 (1993). In *Daubert v. Merrell Dow Pharmaceuticals, Inc.*, 509 U.S. 579 (1993), the

U.S. Supreme Court held that expert opinion based on a scientific technique is not admissible unless the technique is "generally accepted" as reliable in the applicable scientific community. Courts have not yet addressed whether this standard applies to health care modalities outside biomedicine, which involve techniques foreign to conventional scientific methodologies.

39. An example diagnostic and therapeutic technique that should be offered in this scenario would be the use of pulse diagnosis in acupuncture and oriental medicine to detect imbalances of *chi* and take preventive measures against disease.

40. See chapter 3.

41. For example, "fraud" requires intentional deception and cannot be applied against complementary and alternative medicine providers where appropriate disclosures have been made to voluntary and intelligently consenting patients. Cohen 1998, 104–8.

42. For example, in *Charell*, the patient claimed that the defendant dissuaded her from chemotherapy and radiation (660 N.Y.S.2d at 665).

43. See A. C. Brooks, "Middle Ear Infections in Children," 146 *Sci. News* 332–33 (Nov. 19, 1994); S. Stool et al., *Otitis Media with Effusion*, AHCPR Pub. 94–0622 (Rockville, Md.: U.S. Department of Health and Human Services, Public Health Service, Agency for Health Care Policy Research, 1994).

CHAPTER 3

1. The need to address these issues has become more urgent with congressional creation of a National Center on Complementary and Alternative Medicine within the National Institutes of Health (S. 2440, § 601 [1998] [amending 42 U.S.C. §§ 281 et seq.]); passage of the Dietary Supplement Health and Education Act (Pub. L. 103–417, 108 Stat. 4325, codifed at 21 U.S.C. §§ 301 et seq.), which authorizes widespread consumer access to dietary supplements; introduction of the federal Access to Medical Treatment Act (S. 578 and H.R. 756 [1997]), which would authorize patient access to non-FDA-approved treatments, under certain conditions; and state statutes relieving physicians from discipline solely based on using complementary and alternative medicine (Federation of State Medical Boards, "Federation Bulletin," 84 [3] *Journal of Medical Licensure and Discipline*, 182 [1997]). (Alaska [1990], Washington [1991], North Carolina [1993], Oklahoma [1994], New York [1994], Oregon [1995], Colorado [1997], Georgia [1997], and Texas (1997) have enacted such legislation.) A list of state law developments is maintained at www.healthlobby.com.

2. *Canterbury v. Spence*, 464 F.2d 772 (D.C. Cir. 1972).

3. Barry R. Furrow, Timothy L. Greaney, Sandra H. Johnson, Timothy S. Jost, and Robert L. Schwartz, *Health Law*, 243–47, 268–80 (Minneapolis: West Publishing, 1995).

4. S. Bigos, *Acute Low Back Problems in Adults: Clinical Practice Guidelines*, AHCPR Pub. 95-0643 (Rockville, Md.: U.S. Dept. of Health and Human Ser-

vices, Public Health Service, Agency for Health Care Policy and Research, 1994).

5. J. Helms, "Acupuncture for the Management of Primary Dysmenorrhea," 69 *Obstet. Gynecol.* 51–56 (1987).

6. J. Kleijnen and P. Knipschild, "Ginkgo Biloba for Cerebral Insufficiency," 34 *Br. J. Clin. Pharm.* 352–58 (1992).

7. P. L. Le Bars, M. M. Katz, N. Berman, T. M. Itil, A. M. Freedman, and A. F. Schatzberg, "A Placebo-Controlled, Double-Blind, Randomized Trial of an Extract of Ginkgo Biloba for Dementia," 278 (8) *JAMA* 1327–32 (1997).

8. F. Di Silverio, G. P. Flammia, A. Sciarra, M. Caponera, M. Mauro, M. Buscarini, et al., "Plant Extracts in BPH," 45 *Minerva Urologica e Nefrologica* 143–49 (1993).

9. K. Linde, G. Ramirez, C. D. Mulrow, A. Pauls, W. Weidenhammer, D. Melchart, "St. John's Wort for Depression: An Overview and Meta-Analysis of Randomized Clinical Trials," 313 (7052) *Brit. Med. J.* 253–58 (1996).

10. A. Bensoussan, N. J. Talley, M. Hing, R. Menzies, A. Guo, and M. Ngu, "Treatment of Irritable Bowel Syndrome with Chinese Herbal Medicine: A Randomized Controlled Trial," 280 (18) *JAMA* 1585–89 (1998).

11. Charles Marwick, "Alterations are Ahead at the OAM," 280 (18) *JAMA* 1553–54 (1998).

12. L. A. Vincler and M. F. Nicol, "When Ignorance Isn't Bliss: What Healthcare Practitioners and Facilities Should Know about Complementary and Alternative Medicine," 30 (3) *J. Health and Hosp. L.* 160, 163 (1998).

13. Jay Katz, *The Silent World of Doctor and Patient* (New York: Free Press, 1994).

14. *Schloendorff v. Society of N. Y. Hosp.*, 105 N.E. 92, 93 (N.Y. 1914).

15. Michael H. Cohen, "A Fixed Star in Health Care Reform: The Emerging Paradigm of Holistic Healing," 1 (27) *Ariz. State L.J.* 79, 137–41 (1995).

16. David M. Eisenberg et al., "Unconventional Medicine in the United States: Prevalence, Costs, and Patterns of Use," 328 (4) *N. Engl. J. Med.* 256 (1993).

17. Id.

18. While the physician may feel ethically prohibited from providing a therapy he or she personally feels lacks safety or efficacy, the physician also should be alert to potential claims such as patient abandonment—or even, as suggested, malpractice—if the therapy has efficacy and the physician refuses to provide it. If a physician does choose to provide, rather than refer for, the therapy, the physician should be aware of any legal rules or professional regulations requiring credentialing or training in the therapy (for example, physician use of acupuncture), statutory and FDA rules governing the use of herbs and other dietary supplements, and any applicable medical board decisions; insurance reimbursement implications also must be considered, as well as legal rules governing health care fraud.

19. Stephen Schwartz, "Holistic Health: Seeking a Link between Medicine and Metaphysics," 266 (21) *JAMA* 21 (1991).

20. David Reilly, M. A. Taylor, N. G. Beattie, J. H. Campbell, C. McSharry, T. C. Aitchison, et al., "Is Evidence for Homeopathy Reproducible?" 344 (8937) *Lancet* 1601 (1994).

21. J. H. Lin, "Evaluating the Alternatives," 279 (9) *JAMA* 706 (1998).

22. *Charell v. Gonzales*, 660 N.Y.S.2d 665, 668 (S.Ct., N.Y. County, 1997), affirmed and modified to vacate punitive damages award, 673 N.Y.S.2d 685 (App. Div., 1st Dept., 1998), reargument denied, appeal denied, 1998 N.Y. App. Div. LEXIS 10711 (App. Div., 1st Dept., 1998), appeal denied, 706 N.E.2d 1211 (1998).

23. Robert M. Veatch, *The Patient-Physician Relation: The Patient as Partner* (Bloomington: Indiana University Press, 1991).

24. 574 P.2d 1199, 1203 (Wash. Ct. App. 1978).

25. 431 N.W.2d 855, 861 (Minn. 1988).

26. 634 So.2d 1347, 1351 (La. Ct. App. 1994).

27. Id.

28. Lynn Payer, *Medicine and Culture: Varieties of Treatment in the United States, England, West Germany, and France*, 22 (New York: Henry Holt and Co., 1998).

29. Marjorie Shultz, "From Informed Consent to Patient Choice: A New Protected Interest," 95 *Yale L.J.* 219, 229–33 (1985).

30. 1991 U.S. Dist. LEXIS 14712 (S.D. Ga., Sept. 5, 1991).

31. 989 F.2d 1129, 1132 (11th Cir. 1993).

32. Dean Ornish, L. W. Scherwitz, R. S. Doody, D. Kesten, S. M. McLanahan, S. E. Brown, et al., "Effects of Stress Management Training and Dietary Changes in Treating Ischemic Heart Disease," 24 (1) *JAMA* 54 (1983).

33. See David Spiegel, J. R. Bloom, H. C. Kraemer, and E. Gottheil, "Effect of Psychosocial Treatment on Survival of Patients with Metastatic Breast Cancer," 2 (8668) *Lancet* 888 (1989).

34. See Christina and Stanislav Grof, *The Stormy Search for the Self* (Los Angeles: Jeremy P. Tarcher, 1990); Lee Sannella, *The Kundalini Experience* (Lower Lake, Calif.: Integral Publishing, 1976).

CHAPTER 4

1. Presently, complementary and alternative medicine providers have a duty to refer to physicians when patient conditions exceed the boundaries of the nonmedical providers' expertise. See Michael H. Cohen, *Complementary and Alternative Boundaries: Legal Boundaries and Regulatory Perspectives*, 59, 68–69 (Baltimore: Johns Hopkins University Press, 1998). This rule protects patients against the limited knowledge of nonmedical providers and ensures that they receive appropriate conventional care.

Where domains of knowledge useful to treatment of certain diseases typically lie outside medical expertise and within the fields of practice of complementary and alternative medicine providers, the duty to refer could conceivably run from the physician to such a provider. Further, where sufficient scientific validation and medical acceptance places the complementary and alternative therapy within the standard of care, failing to provide or refer for such a treatment presumably could constitute malpractice. See id., 111.

2. Biomedicine is more open to complementary and alternative therapies than it has been in the past; however, physicians who have turned to complementary and alternative medicine have faced disciplinary proceedings without evidence of patient injury and despite patient testimony that the complementary practices were used as a last resort and resulted in patient improvement. See Cohen 1998, 87–95. Issues of bias, prejudice, and perhaps even persecution continue to plague physicians interested in potential integrative approaches. See Federation of State Medical Boards, "Federation Bulletin," 84 (3) *Journal of Medical Licensure and Discipline* (1997).

3. *Reed v. Bascon*, 530 N.E.2d 417 (Ill. 1988).

4. See, e.g., *Ravo v. Rogatnick*, 514 N.E.2d 1104 (N.Y. 1987).

5. *Stovall v. Harms*, 522 P.2d 353 (Kans. 1974).

6. Cf. *Brooks v. Goldhammer*, 608 So.2d 394 (Ala. 1992) (although the physician breached the standard of care when he made the decision to allow an inexperienced resident to perform intubation, in which case the resident placed a tube in the esophagus rather than intubation, there was insufficient evidence that the patient's death was proximately caused by the physician's decision where it had been established that the resident did not act negligently).

7. *Rouse v. Pitt Memorial Hospital*, 447 S.E.2d 505, review granted, 445 S.E.2d 257 (N.C. 1994).

8. *Johnson v. Ely*, 205 S.W.2d 759 (Tenn. 1947).

9. D. M. Studdert, D. M. Eisenberg, F. H. Miller, D. A. Curto, T. J. Kaptchuk, and T. A. Brennan, "Medical Malpractice Implications of Alternative Medicine," 280 (18) *JAMA* 1610, 1612 (1998).

10. *Stovall v. Harms*, 522 P.2d 353 (Kans. 1974).

11. For example, a family physician who called in a surgeon did not share in malpractice liability for negligence in the operation but nonetheless was held jointly liable to the extent the family physician continued to participate in diagnosis and treatment after the surgeon applied a cast to the patient's arm (*Morrill v. Komasinski*, 41 N.W.2d 620 [Wis. 1950]). However, a physician who admitted a patient to the hospital and continued in charge of the patient's condition was not held liable for the negligence of surgeons resulting in postoperative complications (*Dawson v. Weems*, 352 So.2d 1200 [Fla. App. Dist. 1977]).

12. *Steinberg v. Dunseth*, 631 N.E.2d 809, appeal denied, 642 N.E.2d 1304 (Ill. 1994).

13. *Crump v. Piper*, 425 S.W.2d 924 (Mo. 1968).

14. *Rose v. Sprague*, 59 S.W.2d 554 (Ky. 1933); *Suire v. Lake Charles Mem. Hosp.*, 590 So.2d 619 (La. App. Ct. 1991); *Hammer v. Waterhouse*, 895 S.W.2d 95 (Mo. App. Ct. 1995).

15. *Sawh v. Schoen*, 627 N.Y.S.2d 7 (App. Div. 1995).

16. *Graddy v. New York Medical College,* 243 N.Y.S.2d 940 (N.Y. App. Div., 1st Dept. 1963).

17. *Zuckerman v. Antenucci,* 478 N.S.Y.2d 578 (N.Y. 1984); *Fanelli v. Adder,* 516 N.Y.S.2d 716 (App. Div. 1987).

18. Studdert et al. 1998, 1613.

19. *Jennings v. Burgess,* 917 S.W.2d 790, 796 (Gonzalez, J., concurring in judgment that plaintiffs have a negligent referral cause of action).

20. *Sall v. Eldlfelt,* 662 S.W.2d 517 (Mo. App. 1983). A related doctrine is *res ipsa loquitor,* in which multiple physicians are involved in treating a patient who, because of anesthesia or other circumstances, cannot identify which physician is responsible for a specific act or aspect of the negligence. See *Ybarra v. Spanguard,* 208 P.2d 445 (Cal. 1949); *Crump v. Piper,* 425 S.W.2d 924, 926 (Mo. 1968).

21. See, e.g., *Robinson v. Mt. Sinai Med. Center,* 402 N.W.2d 711 (Wis. 1987) (action alleging joint liability for brain damage to the patient as a result of negligent treatment by physicians at two different hospitals).

22. 962 S.W.2d 473 (Tenn. 1998).

23. Individual defendants can seek severance if prejudice may result from joinder. See Fed. R. Civ. P. 20(b) and 42(b). Courts, however, may be reluctant to sever defendants at the pleading stage and may wait until discovery or even into trial. Further, because plaintiffs' allegations are taken as true for purposes of a motion to dismiss, defendants will remain in the litigation unless and until successful on summary judgment, which requires presentation of evidence. Yet summary judgment will not be granted if any genuine issue of material fact remains to be tried. See Fed. R. Civ. P. 56(c). Although procedural rules aim to protect defendants against frivolous lawsuits, see Fed. R. Civ. P. 11(b)(3), liberal pleading and joinder rules make it easy for plaintiffs to bring a chain of providers into the lawsuit, and the standard for summary judgment makes it difficult to get out of the lawsuit before trial.

24. 694 A.2d 648 (Penn. Super. Ct. 1997), appeal denied, 1998 Pa. LEXIS 177 (February 25, 1998), and appeal denied, 1999 Pa. LEXIS 2147 (July 28, 1999).

25. Id., 656.

26. Id.

27. Id., n. 6.

28. Id., 657.

29. Id., n. 8.

30. Wayne R. LaFave and Austin W. Scott, Jr., *Criminal Law,* 589–90 (2d ed., St. Paul: West Publishing, 1986).

31. Id., 579–84. According to LaFave and Scott, however, this is the exception rather than the rule (id., 584).

32. See Cohen 1998, 31 (citing cases).

33. *State v. Hoffman,* 733 P.2d 502 (1987).

34. *Board of Quality Medical Assurance v. Andrews,* 260 Cal. Rptr. 113 (Cal. App. 1989).

35. Cohen 1998, 27 (citing statutes).

36. See Cohen 1998, 47–49.

37. See Barbara A. Brennan, *Hands of Light: A Guide to Healing through the Human Energy Field*, 143, 157 (New York: Bantam Books, 1988).

38. See also *Alternative Medicine: Expanding Medical Horizons (A Report to the National Institutes of Health on Alternative Medical Systems and Practices in the United States)*, NIH Pub. 94–0666, 133–46 (Dec. 1994) (the Chantilly Report).

39. See chapters 1 and 6 for a brief discussion of the claim that in many medical licensing statutes, spiritual healing fits the exemption for religious worship or prayer.

CHAPTER 5

1. Two examples are Columbia Presbyterian in New York and Boulder Community Hospital in Colorado.

2. 211 N.E.2d 253 (1965).

3. 591 A.2d 703 (Penn. 1991).

4. *Albain v. Flower Hospital*, 553 N.E.2d 1038 (Ohio 1990).

5. See Larry Dossey, *Meaning and Medicine: Lessons From a Doctor's Tales of Breakthrough and Healing* (New York: Bantam Books, 1991) (describing "Era III medicine").

6. See Michael H. Cohen, *Complementary and Alternative Medicine: Legal Boundaries and Regulatory Perspectives*, 70–71 (Baltimore: Johns Hopkins University Press, 1998).

7. Cf. *Boyd v. Albert Einstein Med. Ctr.*, 547 A.2d 1229 (Pa. Super. Ct. 1988) (applying vicarious liability to a health maintenance organization).

8. See, e.g., *Weldon v. Seminole Municipal Hosp.*, 709 P.2d 1058 (Okla. 1985).

9. See *Jennings v. Burgess*, 917 S.W.2d 790, 795 (Tex. 1996) (J. Gonzales concurring) (warning that unless the legislature acts on conflicts in managed care settings between financial incentives and the best interest of the patient, courts "will be forced to re-think traditional notions of duty and standards of care, leading to fundamental doctrinal shifts" in malpractice liability). Courts have shown creativity in extending liability to hospitals and HMOs for patient injuries. See, e.g., *McClelland v. Health Maintenance Organization*, 604 A.2d 1053 (Pa. Super. Ct. 1992) (HMO held to have a nondelegable duty to retain only competent providers); *Elsessor v. Hospital of the College of Osteopathic Medicine*, 802 F. Supp. 1286 (E.D. Pa. 1992) (HMO held negligent under theory of apparent or ostensible agency); *Schleier v. Kaiser Found. Health Plan of the Mid-Atlantic States, Inc.*, 876 F.2d 174 (D.C. Cir. 1989).

10. See R. H. Gracely, R. Dubner, W. R. Deeter, and P. J. Wolksee, "Clinicians' Expectations Influence Placebo Analgesia," 1 (8419) *Lancet* 43 (1985); D. Spiegel and R. Moore, "Imagery and Hypnosis in the Treatment of Cancer," 11 (8) *Oncology* 1179 (1997); David Spiegel, "Healing Words: Emotional Expression and Disease Outcome," 281 (14) *JAMA* 1238 (1999).

11. *Mertens v. Hewitt Associates*, 508 U.S. 248 (1993).

12. 29 U.S.C. § 1144(a). See, e.g., *Blue Cross and Blue Shield Plans v. Travelers Ins. Co.*, 514 U.S. 645 (1995) (ERISA does not preempt a New York statute that requires hospitals to add a surcharge to their rates in order to fund a pool that reimbursed hospitals for the costs of treating patients without insurance).

13. 29 U.S.C. § 1144(b)(2)(A). See, e.g., *Metropolitan Life Insurance Co. v. Massachusetts*, 471 U.S. 724 (1985) (state law mandating the inclusion of mental health benefits in group health insurance falls within the savings clause and therefore is not preempted).

14. 29 U.S.C. § 1144(b)(2)(B).

15. *FMC Corp. v. Holliday*, 498 U.S. 52 (1990).

16. See, e.g., *Corcoran v. United Healthcare, Inc.*, 965 F.2d 1321 (5th Cir. 1992), cert. denied, 502 U.S. 1033 (1992); *Dukes v. U.S. Health Care Systems of Pa., Inc.*, 848 Supp. 39 (E.D. Pa. 1994).

CHAPTER 6

1. *Alternative Medicine: Expanding Medical Horizons (A Report to the National Institutes of Health on Alternative Medical Systems and Practices in the United States)*, NIH Pub. 94–0666, 134–42 (Dec. 1994) (the Chantilly Report).

2. Id., 134.

3. See generally Dolores Krieger, *The Therapeutic Touch: How to Use Your Hands to Help and Heal* (New York : Simon and Schuster, 1992).

4. See Daniel J. Benor, "Healers and a Changing Medical Paradigm," 3 (2) *Center for Frontier Sci.* 38 (1993); Chantilly Report, 142–44 (citing studies).

5. See Beverly Rubik, "Energy Medicine and the Unifying Concept of Information," 1 (1) *Alt. Ther. in Health and Med.* 34 (Mar. 1995); Chantilly Report, 139–42.

6. See Chip Brown, "The Experiments of Dr. Oz," *New York Times Magazine*, 21, 23 (July 30, 1995); see also Chantilly Report, 144–46 (research recommendations).

7. See Chantilly Report, 136–37.

8. Oscar Janiger and Philip Goldberg, *A Different Kind of Healing: Doctors Speak Candidly about Their Successes with Alternative Medicine*, 123, 128–32 (New York: Putnam Publishing Group, 1993).

9. C. Norman Shealy and Caroline Myss, *The Creation of Health: Merging Traditional Medicine with Intuitive Diagnosis*, 74–78 (Walpole: Stillpoint Pub. Co., 1988).

10. Daniel P. Wirth, "The Effect of Non-Contact Therapeutic Touch on the Healing Rate of Full Thickness Dermal Wounds," 1 *Subtle Energies* 2 (1990).

11. See Brown 1995.

12. It is inappropriate to "relegate the entire experience to the realm of mystery," if energy healing indeed will be found to have some scientific basis and definite clinical applications. Michael H. Cohen, "A Fixed Star in Health

Care Reform: The Emerging Paradigm of Holistic Healing," 1 (27) *Ariz. State L.J.* 79, 84 (1995).

13. Dolores Krieger describes the process as turning attention toward interior experience and focusing on "latent senses" (*Living the Therapeutic Touch,* 60–63 [New York: Dodd, Mead, 1987]), which is analogous to the description of intuition or "high sense perception" (Barbara A. Brennan, *Hands of Light: A Guide to Healing through the Human Energy Field,* 10, 38–39, 153–54, 165–67 [New York: Bantam Books, 1988]).

14. A limited number of statutes exclude specific forms of energy healing from massage therapy licensing requirements. See, e.g., 32 Me. Rev. Stat. Ann. § 14307.2 (exempting Rolfing, Trager, reflexology, Shiatsu, Reiki, and Polarity Therapy, provided practitioners do not use the title "massage therapist" or "massage practitioner"). The statute does not, however, exempt these practices from the medical practice act. In states that define massage therapy in terms of touch, pressure, rubbing, or stroking—see, e.g., Utah Code Ann. § 758-47a-2(2)—energy healers without massage therapy licenses conceivably could be prosecuted for the unlawful practice of massage.

15. 349 N.Y.S.2d 604, 612 (N.Y. Sup. Ct. 1973).

16. Id., 611–12.

17. See, e.g., *People v. Steinberg,* 73 N.Y.S.2d 475, 577 (Mag. Ct. 1947); *Amber,* 349 N.Y.S.2d 612.

18. See, e.g., Code Va. Ann. § 54.1–2914.8 (1994) (providing that any practitioner of the healing arts regulated by the state board "shall be considered guilty of unprofessional conduct if he . . . [a]ids or abets, *has professional connection with,* or lends his name to any person known to him to be practicing illegally any of the healing arts" [emphasis added]).

19. See Chantilly Report, 147; Robert H. Blanks, Tonya L. Schuster, and Marnie Dobson, "A Retrospective Assessment of Network Care Using a Survey of Self-Rated Health, Wellness, and Quality of Life," 1 (4) *J. Vertebral Sublux. Research* 11 (1997).

20. Barbara Brennan's work in healing science developed in part out of work by Dr. John Pierrakos, diagnosing and treating psychological disorders based on the chakras, the energy centers within the biofield; Pierrakos's work in turn emerges out of that of Alexander Lowen and Wilhelm Reich. See Brennan 1998, 32; John C. Pierrakos, *Core Energetics: Developing the Capacity to Love and Heal* (Mendocino: Life Rhythm, 1990).

21. Chantilly Report, 135.

22. See generally A. H. Almaas, *The Point of Existence: Transformations of Narcissism in Self-Realization* (Berkeley: Diamond Books, 1996).

23. Rudolph Steiner wrote: "we are continually surrounded by spiritual happenings and beings. Physical phenomena are merely the expression of spiritual deeds, and things that appear to us in material form are the outward sheaths of spiritual beings" (*The Spiritual Hierarchies and Their Reflection in the Physical World,* 15 [Hudson, N.Y.: Anthroposophic Press, 1987]).

24. Evelyn Underhill has written that sharing the contemplative life shared

by artists, poets, and mystics "would mean that we should receive from every flower, not merely a beautiful image to which the label 'flower' has been affixed, but the full impact of its unimaginable beauty and wonder, the direct sensation of life having communion with life: that the scents of ceasing rain, the voice of trees, the deep softness of the kitten's fur, the acrid touch of sorrel on the tongue, should be in themselves profound, complete, and simple experiences, calling forth simplicity of response in our souls" (*Practical Mysticism,* 44–45 [Columbus, Ohio: Ariel Press, 1942]). Underhill posits that the mystical life is every human's birthright.

25. Barbara Brennan (1988, 10) describes "high sense perception" as "a natural evolutionary step for the human race, leading us into the next stage of development where, because of our newly gained abilities, we will have to be deeply honest with others."

26. See Julie Motz, *Hands of Life: From the Operating Room to Your Home, An Energy Healer Reveals the Secrets for Using Your Body's Own Energy Medicine for Healing, Recovery, and Transformation* (New York: Bantam Books, 1998); Mehmet Oz, *Healing from the Heart: A Leading Surgeon Explores the Power of Complementary Medicine* (New York: NAL/Dutton, 1998).

27. See, e.g., Shafica Karagulla and Dora Kunz, *The Chakras and the Human Energy Fields* (Wheaton: Theosophical Publishing House, 1990); Wendy Wetzel, "Healing Touch as a Nursing Intervention: Wound Infection following Cesarean Birth—an Anecdotal Case Study," 11 (30) *J. Hol. Nurs.* 277 (1993). Healers also report consistently good results with post-traumatic stress disorder, irritable bowel syndrome, migraine, anorexia and bulimia, and third-trimester pregnancy and birthing (Chantilly Report, 144).

28. See, e.g., Bonnie Steinbock, *Life before Birth: The Moral and Legal Status of Embryos & Fetuses* 35 (New York: Oxford University Press, 1992).

29. See *People v. Abrams,* 576 N.Y.S.2d 338 (App. Div. 1991) (citing New York Educ. Law. §§ 7601, 7603, 6513[1], and holding that it is not a crime to practice psychology without a license); Wis. Stat. Ann. § 455.02(1)(a) (1994): "This chapter does not restrict exclusively to licensed psychologists the rendering of services included within the practice of psychology, but only an individual licensed . . . may use the title. . . ."

30. These healers typically are exempt from medical practice acts as long as they limit their activities to "praying" over their clients or to delivering their services in a religious context. See Barry Nobel, "Religious Healing in the Courts: The Liberties and Liabilities of Patients, Parents, and Healers," 16 *U. Puget Sound L. Rev.* 599 (1993); see also D.C. Code § 2–3301.4(d)(1) (1994) (exempting any "minister, priest, rabbi, officer, or agent of any religious body or any practitioner of any religious belief *engaging in prayer or any other religious practice* or nursing *practiced solely in accordance with the religious tenets of any church* for the purpose of fostering the physical, mental, or spiritual well-being of any person" [emphasis added]).

31. See, e.g., *Foster v. Board of Chiropractic Examiners,* 359 S.E.2d 877 (Ga. 1987).

32. Rosalyn Bruyere, *Wheels of Light: A Study of the Chakras* 227–28 (Arcadia: Bon Productions, 1989).

33. See, e.g., Del. Code Ann. tit. 24, § 701 (1974); Haw. Rev. Stat. § 455–1(1) (1995 and Supp. 1994).

34. For example, under state licensing statutes, chiropractors are permitted to assess the flow of nerve energy and engage in spinal manipulation but not to diagnose and treat diseases generally.

35. The Chantilly Report presents three major current hypotheses: that the biofield is (1) "metaphysical (outside the four dimensions of space and time and untestable)," (2) an "electromagnetic field effect," and (3) a "presently undefined but potentially quantifiable field effect in physics" (139). The report suggests testing the hypothesis that the biofield is either bioelectromagnetism or a field in physics other than those already known, and it rejects the notion that energy healing is effective solely as a placebo effect (144–46). The report further notes the lack of "true peers" who are capable of "peer review" and suggests that individuals who have a "hands-on understanding" be included on review committees (146).

36. Ted J. Kaptchuk and David M. Eisenberg, "The Persuasive Appeal of Alternative Medicine," 129 (12) *Ann. Int. Med.* 1061, 1062 (1998) (citing sources).

37. Kaptchuk and Eisenberg (1998, 1062) note concerning vitalistic systems: "Truth is experiential and is ultimately accessible to human perceptions. Nature is not separate from human consciousness. . . . The science of alternative medicine, unlike the science component of biomedicine, does not marginalize or deny human experience; rather, it affirms patients' real-life worlds."

38. See Jerome P. Kassirer and Marcia Angell, "Alternative Medicine: The Risks of Untested and Unregulated Remedies," 339 (12) *N. Engl. J. Med.* 839 (1998).

39. Bohm's work is summarized and used as an explanatory model for energy healing in Michael M. Talbot, *The Holographic Universe* (New York: HarperPerennial Library, 1992).

40. In current research, such phenomena are classified under the term *placebo effect* rather than the less respected term *psychic phenomena*. See, e.g., R. H. Gracely, R. Dubner, W. R. Deeter, and P. J. Wolksee, "Clinicians' Expectations Influence Placebo Analgesia," 1 (8419) Lancet 43 (1985).

41. Such a conflict may exist, for example, when acupuncturists receive legislative authorization to use Western diagnostic tests: they may find malpractice liability extended, since courts are likely to apply medical, rather than acupuncture, standards of care. See Cohen 1998, 67.

42. Although the tradition of meditation and contemplation is very much alive in Western mystical tradition, we typically think of prayer as directed outward, toward a Supreme Being, rather than going within. Whatever the strategy, studies of prayer involve a state of "compassion, love, or empathy" with the prayee, or a feeling that prayer and prayee are one (Chantilly Report, 33).

43. See Chantilly Report, 32–34 (citing studies).

44. Curiously, the Chantilly Report classifies prayer as a mind-body ther-

apy but considers biofield therapeutics a manual therapy. However, the report acknowledges that the two fields of therapy overlap, noting that energy healing does not necessarily require contact with the physical body and that "mental healing, psychic healing, distance healing, nonlocal healing, and absent healing" are part of energy healing (135).

45. Id., 33.

46. Id., 34.

47. Id.

48. One possible avenue for research is the effect of acupuncture on the neuropeptide chemicals involved in the digestive and immune responses (Chantilly Report, 78).

49. Chantilly Report, 148.

50. See Cohen 1998, 44–45 (citing statutes).

51. Id.

52. H. H. Shenphan Dawa Norbu Rinpoche, foreword to H. H. Dudjon Rinpoche, *Sadhana of the Medicine Buddha,* ed. Arthur Mandlebaum, vii (New York: Yeshe Melong, 1998).

53. Id.

54. Rinpoche 1998, viii; John F. Avedon, *In Exile from the Land of Snows,* 143 (New York: HarperCollins, 1997).

55. Rinpoche 1998, viii.

56. Id.

57. See Brennan 1988, 10, 142.

58. Avendon 1997, 155; for an overview of the process for approving new drugs, see Cohen 1998, 73–78.

CHAPTER 7

1. *Alternative Medicine: Expanding Medical Horizons (A Report to the National Institutes of Health on Alternative Medical Systems and Practices in the United States),* NIH Pub. 94–0666, 95 (the Chantilly Report).

2. Id.

3. Id.

4. Id.

5. For a radical vision of such a clinic in the United States, see Patch Adams, *Gesundheit!* (Rochester, Vt.: Healing Arts Press, 1993). Adams's dream of a forty-bed free hospital, with no malpractice insurance and no salaries, and situated on 310 acres in a medically underserved area of West Virginia gained visibility (and funding) through the release of the film *Patch Adams.*

6. See, e.g., Chantilly Report, 99 (describing *curanderismo,* a folk system used in Latin America and among many Hispanic Americans in the United States). *Curanderismo* includes a humoral model for classifying activity, food, drugs, and illnesses, including a series of folk illnesses, such as "evil eye" and "blockage." The Chantilly Report concludes: "Although no formal effective-

ness studies seem to have been done on this system, its wide popularity and the research suggesting the relevance of the folk diagnoses for biomedical practice indicate the need for further demographic and effectiveness studies."

7. Id., 102–3.

8. This was William James's "empiricist criterion" for distinguishing divine experiences from "too patently silly . . . trances and convulsive seizures" (William James, *The Varieties of Religious Experience*, 34 [New York: Collier Books, 1961]).

9. Chantilly Report, 95–98.

10. Id., 95.

11. New York Educ. Law, § 6527.4a.

12. Michael H. Cohen, "A Fixed Star in Health Care Reform: The Emerging Paradigm of Holistic Healing," 1 (27) *Ariz. State L.J.* 79, 84 (1995).

13. *Thomas v. Review Bd. of Ind. Employment Sec. Div.*, 450 U.S. 707 (1981).

14. Id., 717.

15. *U.S. v. Ballard*, 322 U.S. 78 (1944).

16. Id., 86.

17. *Torcaso v. Watkins*, 367 U.S. 488 (1961).

18. Id., 495.

19. *United States v. Seeger*, 380 U.S. 165 (1965).

20. Id., 166.

21. Id., 176.

22. *Wallace v. Jaffree*, 472 U.S. 38 (1985).

23. See *Stone v. Graham*, 449 U.S. 39 (1980); *Abington School Dist. v. Schempp*, 374 U.S. 203 (1963); *Engel v. Vitale*, 370 U.S. 421 (1962).

24. As Charles Tart writes, some believe that most petitionary prayer has almost no effect but that "a consistently held desire for something" can affect "higher levels of reality or higher beings" (*Waking Up: Overcoming the Obstacles to Human Consciousness*, 229 [Boston: Shambhala Publications, 1986]). Tart concludes: "*Effective* petitionary prayer would be much more possible to a person who was genuinely conscious, who, at will and for extended periods, deliberately summoned up the intellectual and emotional intensity to pray consciously without distraction. If he prayed from his more integrated and constructive subpersonalities or from his essence, better yet. Praying from the third level of consciousness, remembering yourself while you pray, is the most effective of all" (230).

25. The Supreme Court has held that a law singling out religious conduct for restriction is constitutionally impermissible unless narrowly tailored to serve a compelling government interest: see *Church of the Lukumi Babalu Aye v. City of Hialeah*, 508 U.S. 520 (1993) (striking down city ordinances that prohibited the ritual sacrifice of animals, because the ordinances discriminated against the worship ceremonies of an Afro-Caribbean religion); *Employment Div. v. Smith*, 494 U.S. 872 (1990) (in a case involving denial of unemployment benefits to drug rehabilitation counselors who were fired for ingesting peyote for sacramental purposes at a Native American ceremony, the court held that

government may restrict religiously motivated conduct if the law generally applies to all citizens and does not single out religion).

26. A related legal concern is the role of abuse and neglect laws, which deter parental reliance on spiritual practices as a substitute for conventional medicine when their children face serious illness or death. See, e.g., *Newmark v. Williams*, 588 A.2d 1108 (Del. 1991) (the court will not order medical treatment of a child over the religious objections of parents where the prognosis with treatment is only slightly better than the prognosis without treatment and where the treatment is highly invasive and painful to the child). The relationship between energy healing, prayer, and religious objections to conventional medical treatments has yet to be untangled.

CHAPTER 8

1. See, e.g., *Report on H.R. 3103, Health Insurance Portability and Accountability Act of 1996*, 142 (115) *Cong. Rec.* H9537–38 (July 31, 1996).

2. Michael H. Cohen, "A Fixed Star in Health Care Reform: The Emerging Paradigm of Holistic Healing," 1 (27) *Ariz. State L.J.* 79 (1995).

3. Federal courts exercising subject-matter jurisdiction based on diversity of citizenship apply state law pursuant to the *Erie* doctrine; see *Erie v. Tompkins*, 304 U.S. 64 (1938).

4. 18 F. Supp. 2nd 117 (D. Mass. 1998).

5. Lon Fuller believed that "[t]he ultimate problem of the law is balance" (Lon Fuller, *Legal Fictions*, 137 [Stanford: Stanford University Press, 1967]).

6. The author here expresses no opinion regarding Amrit Desai or the Kripalu Yoga Fellowship.

CHAPTER 9

1. *Congressional Findings Related to Dietary Supplements Health and Education Act of 1994*, Pub. L. 103–417, 2, 15(a), 108 Stat. 4325, 4326 (1994).

2. Senate Committee on Labor and Human Resources, *Report of the Senate Committee on Labor and Human Resources on the Dietary Supplement Health and Education Act of 1994*, S. Rept. 103–410, 103rd Cong., 2d sess., 14 (1994) (the DSHEA Report). Among other activities, between 1966 and 1973, the FDA issued proposed regulations to classify a vitamin product as an over-the-counter drug if the product exceeded 150 percent of the recommended daily allowance. In the 1970s, the FDA attempted to regulate vitamins by claiming they were toxic. The history is further summarized at DSHEA Report, 15.

3. 21 U.S.C. § 321(ff)(1)(A)–(F).

4. Id., § 321(ff)(2)(A)–(B). The latter would include, for example, powders, bars, and drinks (DSHEA Report, 35).

5. Id., § 321(ff)(2)(C).

6. Id., § 321(s)(4)–(6).

7. Id., § 321(ff).

8. Id., § 321(g)(1)(B).

9. Id., § 350b(a)(2).

10. Id., § 342(f)(1)(A).

11. Id., § 342(f)(1)(C).

12. Id., § 342(f)(1). In contrast, manufacturers bear the burden of proving that food additives, when added to food, are "generally recognized as safe" (id., § 348).

13. Id., § 342(f)(2).

14. Id., § 343(s).

15. Id., § 343(1)(5)(F).

16. Id., § 342(g)(2).

17. Id., § 343–2(a)(1)–(5).

18. Id., § 343–2(b)–(c).

19. Id., § 343(r)(6)(A)–(C).

20. Id., § 343(r). A product is subject to regulation as a "drug" if it is *intended to* "affect the structure or any function of the body of man," unless it is a food; see id., § 321(g)(1)(C). The intended use of the product, as shown by representations made for it in promotional materials, determines whether that product and its ingredients are subject to regulation as a food or drug. If a vitamin or herbal product, for example, is represented for use as a "dietary supplement," it is regulated as food; if it is represented to cure, mitigate, treat, or prevent disease, it is regulated as a drug (DSHEA Report, 20).

21. DSHEA Report, 23–24. The NLEA standard for FDA approval of health claims, "significant scientific agreement," remains in effect for dietary supplements during a two-year period of study by the Dietary Supplement Commission established under the DSHEA.

22. 21 U.S.C. § 343(r)(6)(C).

23. 21 C.F.R. § 101.14(a)(1) (1998).

24. Pub. L. 101–535, 104 Stat. 2353 (1990), codified at 21 U.S.C. § 343(r)(3)(B)(i).

25. Pub. L. 102–571, 106 Stat. 4491 (1992).

26. The FDA proposed to change its definition of such health claims from a definition referring to "damage to an organ, part, structure, or system of the body . . ." to "any deviation from, impairment of, or interruption of the normal structure or function . . . of the body" (FDA Proposed Rule, 63 Fed. Reg. 23624 [April 29, 1998]). The FDA was severely criticized for this proposed change. See, e.g., letter from Rep. Daniel Burton to Michael A. Friedman (August 27, 1998) re FDA Docket No. 98N-044 (suggesting that the new definition would include such conditions as pregnancy, menopause, and aging and make any claim for alleviating symptoms of these states a health claim ["disease claim"]).

27. The commission recommended that the significant scientific agreement standard also be applied to dietary supplements (*Commission on Dietary Supplement Labels React to the President, Congress, and the Secretary of the Depart-*

ment of Health and Human Services, GPO 017–001–00531–2 [Nov. 1997], vii, 31; see also Margaret Gilhooley, "Herbal Remedies and Dietary Supplements: The Boundaries of Drug Claims and Freedom of Choice," 49 *Fla. L. Rev.* 663, 680 (1997). The commission further recommended greater FDA use of outside expert reviewers.

28. 21 U.S.C. § 343, note.

29. 21 C.F.R. §§ 101.14., 101.70. To date, the FDA has authorized only two health claims on dietary supplements, concerning calcium and osteoporosis and concerning folate and neural tube defects; see 21 C.F.R. §§ 101.72(c)(2)(ii)(C), 101.79(c)(2)(ii)(B). The FDA has approved several health claims on foods—for example, concerning fruits and vegetables and cancer and concerning soluble fiber and coronary heart disease; see 21 C.F.R. §§ 101.78, 101.81.

30. Michael H. Cohen, "A Fixed Star in Health Care Reform: The Emerging Paradigm of Holistic Healing," 1 (27) *Ariz. State L.J.* 79, 138 (citing Tom L Beauchamp and James. F. Childress, *Principles of Biomedical Ethics,* 126, 274 [New York: Oxford University Press, 1994]).

31. While this latter scenario is difficult to imagine, the decision to take a dietary supplement would be "involuntary" if, for example, the patient was somehow addicted to the particular supplement.

32. I have argued elsewhere that this regulatory stance reflects the medical control of licensing, educational, and reimbursement mechanisms beginning in the late nineteenth century, which created a medical monopoly and suppressed or excluded competitors in the healing arts under the guise of patient protection. See Michael H. Cohen, *Complementary and Alternative Medicine: Legal Boundaries and Regulatory Perspectives,* 15–23 (Baltimore: Johns Hopkins University Press, 1998).

33. *Hearing of the Oversight and Investigations Subcommittee of the House Commerce Committee: Access to Medical Treatments* (available in LEXIS, LEGIS Library, CNG TST file) (Feb. 29, 1996); see also "FDA Does Not Serve Patients by Denying Treatment of Last Resort Pursued by Terminally Ill Patients," 142 *Cong. Rec.* H. 4115 (April 29, 1996).

34. Id.

35. Id.

36. 438 F. Supp. 1287 (W.D. Okla. 1977), rev'd, 442 U.S. 544 (1979), cert. denied, 449 U.S. 937 (1980).

37. Id., 554.

38. 616 F.2d 457.

39. Although the Southern District of Texas recognized a constitutional right to obtain acupuncture in *Andrews v. Ballard* (498 F. Supp. 1038 [S.D. Tex. 1980]), the holding has by and large been rejected by subsequent courts; see, e.g., *New York State Ophthalmological Society v. Bowen,* 854 F.2d 1379 (D.C. Cir. 1988). But see *Suenram v. Society of the Valley Hospital,* in which the New Jersey Superior Court held that a terminally ill cancer patient, having tried chemotherapy, had a fundamental right to choose laetrile as a last resort.

According to the court, "[w]here a person is terminally ill . . . and unresponsive to other treatments, the public harm is considerably reduced" (383 A.2d 143 [Superior Ct. N.J. 1977]).

40. Gilhooley 1997, 702.

41. *Dietary Supplement Statements of Nutritional Support*, Tan Sheet 11-15 (Jan. 15, 1996), cited in Gilhooley 1997, 686. Gilhooley (724) notes that while the FDA receives notification of such statements pursuant to 21 U.S.C. § 343(r)(6), prior FDA approval for such statements is not required.

42. For example, the suggestion has been made that the test should be "claim-specific" and should relate to "whether a consumer would be able to understand how the supplement is to be used to obtain effects normally associated with the use of foods" (Gilhooley 1997, 690). An alternative proposal is that claims "should not refer to uses that require professional supervision and a prescription" (id., 692). The FDA recently released final regulations defining the types of statements that can be made concerning the effect of a dietary supplement on the structure or function of the body and establishing criteria for determining when a statement about a dietary supplement is a claim to diagnose, cure, mitigate, treat, or prevent disease and thus requires FDA approval. 21 CFR Part 101, Regulation on Statements, Made for Dietary Supplements Concerning the Effect of the Product on the Structure or Function of the Body, 65:4 Fed. Reg. 1000 (Jan. 6, 2000). Among other things, the regulations retain the definition of "disease or health-related condition" in 21 CFR § 101.14(a)(5), which was part of the Nutrition Labeling and Education Act, and provide that common conditions associated with natural states or processes that do not cause significant or permanent harm (such as hot flashes, premenstrual syndrome, and mild memory problems associated with aging) will not be treated as diseases under this provision.

43. Cohen 1998, 2.

44. See Cohen 1998, 2–8.

45. See generally *Alternative Medicine: Expanding Medical Horizons (A Report to the National Institutes of Health on Alternative Medical Systems and Practices in the United States)*, NIH Pub. 94–0666, xi–xxii (Dec. 1992). To some extent, these dichotomies are shifting. As integrative medicine is beginning to take preliminary shape in clinical practice, biomedicine is selectively incorporating mind-body technologies. At the same time, complementary and alternative medicine is moving toward mechanism and reductionism as providers and professional organizations attempt to deepen their foothold in the mainstream (for example, by emphasizing increasingly rigorous and standardized credentialing mechanisms and by striving to increase third-party reimbursement mechanisms). Thus, biomedicine can be practiced in a holistic fashion, and complementary and alternative medicine can be practiced in a reductionistic and mechanistic manner.

46. 164 F.3d 650 (D.C. Cir. 1999), reh'g en banc denied, 172 F.3d 72.

47. Id., 655.

48. Id., 655–60.

49. Id.

50. The court's disposition in *Pearson v. Shalala* was to hold invalid the FDA's interpretation of its general regulation and rejection of the four proposed health claims and remand the case to the district court with instructions that the FDA "must explain what it means by significant scientific agreement or, at minimum, what it does not mean" (Id., 661).

51. See Cohen 1998, 28–29.

52. In *Meza v. Southern Calif. Physicians Ins. Exchg.*, 73 Cal. Rptr. 91 (Ct. App. 1998), a California appeals court considered whether an injection of tea tree oil into plaintiff's left index finger constituted use of "any drug . . . disapproved or not yet approved" by the FDA. Plaintiff had received the injection to treat a wart; within 24 hours, necrosis and infection forced partial amputation of the finger. Plaintiff sued her physician for malpractice. The physician declared bankruptcy; the insurer, who was defending the physician, then denied coverage based on a policy exclusion containing the above-quoted language. Plaintiff argued that since no therapeutic claims had been made for the substance, it was not a drug. The court reasoned that the tea tree oil was used for a medical *purpose* and, therefore, both under the ordinary, dictionary definition of the word *drug* and, the definition in the federal Food, Drug, and Cosmetic Act, the tea tree oil was a drug. The court further noted that the oil was a homeopathic remedy, even though not listed in the Homeopathic Pharmacopoeia, and as such fell within the definition of "drug." Finally, the court observed that the physician used the oil with the express intent of curing, mitigating, or treating plaintiff's wart, thus again fitting the legal definition of a drug.

CHAPTER 10

1. See Tom L. Beauchamp, "The Principles Approach," 23 (6) *Hastings Center Rep.* S9 (1993).

2. See, e.g., Ronald M. Green, "Method in Bioethics: A Troubled Assessment," 15 *J. Med. and Phil.* 179 (1990).

3. See, e.g., Susan Wolf, "Ethics Committees and Due Process: Nesting Rights in a Community of Caring," 50 *Md. L. Rev.* 798, 840 (1991).

4. Tom L. Beauchamp and James F. Childress, *Principles of Biomedical Ethics*, 121 (4th ed., New York: Oxford University Press, 1994).

5. Id., 189.

6. Id., 259.

7. Id., 327.

8. Id., 462.

9. Beauchamp and Childress write, "Principles and rules cannot fully encompass what occurs when parents lovingly play and nurture their children, or when physicians and nurses provide palliative care for a dying patient and comfort to the patient's distressed spouse" (id., 462).

10. See Eric J. Cassell, *Talking With Patients*, 2:1–3 (Cambridge, Mass.: MIT Press, 1985). Cassell argues that "scientific doctors who lack developed personal powers are inadequately trained." According to Cassell, the art of medicine includes not only scientific competence but also the ability to acquire and integrate subjective information. Cassell gives the example of a medical intern whose care is limited by his feeling of hopelessness, which he has unconsciously adopted from the patient.

11. Id., 16–17. Cassell notes: "History taking is often taught as if the object is to strip away all the confusion heaped on the facts by patients in order to get at the diagnosis" (17).

12. See, e.g., Rosanne M. Radziewicz and Susan Moeller Schneider, "Using Diversional Activity to Enhance Coping," 15 (4) *Cancer Nurs.* 293, 294 (1992).

13. See generally Jay Katz, *The Silent World of Doctor and Patient* (New York: Free Press, 1984). The view that only physicians heal is reflected in state statutes for physician licensing, which typically criminalize the unlicensed practice of medicine, and which arguably overbroadly define practicing medicine. See, e.g., Mich. Comp. Laws Ann., § 333.17001 (West 1992) (defining the practice of medicine as "diagnosis, treatment, prevention, cure, or relieving of a human disease, ailment, defect, complaint or other physical or mental condition, by attendance, advice, device, diagnostic test, or other means").

14. Katz 1984, 209.

15. Eric J. Cassell, "The Sorcerer's Broom: Medicine's Rampant Technology," 23 (6) *Hastings Center Rep.* 32 (1993). Cassell quotes Emerson: "Things are in the saddle and ride mankind."

16. David A. Grimes, "Technology Follies: The Uncritical Acceptance of Medical Innovation," 269 *JAMA* 3030 (1993) (citing examples). For instance, electronic fetal monitoring during labor was widely disseminated during the 1970s but was criticized when randomized controlled trials showed that the monitoring conferred no demonstrable benefit to the fetus yet posed significantly increased risks of operative delivery (id.).

17. Patricia L. Starck and John P. McGovern, foreword to *The Hidden Dimension of Illness: Human Suffering*, xi, Patricia L. Stark and John P. McGovern, eds. (New York: National League for Nursing Press, 1992).

18. Eric J. Cassell, "The Nature of Suffering: Physical, Psychological, Social, and Spiritual Aspects," in id., 1.

19. Timothy E. Quill, "Risk Taking by Physicians in Legally Gray Areas," 57 *Albany L. Rev.* 693, 697 (1994).

20. Katz 1984, 208–9. Physicians thus "deprive patients of vital information, or pat patients on the back and assure them that everything will be all right." This in turn makes patients feel "disregarded, ignored, patronized, and dismissed" (id., 210)

21. Id., 209. Katz provides the example of a cardiology patient's initial meeting with Dr. Chris Barnard regarding a heart transplant operation; the patient compares Barnard to a "handsome Smuts" and then to a "martyred

Christ" (id., 131–32, quoting P. Blaiberg, *Looking at My Heart*, 65–66 [New York: Stein and Day, 1968]).

22. These include fiduciary, partner, accommodator, contractor, technician, friend, teacher, and bureaucrat. See James F. Childress, *Who Should Decide: Paternalism in Health Care*, 6 (New York: Oxford University Press, 1982).

23. Id., 4–5.

24. For an interesting account of Erickson's work, see Milton H. Erickson and Ernest L. Rossi, *The February Man: Evolving Consciousness and Identity in Hypnotherapy* (New York: Brunner/Mazel, 1989).

25. See David Cheek, "Unconscious Perception of Meaningful Sounds during Surgical Anaesthesia as Revealed under Hypnosis," 1 *Am. J. Clin. Hypnosis* 101, 109 (1959) (reporting hypnotic subjects' auditory impressions of surgeries experienced under anesthesia).

26. The American Medical Association has noted: "Disclosing the death of a patient is a duty which goes to the very heart of the physician-patient relationship. . . . The emotional needs of the family . . . must at all times be given foremost consideration" (American Medical Association, *Code of Medical Ethics: Current Opinions with Annotations,* opin. 8.18 [1994]).

27. Cf. Robert M. Veatch, *The Patient-Physician Relation: The Patient as Partner*, 2:2 (Bloomington: Indiana University Press, 1991): "The term patient is not a good one. Etymologically it implies suffering, the connotation of passivity. But patients can be passive no longer."

28. The author witnessed one surgery of a diabetic ten year old who had undergone a dozen such procedures in the past few years. The staff knew the situation and knew the child. One of the surgeons appeared to comfort the child, calling him by name, even though the child was anesthetized. This gave the impression of caring and of valuing the child's dignity and integrity.

29. If competent, the patient has a legal right to refuse lifesaving treatment. See *Cruzan v. Director, Missouri Dept. of Public Health*, 497 U.S. 261 (1990).

30. Informed consent only requires the physician to disclose information material to the patient's decision to submit to a particular medical procedure. See *Canterbury v. Spence*, 464 F.2d 772, 786–87 (D.C. Cir.), cert. denied, 409 U.S. 1064 (1972).

31. *Cruzan*, 497 U.S. 279–80.

32. T. S. Eliot, "The Love Song of J. Alfred Prufrock," in *Norton Anthology of Poetry*, ed. Richard Ellman and Robert O'Clair (New York: W. W. Norton and Co., 1973). See Cruzan, 497 U.S. at 286 (observing that family members "do not wish to witness the . . . [condition] of a loved one which they regard as hopeless, meaningless, and even degrading").

33. The challenged legislation in *Cruzan* required a guardian seeking to discontinue nutrition and hydration of a person in a persistent vegetative state, to provide "clear and convincing evidence" of what the individual's decision would have been (497 U.S. 284–86).

34. Given the imbalance of power and the "hopeless . . . and even degrading" (*Cruzan*, 497 U.S. 286) position into which Mattie was thrust, one wonders whether Mattie was capable of disclosing her suffering to a hostile interrogator on whom she was dependent for life support.

35. See, e.g., Richard M. Zaner, *Ethics and the Clinical Encounter,* 3 (Englewood Cliffs, N.J.: Prentice Hall, 1988) (describing the bureaucratic, fragmented, and dehumanizing nature of modern health services).

36. See Katz 1984. Veatch (1991, 2–3) observes that increasingly, patients visiting physicians are in fact healthy. They come for physical examinations, for example, or for immunizations or other services that do not suggest illness; or patients may have illnesses that are chronic and stable. Veatch notes that none of these patients is sick "to the extent of being incapable of participating actively in an ongoing patient-physician relation." Veatch thus proposes the model of the active bargaining process for the physician-patient relationship.

37. See generally Susan Sherwin, *No Longer Patient: Feminist Ethics and Health Care* (Philadelphia: Temple University Press, 1992).

38. Donald Konold and Robert M. Veatch, "Codes of Medical Ethics," in Warren T. Reich, ed., *Encyclopedia of Bioethics,* 3:162, 166 (New York: The Free Press, 1978).

39. Sogyal Rinpoche, *The Tibetan Book of Living and Dying,* 221–22 (San Francisco: Harper SanFrancisco, 1992) (quoting Shantideva, *A Guide to the Bodhisattva's Way of Life,* trans. Stephen Batchelor, 30–32 [Dharamsala: Library of Tibetan Works and Archives, 1979]). Cf. Cassell 1992, 9: "There is one more way by which we can know that others suffer—by directly experiencing within ourselves their feelings of desperation and disintegration, in the same manner that parents frequently experience the emotions of their children and psychiatrists of their patients. . . . Directly experiencing the emotions of others is . . . not part of our everyday language nor of medical discourse . . . [but] this basis for compassion . . . is part of the everyday world."

40. Larry Dossey, *Meaning and Medicine: Lessons From a Doctor's Tales of Breakthrough and Healing,* 24 (New York: Bantam Books, 1991).

41. Cf. Roger J. Bulger, *In Search of the Modern Hippocrates,* 153 (Iowa City: University of Iowa Press, 1987): "The day [in the hospital] is dominated by mechanical worries, dials, buttons, and computers, all of which are essential and even vital, but none gives access to a patient's feelings. . . . [S]cientific care has eroded the human care which has always been a part of the healing process."

42. See John Arras, "Principles and Particularity: The Role of Cases in Bioethics," 60 *Ind. L.J.* 983, 1004 (1994) (describing the notion that "story or history," as opposed to "a top-down 'applied ethics' model," is the "most appropriate form of representing moral problems").

43. See Joel Feinberg, III, *The Moral Limits of Criminal Law,* chap. 19 (New York: Oxford University Press, 1986), cited in Beauchamp and Childress 1994, 410. Feinberg defines autonomy with reference to a zone of "breathing space" around the body.

44. See Ken Wilber, *No Boundary: Eastern and Western Approaches to Personal Growth,* 1–14 (Boston: Shambhala Publications, 1979).

45. See, e.g., Ben Rich, "Postmodern Medicine: Reconstructing the Hippocratic Oath," 65 *U. Colo. L. Rev.* 77 (1993).

46. Michael Polanyi and Harry Prosch, *Meaning,* 66 (Chicago: University of

Chicago Press, 1975). Polanyi adds (loc. cit.), "Men believe in the reality of these meanings whenever they perceive them—unless some intellectual myth in which they also come to believe denies reality to some of them."

47. Cf. Milner S. Ball, *Lying Down Together: Law, Metaphor, and Theology,* 17 (Madison: University of Wisconsin Press, 1985): "Conceptual metaphors for law can circulate, diversify, increase, stimulate the creating of other metaphors, and challenge the hegemony of monolithic conceptual thinking."

48. Id.

49. Communication is said to occur on many levels, most nonverbal and subtle. See David Cheek, "Communication with the Critically Ill," 12 (2) *Am. J. Clin. Hypnosis* 75 (1969). Indeed, hypnosis uses such tools as ideomotor signals—tiny, unconscious movements of the head or fingers—to communicate with the subject. See, e.g., Ernest Rossi, *The Psychobiology of Mind-Body Healing: New Concepts of Therapeutic Hypnosis,* 89–91 (New York: W. W. Norton and Co., 1993); Stephen Gilligan, *Therapeutic Trances: The Cooperation Principle in Ericksonian Hypnotherapy,* 337 (New York: Brunner/Mazel Publisher, 1987). Even if Mattie had not said, "I want to cry," she still communicated—through gesture, movement, emotion, and silence. Dr. S's description of his patients as "noncommunicative" made a discussion of substituted judgment (see *Cruzan,* 497 U.S. 284–86) infinitely more inviting but actually substituted banter for communication. Cf. Gilligan 1987, 261 (observing that a trance state can occur when "the ensuing confusion is amplified to create more uncertainty. . . ."); Michael Yapko, *Trancework: An Introduction to the Practice of Clinical Hypnosis,* 139 (New York: Irvington Publisher, 1990) (describing "trance logic" as the "voluntary state of accepting suggestions . . . without the critical evaluation that would, of course, destroy the validity of meaningfulness of provided suggestions").

50. Cf. Violet de Laszlo, ed., *The Basic Writings of Carl Jung,* 158–62 (Princeton: Princeton University Press, 1959) (Jung describes the anima, or universal feminine archetype, within human consciousness); Joseph Campbell, *The Hero with a Thousand Faces* (New York: Fine Communications, 1996) (describing the archetype of the universal mother); William Blank, *Torah, Tarot, and Tantra,* 39 (Gloucester: Sigo Press, 1991) (describing the Shechinah, or receptive, feminine archetype defining the presence of God in the world).

51. Multiple fertilized eggs result in three cases: (1) naturally, when the egg splits; (2) as a side effect of infertility medication; and (3) when the obstetrician, to increase the odds of a successful pregnancy, implants additional eggs. See M. I. Evans et al., "Selective First-Trimester Termination in Octuplet and Quadruplet Pregnancies: Clinical and Ethical Issues," 71 *Obstet. and Gynecol.* 289 (1988) (observing that "[t]he induction of grand multiple gestations is a known complication of infertility treatments").

52. With "quadruplets or multifetal gestations of more than five fetuses"— in other words, when four or more embryos are present—and "in multiple pregnancies bearing more than one anomalous fetus," "selective termination" of excess fetuses is deemed ethically appropriate (M. I. Evans et al., "Attitudes on the Ethics of Abortion, Sex Selection, and Selective Pregnancy among Health

Care Professionals, Ethicists, and Clergy Likely to Encounter Such Situations," 164 (4) *Am. J. Obstet. and Gynecol.* 1092 [1991]).

53. J. C. Fletcher, "Ethical Aspects of Prenatal Diagnosis: Views of U.S. Medical Geneticists," 14 (2) *Clin. Pernatol.* 293 (1987) (calling for greater study). Obstetricians view MFPR not as destroying life but as lifesaving: the object is to allow the mother to have one, two, or possibly three healthy babies, rather than four to nine sick ones. For this reason, even "right-to-life" patients have requested the technology (Ashmead, interview). Cf. F. N. L. Poynter, "Hunter, Spallanzani, and the History of Artificial Insemination," in Lloyd Stevenson and Robert Multhauf, eds., *Medicine, Science, and Culture,* 97–113 (Baltimore: Johns Hopkins University Press, 1968) (historical overview of the public controversy over artificial insemination).

54. See The American College of Obstetricians and Gynecologists Committee on Ethics, *Patient Choice: Maternal-Fetal Conflict,* opin. 55 (1987) (noting the increase in the possibility for such conflicts, given the increasing accessibility of the fetus to diagnostic and treatment procedures); Rosa Kim, "Reconciling Fetal/Maternal Conflicts," 27 *Idaho L. Rev.* 223 (1990–91).

55. Individual rights are "political trumps held by individuals" and exist to protect individuals from collective decisions that deny them what they wish to have or do or that impose some loss or injury on them (Ronald Dworkin, *Taking Rights Seriously,* xi [Cambridge, Mass.: Harvard University Press, 1978]). According to legal positivism, rights thus do not have "some special metaphysical character" but rather exist "only insofar as th[ey] have been created by explicit political or social practice" (id., xii). Dworkin (loc. cit.) argues that some rights are, however, "fundamental and even axiomatic," such as the "right to equal concern and respect." See David Blickenstaff, "Defining the Boundaries of Personal Privacy: Is There a Paternal Interest in Compelling Fetal Surgery?" 88 (3) *Nw. U. L. Rev.* 1157 (1994) (arguing for a woman's right to refuse fetal surgery).

56. Cf. Abraham Joshua Heschel, *The Sabbath: Its Meaning for Modern Man,* 3 (New York: Farrar, Straus and Giroux, 1983): "Technical civilization is man's conquest of space. . . . But time is the heart of existence. To gain control of the world of space is certainly one of our tasks. The danger begins when in gaining power in the realm of space we forfeit all aspirations in the realm of time . . . where the goal is not to have but to be, not to own but to give, not to control but to share, not to subdue but to be in accord."

57. Cf. Scott Altman, "(Com)modifying Experience," 65 *S. Cal. L. Rev.* 293, 302 (1991): "medical technologies that shorten or risk the life of a person, or something that resembles a person, for the benefit of another . . . demonstrate that persons have noninfinite value and that people treat others as objects that can be used solely as means." See also Margaret Radin, "Reflections on Objectification," 65 *S. Cal. L. Rev.* 341 (1994).

58. Gilligan (1987, 337) notes that "trance is an experiential continuum of involvement rather than an 'all or none' phenomenon." Charles Tart goes further, arguing that "enlightenment" is a "continuum of development rather than

an all-or-none state," with altered states such as hypnosis creating "jumps" in the continuum (*Waking Up: Overcoming the Obstacles to Human Potential,* 7 [Boston: Shambhala Press, 1987]). Tart observes that since childhood, his subjective experience has contradicted the Western view that such states as dreaming are "not real" (5); he uses the term "consensus consciousness" to suggest that "ordinary consciousness" does not connote "naturalness and normality" but rather is a trance state shaped by the "consensus of belief" of Western culture (11).

59. The opinion of the American College of Obstetricians and Gynecologists Committee on Ethics (1987) speaks in terms of "jeopardiz[ing] the fetus," "distress or deterioration," "fetal interests, "fetal needs," and "welfare of the fetus."

60. Cf. Swami Muktananda, *Play of Consciousness,* 5 (South Fallsburg, N.Y.: SYDA Foudnation 1978) (describing all creation as conscious); Walt Whitman, *Leaves of Grass* (1855): "I bequeath myself to the dirt to grow from the grass I love, / If you want me again look for me under your boot-soles" (quoted in the *Norton Anthology of Modern Poetry,* ed. Richard Ellman and Robert O'Clair [New York: W. W. Norton and Co., 1973]).

61. Cf. Guido Calabresi and Philip Bobbit, *Tragic Choices,* 26 (New York: W.W. Norton and Co., 1978): "Though subterfuge may bring us peace, for a while, it is honesty which causes the tragic choice to reappear . . . [and] permits us to know what is to be accepted and, accepting, to reclaim our humanity and struggle against indignity."

62. Cf. Hannah Arendt, *Totalitarianism,* 111 (San Diego: Harcourt Brace and Co., 1968): "Systematic lying to the whole world can be safely carried out only under the conditions of totalitarian rule, where the fictitious quality of everyday reality makes propaganda largely superfluous."

63. For differing religious views, see Laura Bishop and Mary Coutts, "Religious Perspectives on Bioethics," 4 (2) *Kennedy Inst. of Ethics J.* 155 (1994) (describing attitudes toward reproductive and other technologies in African religious traditions, the Bahai faith, Buddhism and Confucianism, Eastern Orthodoxy, Hinduism, Islam, Jainism, Judaism, Native American religious traditions, Protestantism, and Roman Catholicism). Cf. American Medical Association, *Code of Medical Ethics: Current Opinions with Annotations,* opin. 2.01 (1994): "the Principles of Medical Ethics of the AMA do not prohibit a physician from performing an abortion in accordance with good medical practice and under circumstances that do not violate the law."

64. Indeed, one can hardly frame the language of "rights" to this analysis. On one side is the couple's interest in a healthy baby; on the other side is the egg's right to avoid being fertilized only to be "selectively terminated." "Egg rights" arguably are no less compelling than "fetal rights," particularly in light of the difficulty in determining the moment at which the latter rights attach. See Charles Kester, "Is There a Person in That Body? An Argument for the Priority of Persons and the Need for a New Legal Paradigm," 82 *Geo. L.J.* 1643, 1650, 1681–83 (1994) (rejecting "viability" as a criterion for granting legal standing to

the fetus, and arguing that once they develop brain function, fetuses should be "presumed to possess . . . consciousness" and hence should be recognized as persons with legal standing).

65. Mattie probably received the standard of care customary in the locality. See *Smith v. Menet,* 530 N.E.2d 277 (Ill. App. 2 Dist. 1988) (describing the standard of care in medical malpractice).

66. There is no suggestion here that we do away with modern Western science. On the contrary, the notion of "integrative medicine" is explicated as a health care system in which complementary and alternative medicine modalities are integrated, as *safe, effective,* and *appropriate,* and *in the best interest of the patient,* into conventional care. Thus, the perspective is to consider the benefits and the limitations of conventional medicine, with its scientific underpinnings, as well as of complementary and alternative medicine, with its vitalistic or quasi-mystical side. In this light, the indigenous healer mentioned in chapter 7, the overreaching spiritual healer mentioned in chapter 8, and the appropriate or inappropriate reliance on herbal medicine mentioned in chapter 9 each crystallize the problems associated with a pendulum swing from modern Western science to ancient medical traditions and healing on the spiritual level.

67. Cf. Huston Smith, *The Religions of Man,* 148 (New York: Harper and Row, 1989) (describing Buddha's First Noble Truth, that life is suffering). In Sanskrit the word *budh* means both "to wake up" and "to know"; hence, Buddha is the "Awakened One" (id., 122).

68. See Eric Cassell, "The Sorcerer's Broom: Medicine's Rampant Technology" 23 (6) *Hastings Center Rep.* 32 (1993) (describing the reduction of "human illness" to "the biological problem of disease").

69. An obstetrician who attempts to commune, on an inner level, with embryos—to inform himself of their experience and inform them of medical alternatives, might be regarded in the same vein as a person who talks to plants, to pets (which may be more common), or to themselves (which most of us do mentally rather than out loud, thus avoiding a diagnosis under the DSM-IV (Diagnostic and Statistical Manual of Mental Disorders, 4th ed.), a system of codes maintained by the American Psychiatric Association. Cf. R. D. Lang, *The Politics of Experience,* 121 (New York: Pantheon Books, 1983) (describing schizophrenia as a "political event," a "social prescription that rationalizes a set of social actions whereby the labeled person is annexed by others . . . into a role"); Mircea Eliade, *The Sacred and the Profane,* 209 (New York: Harcourt, Brace and World, 1957): "A purely rational man is an abstraction; he is never found in real life."

70. Arras 1994, 997.

71. For example, in Mattie's situation, the ethical issue is not whether someone else has the right to disconnect her life support but whether someone has the right to pronounce her as good as dead. Cf. Kester 1994, 1667 (proposing that "[a]n individual whose body is irreversibly . . . incapable of sustaining the functions necessary for consciousness is not a person").

72. See Arras 1994, 997–98 (describing such a shift in Robert Burt, *Taking*

Care of Strangers: The Rule of Law in Doctor-Patient Relations [New York: The Free Press, 1979]). Arras notes that Burt "enlarged the understanding" of autonomy by "attempting to place the patient's treatment refusal in an emotional context," rather than resorting to "a mechanical application of the principle."

73. This is the position taken by those who practice *phowa*, the transference of consciousness at the moment of death: prolonging life is less important than providing a peaceful atmosphere for the dying process. See Rinpoche 1992, 231–35, 372.

74. See Quill 1994. Indeed, according to Rinpoche (1994, 372), what happens just before, during, and after death is of "immense importance": life-sustaining treatment that "merely prolongs the dying process may only kindle unnecessary grasping, anger, and frustration in a dying person." Rinpoche argues that "[p]eaceful death is really an essential human right" Cf. Daniel Callahan, "Pursuing a Peaceful Death," 23 (4) *Hastings Center Rep.* 33, 34 (1993) (observing that the process of dying is "deformed" by "technological brinksmanship").

75. See, e.g., American Medical Association, *Code of Medical Ethics: Reports*, rep. 59 (1994) (rejecting "physician-assisted suicide" as "fundamentally inconsistent with the professional role of physicians as healers").

76. See, e.g., Nel Noddings, *Caring: A Feminine Approach to Ethics and Moral Education*, 79–103 (Berkeley: University of California Press, 1984); Birgit Victor, "Theoretical Discussion of a Model of Caring for Persons with HIV Infection," 7 *Scand. J. Caring Sci.* 243 (1993).

77. In fact, the intervention determines which of the embryos within the family will develop into "persons," thus eliminating future siblings and initiating a whole array of family dynamics. Since courts have imposed a duty on the physician to avoid injury to the fetus (see Jeffrey Phelan, "The Maternal Abdominal Wall: A Fortress against Fetal Health Care?" 65 *S. Cal. L. Rev.* 461, 472 [1991] [citing cases]), if embryos are considered persons, a conflict of interest arises between the various candidates.

78. Cf. Arras 1994, 997: "Is the withholding of artificial nutrition through a nasogastric tube an example of intentional 'killing' or an example of a humble, merciful withdrawal of ineffective medical treatments?"

79. See generally Ernest Becker, *Escape from Evil* (New York: The Free Press, 1975) (describing the denial of death in American culture); Elizabeth Kubler-Ross, *On Death and Dying* (New York: Macmillan Publishing Company, 1969).

80. See generally Dossey 1991 (describing meaning in medicine); Kenneth Pelletier, *Holistic Medicine*, 23–39 (New York: Delacourte Press, 1979) (critiquing the Newtonian view of disease as mechanical and reductionist and advocating a new medical model that would integrate prevention, lifestyle modification, and psychological counseling and support patient responsibility for self-care).

81. See Arras 1994, 995 (noting the effect of culture on bioethical principles and theorizing).

82. Indeed, the "universal" experience of death—as expressed in dreams, poetry, and recurrent world myths—is that death "is never seen to stand alone

as a final act of annihilation" but rather occurs in a cycle of death and rebirth, with initiation from one stage of development to another, and hence redemption (Joseph Henderson and Maud Oakes, *The Wisdom of the Serpent: The Myths of Death, Rebirth, and Resurrection,* 4 [Princeton: Princeton University Press, 1963]. Thus, the compassion or consciousness with which one ends life matters to the organism, just as the compassion or consciousness that attends birth is significant. Cf. Wilhelm Reich, *Children of the Future: On the Prevention of Sexual Pathology,* 3–4 (New York: Farrar, Strauss and Giroux, 1983) (describing birth-related trauma).

83. Cf. Stefano Rodota, "Cultural Models and the Future of Bioethics," 10 *J. Contemp. Health L. and Pol'y* 33 (1994) (referring to stances, such as that of the Catholic Church, which "bundl[e] together abortion, contraception, euthanasia and reproduction technologies and rejec[t] them wholesale"); Kester 1994, 1676 (citing "sincerely held but incompatible views" as to whether fetuses are "persons").

84. Cf. Gopi Krishna, *Reason and Revelation,* 43 (New Delhi: Kundalini Research and Publication Trust, 1979): "It is the human ego, with its intolerance of others' views, that is often responsible for the battles and wrangles in the domain of knowledge. Almost every great thinker, skilled in penmanship, with appropriate arguments tries to win finality for his views. This is an incorrigible habit of reason. It can never be stilled into that perfect calm which knows that the search is over."

85. See generally Smith 1989.

86. See, e.g., Alexander Capron, "Easing the Passing," 24 (4) *Hastings Center Rep.* 25 (1994) (describing "compassion in dying" as a ground for legalizing medically assisted death).

87. See supra, n. 9 and accompanying text.

88. For examples of this dual identity, see Kyriacos C. Markides, *The Magus of Strovolos: The Extraordinary World of a Spiritual Healer* (New York: Viking Penguin, 1989) (on a sociology professor's initiation into Christian spirit mysteries); Andrew Harvey, *Hidden Journey: A Spiritual Journey* (New York: Viking Penguin, 1992) (on an Oxford professor's initiation by an Indian guru); Tart 1987 (on a psychology professor's initiation into trance states through systems of knowledge developed by G. I. Gurdjieff).

89. See generally Burton J. Bledstein, *The Culture of Professionalism: The Middle Class and the Development of Higher Education in America* (New York: W.W. Norton and Company, 1976).

90. Michael Harner, *The Way of the Shaman,* xvii–xix (San Francisco: Harper San Francisco, 1990). Shamanism does not require "faith" but rather rests on one's own experience of different states of consciousness (id., xix). Harner notes that it is "unnecessary and even distracting to be preoccupied with achieving a scientific understanding of what 'spirits' may really represent and why shamanism works" (xxiii).

91. Sandra Ingerman, *Soul Retrieval: Mending the Fragmented Self through Shamanic Practice,* 33 (San Francisco: Harper San Francisco, 1991). Eliade notes: "The shaman is, therefore, the man who can die, and then return to life, many

times. . . . Through his initiation, the shaman learns . . . what he must do when his soul abandons his body—and, first of all, how to orient himself in the unknown regions which he enters during his ecstasy" (Mircea Eliade, *Birth and Rebirth*, 95 [New York: Harper and Brothers, 1958], quoted in Henderson and Oakes 1963, 207).

92. Harner 1990, xxiii.

93. Ingerman 1991, 17.

94. Cf. Roger J. Bulger, ed., *In Search of the Modern Hippocrates*, 122 (Iowa City: University of Iowa Press, 1987) (observing that "a real cure emerges by virtue of a relationship that will be beneficial to both patient and doctor"). Bulger emphasizes physicians' reliance on the placebo effect—the "therapy of the word"—as the most powerful healing tool, and he observes that Western medicine's association with action rather than words creates "a most peculiar and persistent separation of medicine from the great healers and healing associated with religion and religious leaders" (121–22).

95. See Harner 1990, xviii.

96. See Patricia King, "Rights within the Therapeutic Relationship," 6 (1) *J. Law and Health* 31 (1991–92) (arguing that conceiving autonomy in terms of a "narrow image of rights . . . independent of care" distorts therapeutic relationships and "makes implementation of rights, as expressed in this individual autonomous model, impossible"). King notes that judicial language, particularly in cases involving mental illness, "tells only part of the truth of the human experience." She argues that each judicial opinion "articulates some dimension of human experience but no one articulates the wholeness of human experience" and that rather than protecting autonomy, this disconnects persons from relationships where "their autonomy might flourish" (57).

97. Campbell 1949, 3.

98. We were told of a physician who spent too much time with her patients. She was told to either increase her efficiency or accept a salary cut; she chose the latter.

99. Rodota 1994, 33.

100. I am also challenging three premises of conventional wisdom that are embedded in the stories, namely, (1) anything not subject to scientific proof (for example, the angel on the necklace) is a matter of personal belief and hence irrelevant to healing and/or rule making; (2) all intersubjective experience (for example, the dream of the lady in blue and white) must fit into a well-defined belief system adopted by a mainstream religious body; and, as a corollary, mystical experience is "religious" and hence not real; (3) all legal rules must be "neutral," free from inner vision, body wisdom, and feeling; distinctions are rational and made on a purely intellectual basis, without regard to unconscious and archetypical elements. Cf. John Herman Randall, Jr., *The Making of the Modern Mind*, 282–307 (New York: Columbia University Press, 1976) (describing the "deification of reason").

101. Martin Buber writes that humans live in "two tidily circled-off provinces, one of institutions and the other of feelings—the province of It and the province of I" (*I and Thou*, 43 [2d ed., New York: Charles Scribner's Sons,

1958]). According to Buber (loc. cit.), feelings are "'within,' where life is lived and man recovers from institutions."

102. The Western notion of personhood dismisses subjectivity and "sharply opposes reality and nonreality," asserting that "imagining, dreaming, and hearing voices, for example, are not 'real'" (Willy DeCraemer, "A Cross-Cultural Perspective on Personhood," 61 *Milbank Fund Q./Health and Soc.* 1, 21 (1983). Central African and Japanese perspectives, by way of contrast, emphasize the "'inner,' emotive, symbolic, and ritual aspects" of personhood in society (id., 32).

103. See Guido Calabresi, *Ideals, Beliefs, Attitudes, and the Law: Private Law Perspectives on a Public Law Problem*, 95–96 (Syracuse: Syracuse University Press, 1985), quoted in Rodota 1994, 34. Calabresi argues that in *Roe v. Wade* the U.S. Supreme Court should have "simply denied that fetuses were alive," leaving "unprovable, metaphysical arguments" to the people, rather than proclaiming that "anti-abortion beliefs as to commencement of life, whether true or not, are part of our Constitution."

104. Buber (1958, 46) critiques the manipulative, ends-oriented view of life: "If a man lets it have the mastery, the continually growing world of It overruns him and robs him of the reality of his own I, till the incubus over him and the ghost within him whisper to one another the confession of their own non-salvation." Buber describes the I-Thou relationship as one in which the "whole being" participates (3); thus, "[a]ll real living is meeting" (11).

105. See Michael Cohen, "A Fixed Star in Health Care Reform: The Emerging Paradigm of Holistic Healing" 1 (27) *Ariz. State L.J.* 79 (1995).

106. William James, *The Varieties of Religious Experience*, 29 (New York: Collier Books, 1961).

107. An Israeli poet writes: "'Where do you feel your soul?' / Stretched between mouth-hole and ass-hole / a white thread, not transparent mist, / squeezed into a corner between two bones / in pain. / When satiated, vanishing like a cat. / I belong to the last generation / to separate body and soul . . ." Yehuda Amichai, *Travels*, trans. Ruth Nevo, 53 (Bronx: Sheep Meadow Press, 1986).

108. James 1961, 29. James (loc. cit.) calls medical materialism a "simpleminded system of thought," observing that it "finishes up Saint Paul by calling his vision on the road to Damascus a discharging lesion of the occipital cortex, he being an epileptic," and that it "snuffs out Saint Teresa as an hysteric, Saint Francis of Assisi as an hereditary degenerate."

109. Franz Kafka, "Before the Law," in *The Complete Stories*, 3 (New York: Schochen Books, 1971).

CHAPTER 11

1. See Valerie Hunt, *Infinite Mind: Science of the Human Vibrations of Consciousness* (Malibu: Malibu Publishing Company, 1996).

2. Edwin A. Abbot, *Flatland: A Romance of Many Dimensions* (New York: Dover Press, 1952).

3. The *Übermensch* is one who has "overcome his animal nature, organized the chaos of his passions, sublimated his impulses." Walter Kaufmann, *Nietzsche: Philosopher, Phsychologist, Antichrist, 316* (4th ed., Princeton: Princeton University Press, 1974).

4. I Hermas, III:7 in *The Lost Books of the Bible and the Forgotten Books of Eden*, 202 (New York: Meridian, 1974).

5. David R. Blumenthal writes: "Ezekiel's vision is not a mystic vision. . . . Rather, it is God Who has seized the prophet and overwhelmed him with His majesty." *Understanding Jewish Mysticism: A Source Reader—the Merkabah Tradition and the Zoharic Tradition*, 51 (New York: Ktav Publishing House, 1978).

6. Carlos Castaneda, *The Art of Dreaming* (New York: HarperCollins, 1993), viii.

7. *State v. Kellog*, 568 P.2d 514 (Idaho 1977).

8. See *Rogers v. State Bd. of Medical Examiners*, 371 So.2d 1037 (Fla. Dist. Ct. App. 1979), affirmed, 387 So.2d 937 (Fla. 1980).

9. See *Burzynski v. Aetna Life Ins. Co., Inc.*, No. H-89-3976, 1992 U.S. Dist. LEXIS 21300 (S.D. Tex., Mar. 31, 1992).

10. See James S. Gordon, *Manifesto for a New Medicine* (Reading, Mass.: Addison-Wesley, 1996).

11. The same claim was made by Gopi Krishna, who repeatedly asserted that the greatest advancement in human endeavors would come from scientific research into kundalini, which Krishna claimed to be the biological basis for genius and human evolution. See Gopi Krishna, *Kundalini in Time and Space* (New Delhi: Kundalini Research and Publication Trust, 1979).

12. Ravi Ravindra, *Whispers from the Other Shore: A Spiritual Search—East and West*, 25 (Wheaton, Ill.: Theosophical Publishing House, 1984).

13. Wayne B. Jonas, "Alternative Medicine: Learning from the Past, Examining the Present, and Advancing to the Future," 280 (18) *JAMA* 1616–17 (1998).

14. See Michael M. Talbot, *The Holographic Universe* (New York: Harper-Perennial Library, 1992) (describing the concept of enfolded realities postulated by physicist David Bohm).

15. Another plausible interpretation of the narrator's vision of the Sphere is that experience derives from the "other" realm, also known in various traditions as the devil, Satan, the astral tramps of the lower netherworlds, or, in popular imagination, the "Dark Side of the Force." See, e.g., Gershom G. Scholem, *Major Trends in Jewish Mysticism*, 177 (New York: Schocken Books, 1974) (describing the Gnostic idea—found in the *Zohar*, a Jewish mystical text—of a "'left emanation,' i.e. of an ordered hierarchy of the potencies of evil"). Presumably, however, legal rules, ethical codes, internal professional self-regulation, and National Institutes of Health guidelines help prevent abuses of claims to knowledge deriving from these "other" realms of thought. See, e.g., *Basic Department of Health and Human Services Policy for Protection of Human Research Subjects*, 45 C.F.R. § 46.101(a), (f).

16. Daniel Callahan, "Pursuing a Peaceful Death," 23 (4) *Hastings Center Rep.* 33, 34 (1993).

CHAPTER 12

1. See Dorothy Nelkin and Lori Andrews, "Homo Economicus: Commercialization of Body Tissue in the Age of Biotechnology," 28 (5) *Hastings Center Rep.* 30, 34 (1998).
2. See, e.g., Valerie Hunt, *Naibhu* (Malibu: Malibu Publishing Company, 1998).
3. See Sandra Ingerman, *Soul Retrieval: Mending the Fragmented Self* (San Francisco: Harper San Francisco, 1991).
4. See Glenn McGee and Arthur Caplan, "What's in the Dish?" 20 (2) *Hastings Center Rep.* 36 (1999) (calling for "broad, nonpartisan, and theologically informed public discussion" concerning the fate of primordial stem cells).
5. Barbara A. Brennan predicts that with the cultivation of heightened intuitive abilities, our "feelings and private realities will no longer be hidden from others." She adds that "[t]hey already are automatically communicated through our energy fields" (*Hands of Light: A Guide to Healing through the Human Energy Field*, 10 [New York: Bantam Books, 1988]).
6. See Valerie Hunt, *Infinite Mind: Science of the Human Vibrations of Consciousness* (Malibu: Malibu Publishing Company, 1996).

CONCLUSION

1. Patanjali, *How to Know God: The Yoga Aphorisms of Patanjali*, trans. Swami Prabhavananda and Christopher Isherwood, 15–22 (pt. 1, 2nd sutra) (Hollywood: Vedanta Press, 1981). *Sutra*, referring to an aphorism, means "thread."
2. Id., 22 (3rd sutra).
3. When the "obstructions and impurities" of the mind are purified, then the essence of the human being, which is bliss, "shines forth in its own pristine nature, as pure consciousness" (id., 220–21 [pt. 4, 31st and 34th sutra]). For a modern analogue based on initiation into one's essential creativity, see Julia Cameron, *The Artist's Way: A Spiritual Path to Higher Creativity* (New York: Putnam, 1992). Thus, "[t]he yogi who knows that the entire splendor of the universe is his, who rises to the awareness of unity with the universe, retains his divinity even in the midst of various thoughts and fancies." *Isvarapratyabhijna* 2.12, in Swami Muktananda, *Nothing Exists That Is Not Shiva*, 68 (South Fallsburg, N.Y.: SYDA Foundation, 1997).
4. New York Educ. L., § 6521.
5. Mich. Comp. Laws Ann., § 333.17001(d).
6. In Patanjali's system, the eight limbs of yoga are: "the various forms of

abstention from evil-doing *(yama)*, the various observances *(niyamas)*, posture *(asana)*, control of the prana *(pranayama)*, withdrawal of the mind from sense objects *(pratyahara)*, concentration *(dharana)*, meditation *(dhyana)* and absorption in the Atman *(samadhi)*" (Patanjali 1981, 140–41 [pt. 2, 29th sutra]). Like the Tibetan Book of the Dead, Patanjali's text is written less as a religious document than as a manual for enlightenment.

Index